ARIS & PHILLIPS CLASSICAL TEXTS

THUCYDIDES
PYLOS 425 BC
BOOK IV 2-41
A HISTORICAL & TOPOGRAPHICAL STUDY
OF THUCYDIDES' ACCOUNT OF THE CAMPAIGN

with a Translation and Historical Notes by

J.B. Wilson

T0366688

Aris & Phillips is an imprint of Oxbow Books
10 Hythe Bridge Street, Oxford OX1 2EW

First published 1979. Reprinted 2007.

ISBN 978-0-85688-179-0

A CIP record for this book is available from the British Library

Greek text reproduced by permission of Oxford University Press from the Oxford Classical Texts edition of Thucydides' *Histories* edited by H. Stuart Jones and J.E. Powell (2nd ed. 1942).

Printed and bound by CPI Group (UK) Ltd, Croydon, CR0 4YY

Contents

PREFACE

This book is a historical and topographical study in detail of τὰ περὶ Πύλον in 425 B.C., with a brief consideration also of the subsequent history of Pylos up to and including its recapture by Sparta in 409. It is the result of topographical research over five successive summers, combined with a close analysis of the Thucydidean text and other sources. I stand (sometimes heavily) on the shoulders of other scholars, notably Gomme and Pritchett : if I criticise these authors' conclusions at not a few points, this is because they have given us something worth criticising.

The book is meant primarily for those who already have some general knowledge of the topic, or at least of the historical period within which it falls. But I hope it may also illustrate the degree to which this methodology, if used with intensity and precision, may cause us to repaint the received pictures of particular campaigns or other events. If the case of Pylos is at all typical, there is a great deal more work to be done along these lines.

How much longer such work will be possible at Pylos itself is, however, a distressingly open question. Its comparative inaccessibility has so far preserved the area from human spoliation: deservedly so, since it is an area not only of remarkable natural beauty - remarkable even in Greece - but also of enormous historical and archaeological interest for almost any period. Indeed it is hard to think of any part of the world more appealing, or more potentially fruitful, for the historical enquirer, whether professional or amateur. But plans have recently been put forward to turn the Bay of Navarino into a full-scale modern harbour, and to industrialise the area generally. It is not, perhaps, for the historian to balance the potential economic advantages of such a scheme against the cultural losses: but losses there will certainly be, if the scheme comes off. It must at least be said that the next few years may represent the last chance available to archaeologists, topographers and all those interested in Pylian history to pursue their enquiries with much chance of success.

I should like to offer thanks and acknowledgements to Tim Beardsworth, who assisted me in some of the original research, and was co-author of some of the articles originally published on the topic: to the editors of those journals from which I have reprinted some portions of the articles : to Mr. T. Braun and Professor Westlake for much helpful and detailed criticism: to Mr. Christos Christophilopoulos of Koryphasion for a great deal of practical assistance on the site: and not least to Professor A. Andrewes, whose expert tuition in the past is probably responsible for whatever merit there may be in the present work. I am also very grateful to Jeremy Rossiter for drawing the maps so skilfully.

J. B. W.
Oxford, 1978.

iv

SHORT BIBLIOGRAPHY

R. M. Burrows, 'Pylos and Sphacteria', in *Journal of Hellenic Studies* for 1896 (No. 16).
'Pylos and Sphacteria', in *Journal of Hellenic Studies* for 1898 (No. 18).
'Mr. G. B. Grundy on Pylos and Sphacteria', in *Journal of Hellenic Studies* for 1898 (No. 18).

A. W. Gomme, *Commentary on Thucydides* (Oxford University Press, 1956).

G. B. Grundy, 'An Investigation of the Topography of the Region of Sphacteria and Pylos', in *Journal of Hellenic Studies* for 1896 (No. 16).

W. M. Leake, *Travels in the Morea* (London, 1830).

P. Levi, *Pausanias' Guide to Greece* (Penguin, 1971)

T. R. Mills, *Thucydides Bk. IV* (edition) (Oxford University Press, 1930).

J. S. Morrison and R. T. Williams, *Greek Oared Ships* (Cambridge University Press, 1968).

N. D. Papahadzis, Παυσανίου Ελλάδος Περιήγησις (Athens, 1963).

W. K. Pritchett, *Studies in Ancient Greek Topography* (University of California, Berkeley, 1965).

N. S. Valmin, *La Messenie Ancienne* (Lund, 1930).

PRELIMINARY NOTES

Lay-out

Text and translation. Partly for convenient reference, I begin with a page-for-page translation of relevant texts. These consist almost wholly of those parts of Bk. IV of Thucydides which deal with Pylos. I shall take it for granted that Thucydides is the only ancient authority worthy of close analysis. For nearly all the points with which we shall be dealing, other authors add little reliable: the (minor) additions of Plutarch and others are well summarised by Gomme.[1] Where the ultimate capture of Pylos is concerned, however, I have found it necessary (for lack of Thucydides) to give the text and translation of two short extracts, one from Diodorus and one from Xenophon.

At many points the MSS readings, and possible emendations, are relevant to questions of historical fact. As it turns out, historical grounds have led me to come down in favour of the manuscript readings to a far greater extent than most editors (I have marked in the text where my reading is found in none of the MSS). I differ from the Oxford text very rarely. Several other passages which editors have been anxious to emend seem to me entirely satisfactory, for reasons which will be discussed fully in the Notes. It is perhaps worth remarking that, if this is at all typical of Thucydides, his text elsewhere is likely to require much less emendation on historical grounds than is normally supposed.

On the other hand, traditional translations (as well as interpretations) of the text seem to me to have gone seriously astray at many points. So I have made my own translation, using the criteria of clarity and closeness to the text (and, I believe, to historical fact), rather than aesthetic merit.

The reader should not, however, expect from this anything like a general edition even of the excerpted parts of Bk. IV: I am concerned only with historical and topographical fact.

Historical Notes. These follow, roughly, the chronological progress of the campaign, and therefore the order of the text; but many problems are interconnected and relate to different chronological points in it. It has been possible to divide the Notes under a number of main headings, but the reader will need to take up several cross-references.

I shall assume a reasonable amount of background knowledge, and sufficient general familiarity with the campaign, on the part of the reader.

---

1. Gomme, p. 486.

1

Appendix. I have added an Appendix on the existing literature about the campaign, both ancient and modern, and on the general topography.

Maps

I have not found any map of the area which is satisfactory for our purposes. All those I have seen are either too small-scale or too inaccurate (usually both); and there is really nothing for it but to inspect the terrain oneself. Readers may however like to know of the War Office G.S.G.S. 1 : 100,000 Series, prepared during the Second World War, and available most readily at the Library of the Societies for the Promotion of Hellenic and Roman Studies (31-4, Gordon Square, London W.C. 1): of the *Karta Nomos* 1 : 200,000 official Greek survey (best obtained from Edward Stanford Ltd., 12-14 Long Acre, London W.C. 2): and of the (comparatively new) Greek Staff maps at 1 : 50,000. These latter are accurate, though still too small-scale for the details of the campaign: but unfortunately they are - at least officially - inaccessible for reasons of security.

Maps and sketches produced by various editors and commentators are, in nearly every case, untrustworthy: anyone who wants to check them should compare them with Pritchett's aerial photograph. For this book I have used the maps of Grundy and Burrows [2] as a basis, since they are at least on the kind of scale we need: but I have had to have them redrawn and altered in various details - most obviously, to conform to Pritchett's evidence concerning the sea-level (see below). I have checked the final results with the terrain, and am reasonably satisfied as to their accuracy.

Other expertises

The present study is essentially topographical and historical: naturally any such study runs up against problems belonging to other fields within the general area of ancient history. Among these are problems of textual criticism and transmission, Thucydidean usage and linguistics, the nature of the trireme, Spartan hoplite equipment, and so forth. Here I can only refer the reader at relevant points to the best authorities on the subject.

Topography also rubs up against such expertises as hydrography, seismology, meteorology and palaeobotany. Fortunately very few points in the Notes turn on any assumption stemming from these sciences: where they are relevant, I have made this clear. I have put the points affected to experts in informal conversation, and am satisfied that none are demonstrably falsified or even to be regarded as very improbable: more I do not wish to claim. It will be appreciated that these are still very inexact sciences, and likely to remain so for some time.

---

2. See Appendix.

Sea-level

A rise in sea-level is the only point of importance that I shall take for granted. Almost all commentators assume that the land in the Pylos area has risen, at least within the so-called 'Osmyn Aga lagoon'[3] Pritchett [4] has shown, as conclusively as such things can be shown, that the reverse is the truth: in brief, it seems sensible to assume a rise in sea-level of something like 2.5 metres. There are various arguments in Pritchett: those dependent on personal observation I can confirm.

Use of the text

Finally, a brief word on the analysis of the Thucydidean text, which in what follows goes hand in hand with topographical considerations. Some may feel that this is too intensive and detailed, and that I am pressing Thucydides beyond what any author can be expected to bear. Against this one could point to the opposite temptations, presumably more alluring because more commonly yielded to, of over-hastily dismissing what Thucydides says on some grounds or other; wrong information by sources, lack of personal topographical knowledge, various types of 'bias' or 'prejudice', and so on.

I do not think that such arguments can be profitably conducted *a priori*. It is better to see whether the question *solvitur ambulando*, by discovering what actually happens if we press the text to this extent. Either it makes for more vagueness and inaccuracy; or else, as I am quite sure is true in the case of Pylos, the more seriously we take it the more enlightenment we get about the historical and topographical facts. I am not here thinking of cases where editors and commentators have just not bothered to *read* the text properly: for instance, where they have taken Thucydides' διάπλους ship-numbers as if they were blockship-numbers (8.6: see Note F, p. 74). The point is rather that, by a very close scrutiny of the text (in conjunction with the terrain), not only are a number of known problems resolved, but a number of problems that we ought to have raised become apparent, though these too are capable of solution.

I mention all this not primarily by way of justification for the methods employed in the Notes which follow, but to make the suggestions that (a) these methods might be found to yield results in other historical areas: the Pylos campaign had, after all, been studied a good deal in the past and no-one was more surprised than myself when I began to realise how little we in fact knew about it; (b) if Thucydides is as reliable in other cases as he is about Pylos (I can convict him of only one mistake: see Note F, p. 83), we might well be inclined to give his words more weight. In topographical history, at least, it seems to me unreasonable to hold any strong *a priori* views about his reliability and detailed accuracy before subjecting what he says to the sort of methods employed in this book.

---

3. See Appendix.   4. Pritchett, pp. 6 - 17.

References to other literature (see also Appendix)

Because of the complexities of the subject-matter, the reader will find himself obliged to refer to the Thucydidean text, to the maps, to other (cross-referenced) notes and so forth. I have preferred not to add to this burden by frequent references to other writers on Thucydides - for instance, to the very numerous editors and commentators whose work would normally require some acknowledgement. I have, in fact, referred often to Gomme, to authors of particular topographical importance (notably Pritchett), and to a few other scholars whose works are given in the Short Bibliography. I think that the reader will find it easiest to elicit other references from Gomme and from other works mentioned in the bibliography: these works are briefly discussed and evaluated in the Appendix. This seems better than the alternative of giving full references myself: almost every line of Thucydides has been exhaustively discussed, and such references would have enormously increased the length and complexity of this book. I hope that neither contemporary scholars nor the shades of those now in Elysium will feel slighted by this procedure, which is purely one of convenience.

TEXT AND TRANSLATION

TEXT

ΘΟΥΚΥΔΙΔΟΥ ΙΣΤΟΡΙΩΝ Δ

2 Ὑπὸ δὲ τοὺς αὐτοὺς χρόνους τοῦ ἦρος, πρὶν τὸν σῖτον ἐν ἀκμῇ εἶναι, Πελοποννήσιοι καὶ οἱ ξύμμαχοι ἐσέβαλον ἐς τὴν Ἀττικήν (ἡγεῖτο δὲ Ἆγις ὁ Ἀρχιδάμου Λακεδαιμονίων 2 βασιλεύς), καὶ ἐγκαθεζόμενοι ἐδῄουν τὴν γῆν. Ἀθηναῖοι δὲ τάς τε τεσσαράκοντα ναῦς ἐς Σικελίαν ἀπέστειλαν, ὥσπερ παρεσκευάζοντο, καὶ στρατηγοὺς τοὺς ὑπολοίπους Εὐρυμέδοντα καὶ Σοφοκλέα· Πυθόδωρος γὰρ ὁ τρίτος αὐτῶν ἤδη 3 προαφῖκτο ἐς Σικελίαν. εἶπον δὲ τούτοις καὶ Κερκυραίων ἅμα παραπλέοντας τῶν ἐν τῇ πόλει ἐπιμεληθῆναι, οἳ ἐλῃστεύοντο ὑπὸ τῶν ἐν τῷ ὄρει φυγάδων· καὶ Πελοποννησίων αὐτόσε νῆες ἑξήκοντα παρεπεπλεύκεσαν τοῖς ἐν τῷ ὄρει τιμωροὶ καὶ λιμοῦ ὄντος μεγάλου ἐν τῇ πόλει νομίζοντες 4 κατασχήσειν ῥᾳδίως τὰ πράγματα. Δημοσθένει δὲ ὄντι ἰδιώτῃ μετὰ τὴν ἀναχώρησιν τὴν ἐξ Ἀκαρνανίας αὐτῷ δεηθέντι εἶπον χρῆσθαι ταῖς ναυσὶ ταύταις, ἢν βούληται, περὶ τὴν Πελοπόννησον.

3 Καὶ ὡς ἐγένοντο πλέοντες κατὰ τὴν Λακωνικὴν καὶ ἐπυνθάνοντο ὅτι αἱ νῆες ἐν Κερκύρᾳ ἤδη εἰσὶ τῶν Πελοποννησίων, ὁ μὲν Εὐρυμέδων καὶ Σοφοκλῆς ἠπείγοντο ἐς τὴν Κέρκυραν, ὁ δὲ Δημοσθένης ἐς τὴν Πύλον πρῶτον ἐκέλευε σχόντας αὐτοὺς καὶ πράξαντας ἃ δεῖ τὸν πλοῦν ποιεῖσθαι· ἀντιλεγόντων δὲ κατὰ τύχην χειμὼν ἐπιγενόμενος 2 κατήνεγκε τὰς ναῦς ἐς τὴν Πύλον. καὶ ὁ Δημοσθένης εὐθὺς ἠξίου τειχίζεσθαι τὸ χωρίον (ἐπὶ τοῦτο γὰρ ξυνεκπλεῦσαι), καὶ ἀπέφαινε πολλὴν εὐπορίαν ξύλων τε καὶ λίθων, καὶ φύσει καρτερὸν ὂν καὶ ἐρῆμον αὐτό τε καὶ ἐπὶ πολὺ τῆς χώρας· ἀπέχει γὰρ σταδίους μάλιστα ἡ Πύλος τῆς Σπάρτης τετρακοσίους καὶ ἔστιν ἐν τῇ Μεσσηνίᾳ ποτὲ οὔσῃ γῇ, καλοῦσι δὲ αὐτὴν οἱ Λακεδαιμόνιοι Κορυφάσιον. 3 οἱ δὲ πολλὰς ἔφασαν εἶναι ἄκρας ἐρήμους τῆς Πελοποννήσου, ἢν βούληται καταλαμβάνων τὴν πόλιν δαπανᾶν. τῷ δὲ διάφορόν τι ἐδόκει εἶναι τοῦτο τὸ χωρίον ἑτέρου μᾶλλον, λιμένος τε προσόντος καὶ τοὺς Μεσσηνίους οἰκείους ὄντας αὐτῷ τὸ ἀρχαῖον καὶ ὁμοφώνους τοῖς Λακεδαιμονίοις πλεῖστ’ ἂν βλάπτειν ἐξ αὐτοῦ ὁρμωμένους, καὶ βεβαίους ἅμα τοῦ

6

TRANSLATION

THUCYDIDES Bk. IV, Section 2 onwards

About the same time in spring, before the corn was fully ripe, the Peloponnesians and allies invaded Attica: their leader was Agis the son of Archidamos, one of the kings of the Lacedaimonians. They settled down and ravaged the land. The Athenians sent off the 40 ships to Sicily, as they had made preparations to do, and with them the remaining generals, Eurymedon and Sophocles: for Pythodorus, the third general, had already arrived in Sicily. They further instructed these generals to sail via Corcyra, and look after the Corcyreans in the city, who were being plundered by the exiles in the mountains: moreover, 60 Peloponnesian ships had already sailed there to support the exiles in the mountains, and the Peloponnesians thought that they would easily gain control of affairs, since there was a great famine in the city. Demosthenes held no official position since his return from Acarnania; but at his own request the Athenians instructed him to use these 40 ships, if he thought fit, for operations round the Peloponnese.

As they were sailing off the coast of Laconia, they learned that the Peloponnesian ships were already at Corcyra. Eurymedon and Sophocles were pressing on to Corcyra; but Demosthenes told them to put in at Pylos first, do what was necessary, and then sail on. They objected; but by chance a storm arose, and carried the ships to Pylos. Demosthenes said at once that they ought to fortify the place (for that was why he had sailed with them). He pointed out that there was plenty of wood and stone, and that the place was naturally a strong one, and deserted - both Pylos itself and the country for some distance around. For Pylos is about 400 stades from Sparta; it is in what was once the land of Messenia. The Spartans call it Koryphasion. The generals said that there were plenty of deserted promontories in the Peloponnese, if he wanted to occupy one and put the city to expense; but Demosthenes thought that this place had important differences when compared with any other. There was a harbour next to it, and the Messenians had been natives of the land in the old days: they spoke a dialect similar to the Lacedaimonians', and would be able to do them a great deal of damage if they used Pylos as a base - also, they would make a reliable garrison for it.

I prefer to omit οὔτε τοὺς στρατιώτας. See Note C, pp. 62 - 64.

4 χωρίου φύλακας ἔσεσθαι. ὡς δὲ οὐκ ἔπειθεν οὔτε τοὺς στρατηγοὺς οὔτε τοὺς στρατιώτας, ὕστερον καὶ τοῖς ταξιάρχοις κοινώσας, ἡσύχαζεν ὑπὸ ἀπλοίας, μέχρι αὐτοῖς τοῖς στρατιώταις σχολάζουσιν ὁρμὴ ἐνέπεσε περιστᾶσιν ἐκτειχίσαι

2 τὸ χωρίον. καὶ ἐγχειρήσαντες εἰργάζοντο, σιδήρια μὲν λιθουργὰ οὐκ ἔχοντες, λογάδην δὲ φέροντες λίθους, καὶ ξυνετίθεσαν ὡς ἕκαστόν τι ξυμβαίνοι· καὶ τὸν πηλόν, εἴ που δέοι χρῆσθαι, ἀγγείων ἀπορίᾳ ἐπὶ τοῦ νώτου ἔφερον, ἐγκεκυφότες τε, ὡς μάλιστα μέλλοι ἐπιμένειν, καὶ τὼ χεῖρε

3 ἐς τοὐπίσω ξυμπλέκοντες, ὅπως μὴ ἀποπίπτοι. παντί τε τρόπῳ ἠπείγοντο φθῆναι τοὺς Λακεδαιμονίους τὰ ἐπιμαχώτατα ἐξεργασάμενοι πρὶν ἐπιβοηθῆσαι· τὸ γὰρ πλέον τοῦ

5 χωρίου αὐτὸ καρτερὸν ὑπῆρχε καὶ οὐδὲν ἔδει τείχους. οἱ δὲ ἑορτήν τινα ἔτυχον ἄγοντες καὶ ἅμα πυνθανόμενοι ἐν ὀλιγωρίᾳ ἐποιοῦντο, ὡς, ὅταν ἐξέλθωσιν, ἢ οὐχ ὑπομενοῦντας σφᾶς ἢ ῥᾳδίως ληψόμενοι βίᾳ· καί τι καὶ αὐτοὺς

2 ὁ στρατὸς ἔτι ἐν ταῖς Ἀθήναις ὢν ἐπέσχεν. τειχίσαντες δὲ οἱ Ἀθηναῖοι τοῦ χωρίου τὰ πρὸς ἤπειρον καὶ ἃ μάλιστα ἔδει ἐν ἡμέραις ἓξ τὸν μὲν Δημοσθένη μετὰ νεῶν πέντε αὐτοῦ φύλακα καταλείπουσι, ταῖς δὲ πλείοσι ναυσὶ τὸν ἐς τὴν Κέρκυραν πλοῦν καὶ Σικελίαν ἠπείγοντο.

6 Οἱ δ' ἐν τῇ Ἀττικῇ ὄντες Πελοποννήσιοι ὡς ἐπύθοντο τῆς Πύλου κατειλημμένης, ἀνεχώρουν κατὰ τάχος ἐπ' οἴκου, νομίζοντες μὲν οἱ Λακεδαιμόνιοι καὶ Ἆγις ὁ βασιλεὺς οἰκεῖον σφίσι τὸ περὶ τὴν Πύλον· ἅμα δὲ πρῷ ἐσβαλόντες καὶ τοῦ σίτου ἔτι χλωροῦ ὄντος ἐσπάνιζον τροφῆς τοῖς πολλοῖς, χειμών τε ἐπιγενόμενος μείζων παρὰ τὴν καθεστη-

2 κυῖαν ὥραν ἐπίεσε τὸ στράτευμα. ὥστε πολλαχόθεν ξυνέβη ἀναχωρῆσαί τε θᾶσσον αὐτοὺς καὶ βραχυτάτην γενέσθαι τὴν ἐσβολὴν ταύτην· ἡμέρας γὰρ πέντε καὶ δέκα ἔμειναν ἐν τῇ Ἀττικῇ.

* * *

8 Ἀναχωρησάντων δὲ τῶν ἐκ τῆς Ἀττικῆς Πελοποννησίων οἱ Σπαρτιᾶται αὐτοὶ μὲν καὶ οἱ ἐγγύτατα τῶν περιοίκων εὐθὺς ἐβοήθουν ἐπὶ τὴν Πύλον, τῶν δὲ ἄλλων Λακεδαιμονίων βραδυτέρα ἐγίγνετο ἡ ἔφοδος, ἄρτι ἀφιγμένων ἀφ'

2 ἑτέρας στρατείας. περιήγγελλον δὲ καὶ κατὰ τὴν Πελοπόννησον βοηθεῖν ὅτι τάχιστα ἐπὶ Πύλον καὶ ἐπὶ τὰς ἐν τῇ Κερκύρᾳ ναῦς σφῶν τὰς ἑξήκοντα ἔπεμψαν, αἳ ὑπερενεχθεῖσαι τὸν Λευκαδίων ἰσθμὸν καὶ λαθοῦσαι τὰς ἐν Ζακύνθῳ Ἀττικὰς ναῦς ἀφικνοῦνται ἐπὶ Πύλον· παρῆν δὲ ἤδη καὶ ὁ πεζὸς

8

However, he failed to persuade the generals, and also the taxiarchs when he talked to them afterwards; so, since they could not sail, he did nothing - until the soldiers themselves, who were unoccupied, took the initiative and posted themselves around Pylos so as to fortify it. They took this task in hand and worked away at it; they had no iron tools for shaping stones, but they selected the stones, carried them, and put them together as each one happened to fit. When they needed to use mortar anywhere, they carried it on their backs (since they had nothing to hold it in), bending double so that it would stay on better, and clasping their hands together behind them so that it should not fall off. They made haste by every means in their power to finish fortifying the most vulnerable parts before the Spartans could bring up their forces: though most of the place was naturally strong and needed no fortifying.

The Spartans were holding a festival at the time, and anyway did not take the news seriously when they heard it: they thought that, when they marched out against Pylos, either the Athenians would leave or they would easily capture it by an assault. The fact that their army was still in the vicinity of Athens also held them back to some extent. The Athenians fortified the place in those parts which faced the mainland, and the other most important parts, in 6 days. They left Demosthenes there with 5 ships to guard it, and hurried on with the majority of their fleet on the route to Corcyra and Sicily.

When the Peloponnesians who were in Attica learned that Pylos had been captured, they returned home at once. The Spartans, and Agis their king, thought that the events concerned them closely; also, they had invaded Attica early while the corn was still green, and most of their troops were short of provisions. Moreover, the weather was unusually stormy for the time of year, and this caused hardship to the army. Hence it came about, from many causes, that they retired more quickly than usual, and that this invasion was very short: for they only stayed 15 days in Attica.

*   *   *

When the Peloponnesians had retired from Attica, the Spartiates and those of the perioikoi who lived nearest went off immediately to cope with the situation at Pylos. The other Lacedaimonians, having just returned from another expedition, arrived more slowly. They also sent messages around the Peloponnese for reinforcements to come to Pylos as soon as possible, and had already sent a message to their fleet of 60 ships at Corcyra. These latter were dragged over the Leucadian isthmus, passed by the Attic fleet at Zacynthos unseen, and thus reached Pylos, where the land army had already arrived.

3 στρατός. Δημοσθένης δὲ προσπλεόντων ἔτι τῶν Πελοποννησίων ὑπεκπέμπει φθάσας δύο ναῦς ἀγγεῖλαι Εὐρυμέδοντι
καὶ τοῖς ἐν ταῖς ναυσὶν ἐν Ζακύνθῳ Ἀθηναίοις παρεῖναι ὡς
4 τοῦ χωρίου κινδυνεύοντος. καὶ αἱ μὲν νῆες κατὰ τάχος
ἔπλεον κατὰ τὰ ἐπεσταλμένα ὑπὸ Δημοσθένους· οἱ δὲ
Λακεδαιμόνιοι παρεσκευάζοντο ὡς τῷ τειχίσματι προσ-
βαλοῦντες κατά τε γῆν καὶ κατὰ θάλασσαν, ἐλπίζοντες
ῥᾳδίως αἱρήσειν οἰκοδόμημα διὰ ταχέων εἰργασμένον καὶ
5 ἀνθρώπων ὀλίγων ἐνόντων. προσδεχόμενοι δὲ καὶ τὴν ἀπὸ
τῆς Ζακύνθου τῶν Ἀττικῶν νεῶν βοήθειαν ἐν νῷ εἶχον, ἢν
ἄρα μὴ πρότερον ἕλωσι, καὶ τοὺς ἔσπλους τοῦ λιμένος
ἐμφάρξαι, ὅπως μὴ ᾖ τοῖς Ἀθηναίοις ἐφορμίσασθαι ἐς
6 αὐτόν. ἡ γὰρ νῆσος ἡ Σφακτηρία καλουμένη τόν τε
λιμένα παρατείνουσα καὶ ἐγγὺς ἐπικειμένη ἐχυρὸν ποιεῖ καὶ
τοὺς ἔσπλους στενούς, τῇ μὲν δυοῖν νεοῖν διάπλουν κατὰ τὸ
τείχισμα τῶν Ἀθηναίων καὶ τὴν Πύλον, τῇ δὲ πρὸς τὴν
ἄλλην ἤπειρον ὀκτὼ ἢ ἐννέα· ὑλώδης τε καὶ ἀτριβὴς πᾶσα
ὑπ' ἐρημίας ἦν καὶ μέγεθος περὶ πέντε καὶ δέκα σταδίους

I prefer πέντε καὶ
εἴκοσι. See Note A, p.52.

7 μάλιστα. τοὺς μὲν οὖν ἔσπλους ταῖς ναυσὶν ἀντιπρώροις
βύζην κλήσειν ἔμελλον· τὴν δὲ νῆσον ταύτην φοβούμενοι
μὴ ἐξ αὐτῆς τὸν πόλεμον σφίσι ποιῶνται, ὁπλίτας διεβί-
βασαν ἐς αὐτὴν καὶ παρὰ τὴν ἤπειρον ἄλλους ἔταξαν.
8 οὕτω γὰρ τοῖς Ἀθηναίοις τήν τε νῆσον πολεμίαν ἔσεσθαι
τήν τε ἤπειρον, ἀπόβασιν οὐκ ἔχουσαν (τὰ γὰρ αὐτῆς τῆς
Πύλου ἔξω τοῦ ἔσπλου πρὸς τὸ πέλαγος ἀλίμενα ὄντα οὐχ
ἕξειν ὅθεν ὁρμώμενοι ὠφελήσουσι τοὺς αὑτῶν) σφεῖς δὲ
ἄνευ τε ναυμαχίας καὶ κινδύνου ἐκπολιορκήσειν τὸ χωρίον
κατὰ τὸ εἰκός, σίτου τε οὐκ ἐνόντος καὶ δι' ὀλίγης παρα-
9 σκευῆς κατειλημμένον. ὡς δ' ἐδόκει αὐτοῖς ταῦτα, καὶ
διεβίβαζον ἐς τὴν νῆσον τοὺς ὁπλίτας ἀποκληρώσαντες ἀπὸ
πάντων τῶν λόχων. καὶ διέβησαν μὲν καὶ ἄλλοι πρότερον
κατὰ διαδοχήν, οἱ δὲ τελευταῖοι καὶ ἐγκαταληφθέντες εἴκοσι
καὶ τετρακόσιοι ἦσαν καὶ Εἴλωτες οἱ περὶ αὐτούς· ἦρχε δὲ
αὐτῶν Ἐπιτάδας ὁ Μολόβρου.

9 Δημοσθένης δὲ ὁρῶν τοὺς Λακεδαιμονίους μέλλοντας
προσβάλλειν ναυσί τε ἅμα καὶ πεζῷ παρεσκευάζετο καὶ αὐτός,
καὶ τὰς τριήρεις αἳ περιῆσαν αὐτῷ ἀπὸ τῶν καταλειφθεισῶν
ἀνασπάσας ὑπὸ τὸ τείχισμα προσεσταύρωσε, καὶ τοὺς
ναύτας ἐξ αὐτῶν ὥπλισεν ἀσπίσι [τε] φαύλαις καὶ οἰσυΐναις
ταῖς πολλαῖς· οὐ γὰρ ἦν ὅπλα ἐν χωρίῳ ἐρήμῳ πορίσασθαι,
ἀλλὰ καὶ ταῦτα ἐκ λῃστρικῆς Μεσσηνίων τριακοντόρου καὶ
κέλητος ἔλαβον, οἳ ἔτυχον παραγενόμενοι. ὁπλῖταί τε

10

While the Peloponnesian fleet was still on its way, Demosthenes anticipated its arrival and secretly sent off two ships to tell Eurymedon and the fleet at Zacynthos to come to Pylos, as the place was in danger.

The Athenian fleet, then, was hastening on its way according to Demosthenes' instructions; and the Lacedaimonians were preparing to make an attack on the fort by land and by sea. They thought they would capture such a construction easily, since it had been built quickly and was manned by only a few troops. They also expected the Attic fleet from Zacynthos to come to the rescue, and intended - if they had not captured Pylos by that time - to block up the entrances to the harbour, so that the Athenians could not sail in and use it as an anchorage. (The island called Sphacteria extends alongside the harbour, and lies close to it: hence the anchorage is safe and the entrances narrow - the entrance by Pylos and the Athenian fortifications giving a passage for two ships through the channel, and the entrance by the mainland on the other side a passage for eight or nine. Being uninhabited, it was wholly covered with thickets and had no paths: and it is about 25 stades in length.)

These entrances, then, they intended to block up tightly with ships lying parallel to each other, prows to the enemy: and since they were frightened that the Athenians might use Sphacteria as a military base, they ferried hoplites across to it, and stationed others along the mainland. By this plan, they thought, the Athenians would find both the island to be enemy-occupied and the mainland, which gave them no chance of landing (for the coast of Pylos itself, outside the entrance and towards the open sea, is harbourless, and would give them no base of operations to help their troops); and equally they themselves would probably be able to capture the place by siege, without a sea-battle or any unnecessary danger - there was no food in it, and it had not been properly prepared for a siege. This, then, was their agreed plan: and they took the hoplites across to the island, selecting them by lot from all the companies. Different relays of troops succeeded each other at the beginning: but the ones who were there at the end, and were cut off, numbered 420, not counting the attendant helots. Their commander was Epitadas, son of Molobros.

Demosthenes saw that the Lacedaimonians were going to attack with their fleet and their land army at the same time, so he made his preparations too. Of the original triremes that had been left behind, he dragged up those that still remained under the fortifications, and erected a palisade in front of them. The crews that had been in them he armed with shields - poor-quality ones made of wickerwork for the most part: for there was no chance of getting weapons in this uninhabited territory. Even these were obtained from a thirty-oared privateer and a light boat belonging to some Messenians, who had just arrived. There were about 40 hoplites among these Messenians, and he used them with the rest of the hoplites.

τῶν Μεσσηνίων τούτων ὡς τεσσαράκοντα ἐγένοντο, οἷς
2 ἐχρῆτο μετὰ τῶν ἄλλων. τοὺς μὲν οὖν πολλοὺς τῶν τε
ἀόπλων καὶ ὡπλισμένων ἐπὶ τὰ τετειχισμένα μάλιστα καὶ
ἐχυρὰ τοῦ χωρίου πρὸς τὴν ἤπειρον ἔταξε, προειπὼν ἀμύνασθαι τὸν πεζόν, ἢν προσβάλῃ· αὐτὸς δὲ ἀπολεξάμενος ἐκ
πάντων ἑξήκοντα ὁπλίτας καὶ τοξότας ὀλίγους ἐχώρει ἔξω
τοῦ τείχους ἐπὶ τὴν θάλασσαν, ᾗ μάλιστα ἐκείνους προσεδέχετο πειράσειν ἀποβαίνειν, ἐς χωρία μὲν χαλεπὰ καὶ
πετρώδη πρὸς τὸ πέλαγος τετραμμένα, σφίσι δὲ τοῦ τείχους
ταύτῃ ἀσθενεστάτου ὄντος ἐσβιάσασθαι αὐτοὺς ἡγεῖτο προ-
3 θυμήσεσθαι· οὔτε γὰρ αὐτοὶ ἐλπίζοντές ποτε ναυσὶ κρατήσεσθαι οὐκ ἰσχυρὸν ἐτείχιζον, ἐκείνοις τε βιαζομένοις τὴν
4 ἀπόβασιν ἁλώσιμον τὸ χωρίον γίγνεσθαι. κατὰ τοῦτο οὖν
πρὸς αὐτὴν τὴν θάλασσαν χωρήσας ἔταξε τοὺς ὁπλίτας ὡς
εἴρξων, ἢν δύνηται, καὶ παρεκελεύσατο τοιάδε.

10   'Ἄνδρες οἱ ξυναράμενοι τοῦδε τοῦ κινδύνου, μηδεὶς ὑμῶν
ἐν τῇ τοιᾷδε ἀνάγκῃ ξυνετὸς βουλέσθω δοκεῖν εἶναι,
ἐκλογιζόμενος ἅπαν τὸ περιεστὸς ἡμᾶς δεινόν, μᾶλλον ἢ
ἀπερισκέπτως εὔελπις ὁμόσε χωρῆσαι τοῖς ἐναντίοις καὶ ἐκ
τούτων ἂν περιγενόμενος. ὅσα γὰρ ἐς ἀνάγκην ἀφῖκται
ὥσπερ τάδε, λογισμὸν ἥκιστα ἐνδεχόμενα κινδύνου τοῦ
2 ταχίστου προσδεῖται. ἐγὼ δὲ καὶ τὰ πλείω ὁρῶ πρὸς ἡμῶν
ὄντα, ἢν ἐθέλωμέν τε μεῖναι καὶ μὴ τῷ πλήθει αὐτῶν κατα-
3 πλαγέντες τὰ ὑπάρχοντα ἡμῖν κρείσσω καταπροδοῦναι. τοῦ
τε γὰρ χωρίου τὸ δυσέμβατον ἡμέτερον νομίζω, ὃ μενόντων
μὲν ἡμῶν ξύμμαχον γίγνεται, ὑποχωρήσασι δὲ καίπερ χαλεπὸν ὂν εὔπορον ἔσται μηδενὸς κωλύοντος, καὶ τὸν πολέμιον
δεινότερον ἕξομεν μὴ ῥᾳδίας αὐτῷ πάλιν οὔσης τῆς ἀναχωρή-
σεως, ἢν καὶ ὑφ' ἡμῶν βιάζηται (ἐπὶ γὰρ ταῖς ναυσὶ ῥᾷστοί
4 εἰσιν ἀμύνεσθαι, ἀποβάντες δὲ ἐν τῷ ἴσῳ ἤδη), τό τε πλῆθος
αὐτῶν οὐκ ἄγαν δεῖ φοβεῖσθαι· κατ' ὀλίγον γὰρ μαχεῖται
καίπερ πολὺ ὂν ἀπορίᾳ τῆς προσορμίσεως, καὶ οὐκ ἐν γῇ
στρατός ἐστιν ἐκ τοῦ ὁμοίου μείζων, ἀλλ' ἀπὸ νεῶν, αἷς
5 πολλὰ τὰ καίρια δεῖ ἐν τῇ θαλάσσῃ ξυμβῆναι. ὥστε τὰς
τούτων ἀπορίας ἀντιπάλους ἡγοῦμαι τῷ ἡμετέρῳ πλήθει,
καὶ ἅμα ἀξιῶ ὑμᾶς, Ἀθηναίους ὄντας καὶ ἐπισταμένους
ἐμπειρίᾳ τὴν ναυτικὴν ἐπ' ἄλλους ἀπόβασιν ὅτι, εἴ τις
ὑπομένοι καὶ μὴ φόβῳ ῥοθίου καὶ νεῶν δεινότητος κατάπλου
ὑποχωροίη, οὐκ ἄν ποτε βιάζοιτο, καὶ αὐτοὺς νῦν μεῖναί τε
καὶ ἀμυνομένους παρ' αὐτὴν τὴν ῥαχίαν σῴζειν ἡμᾶς τε
5 αὐτοὺς καὶ τὸ χωρίον.'

12

Most of his troops, both the armed and the unarmed, he stationed in the best-fortified and strongest parts of the place, facing the mainland: and he ordered them to repel any attack by the land army. He himself selected 60 hoplites and a few archers out of all his force, and went down outside the wall to the sea, to the point where he thought it most likely that the Lacedaimonians would try to land. The terrain here faced the open sea, and was rough and rocky: but he thought that they would be eager to force an entrance here because the Athenian wall was weakest in this place. (This was because the Athenians had never expected to be inferior in sea-power, and hence had not fortified it strongly.) He realised that if the Lacedaimonians forced a landing, the place could easily be taken. At this point, then, he went right down to the sea and stationed the hoplites there so as to keep the Lacedaimonians off, if he could. Then he addressed them in these terms:

"Men, we are all in this dangerous situation together. In a critical position like this one, none of you must try to be thought clever by calculating all the perils of our position. It is better not to think about them, but just get straight to grips with the enemy, and be confident that we shall survive even these dangers. For in such a crisis as this, calculations are beside the point: we need to act quickly, whatever the dangers. Actually, I myself consider that most of the factors favour us, provided only we stand firm: we must not be frightened of the enemy's numbers and throw away the advantages we have. I would count the difficulty of the terrain for landing in our favour - it is an advantage, anyway, as long as we stand our ground. But if we retreat, the enemy will find it easy enough to cross without anyone stopping them, rough though it is; and even if we do force them back later, they will be much harder to deal with because they will have no easy means of retreat. They are easiest to beat off when they are still on their ships: once they've landed, they will at once be on an equal footing with us.

"There is no reason to worry too much about their numbers: although they are large, they will have to fight in small sections at a time, for lack of anywhere to land nearby. Again, we are not fighting with a land army bigger than ours, on an equal footing: they have to fight from ships, and ships at sea need a lot of good luck. Consequently I think that their disadvantages counterbalance our small numbers. You are Athenians, and know by experience how difficult it is to force a landing against an enemy: you know that if a man stands firm, and does not retreat through fear of the splashing oars and the grim look of a ship bearing down on him, he can never be forced back. I now call on you yourselves, then, to stand firm, beat off this attack right by the water's edge, and save both ourselves and our fort".

11 Τοσαῦτα τοῦ Δημοσθένους παρακελευσαμένου οἱ Ἀθηναῖοι ἐθάρσησάν τε μᾶλλον καὶ ἐπικαταβάντες ἐτάξαντο παρ' αὐτὴν
2 τὴν θάλασσαν. οἱ δὲ Λακεδαιμόνιοι ἄραντες τῷ τε κατὰ γῆν στρατῷ προσέβαλλον τῷ τειχίσματι καὶ ταῖς ναυσὶν ἅμα οὔσαις τεσσαράκοντα καὶ τρισί, ναύαρχος δὲ αὐτῶν ἐπέπλει Θρασυμηλίδας ὁ Κρατησικλέους Σπαρτιάτης. προσέβαλλε
3 δὲ ᾗπερ ὁ Δημοσθένης προσεδέχετο. καὶ οἱ μὲν Ἀθηναῖοι ἀμφοτέρωθεν ἔκ τε γῆς καὶ ἐκ θαλάσσης ἠμύνοντο· οἱ δὲ κατ' ὀλίγας ναῦς διελόμενοι, διότι οὐκ ἦν πλέοσι προσσχεῖν, καὶ ἀναπαύοντες ἐν τῷ μέρει τοὺς ἐπίπλους ἐποιοῦντο, προθυμίᾳ τε πάσῃ χρώμενοι καὶ παρακελευσμῷ, εἴ πως ὠσάμενοι
4 ἕλοιεν τὸ τείχισμα. πάντων δὲ φανερώτατος Βρασίδας ἐγένετο. τριηραρχῶν γὰρ καὶ ὁρῶν τοῦ χωρίου χαλεποῦ ὄντος τοὺς τριηράρχους καὶ κυβερνήτας, εἴ που καὶ δοκοίη δυνατὸν εἶναι σχεῖν, ἀποκνοῦντας καὶ φυλασσομένους τῶν νεῶν μὴ ξυντρίψωσιν, ἐβόα λέγων ὡς οὐκ εἰκὸς εἴη ξύλων φειδομένους τοὺς πολεμίους ἐν τῇ χώρᾳ περιδεῖν τεῖχος πεποιημένους, ἀλλὰ τάς τε σφετέρας ναῦς βιαζομένους τὴν ἀπόβασιν καταγνύναι ἐκέλευε, καὶ τοὺς ξυμμάχους μὴ ἀποκνῆσαι ἀντὶ μεγάλων εὐεργεσιῶν τὰς ναῦς τοῖς Λακεδαιμονίοις ἐν τῷ παρόντι ἐπιδοῦναι, ὀκείλαντας δὲ καὶ παντὶ τρόπῳ
12 ἀποβάντας τῶν τε ἀνδρῶν καὶ τοῦ χωρίου κρατῆσαι. καὶ ὁ μὲν τούς τε ἄλλους τοιαῦτα ἐπέσπερχε καὶ τὸν ἑαυτοῦ κυβερνήτην ἀναγκάσας ὀκεῖλαι τὴν ναῦν ἐχώρει ἐπὶ τὴν ἀποβάθραν· καὶ πειρώμενος ἀποβαίνειν ἀνεκόπη ὑπὸ τῶν Ἀθηναίων, καὶ τραυματισθεὶς πολλὰ ἐλιποψύχησέ τε καὶ πεσόντος αὐτοῦ ἐς τὴν παρεξειρεσίαν ἡ ἀσπὶς περιερρύη ἐς τὴν θάλασσαν, καὶ ἐξενεχθείσης αὐτῆς ἐς τὴν γῆν οἱ Ἀθηναῖοι ἀνελόμενοι ὕστερον πρὸς τὸ τροπαῖον ἐχρήσαντο
2 ὃ ἔστησαν τῆς προσβολῆς ταύτης. οἱ δ' ἄλλοι προυθυμοῦντο μέν, ἀδύνατοι δ' ἦσαν ἀποβῆναι τῶν τε χωρίων χαλεπότητι
3 καὶ τῶν Ἀθηναίων μενόντων καὶ οὐδὲν ὑποχωρούντων. ἐς τοῦτό τε περιέστη ἡ τύχη ὥστε Ἀθηναίους μὲν ἐκ γῆς τε καὶ ταύτης Λακωνικῆς ἀμύνεσθαι ἐκείνους ἐπιπλέοντας, Λακεδαιμονίους δὲ ἐκ νεῶν τε καὶ ἐς τὴν ἑαυτῶν πολεμίαν οὖσαν ἐπ' Ἀθηναίους ἀποβαίνειν· ἐπὶ πολὺ γὰρ ἐποίει τῆς δόξης ἐν τῷ τότε τοῖς μὲν ἠπειρώταις μάλιστα εἶναι καὶ τὰ πεζὰ κρατίστοις, τοῖς δὲ θαλασσίοις τε καὶ ταῖς ναυσὶ πλεῖστον προύχειν.

After Demosthenes had encouraged them in this way, the Athenians felt more confident. They went down to the shore and stationed themselves right along the water's edge. The Lacedaimonians now started to move, and attacked the fort with their land army and with their ships simultaneously. There were 43 ships; the admiral on board was Thrasymelidas, the son of Cratesicles, a Spartiate, and he attacked just where Demosthenes had expected it. The Athenians defended themselves on both sides, land and sea. The Lacedaimonians divided up their fleet into sections of a few ships each, because they could not put in to shore with any more at once: they rested in turn and then attacked. They encouraged each other and showed great spirit in their attempts to force a landing and capture the fort.

Brasidas was the most conspicuous of them all. He was in command of a trireme; and if he saw any of the commanders or helmsmen hesitating (for the shore was hard to land on) and being careful about smashing up their ships, even at places where a landing seemed possible, he shouted to them:"There's no point in sparing timber - our enemies have built a fort on our territory and we can't tolerate it. Wreck the ships completely if you can only force a landing!" To the allies he shouted: "Think of all that the Lacedaimonians have done for you, and don't hesitate to sacrifice your ships for them now! Drive them on shore, make a landing by any possible means, take the fort and the men in it!" With such remarks he spurred on the others; and he made his helmsmen run his own ship aground, and got onto the gangway. He tried to land, but was beaten back by the Athenians and badly wounded: he fainted, and fell back onto the outrigger. His shield fell off into the sea: it was washed ashore, and the Athenians picked it up later and used it for the trophy which they set up to commemorate this attack.

The others were keen enough, but simply could not force a landing, because the terrain was so difficult, and the Athenians stood firm and retreated not at all. In this situation, fortune had reversed the usual circumstances: the Athenians were beating off a Lacedaimonian sea-borne attack from land, and Lacedaimonian land too: the Lacedaimonians were trying to force a landing from ships against the Athenians onto land which was their own, but yet enemy territory! The remarkable thing about this was that the Lacedaimonians' general reputation then was that of a land power, distinguished for military strength, whereas the Athenians were considered to be a sea-power and superior in all naval engagements.

13 Ταύτην μὲν οὖν τὴν ἡμέραν καὶ τῆς ὑστεραίας μέρος τι προσβολὰς ποιησάμενοι ἐπέπαυντο· καὶ τῇ τρίτῃ ἐπὶ ξύλα ἐς μηχανὰς παρέπεμψαν τῶν νεῶν τινὰς ἐς Ἀσίνην, ἐλπίζοντες τὸ κατὰ τὸν λιμένα τεῖχος ὕψος μὲν ἔχειν, ἀποβάσεως

2 δὲ μάλιστα οὔσης ἑλεῖν ⟨ἂν⟩ μηχαναῖς. ἐν τούτῳ δὲ αἱ ἐκ τῆς Ζακύνθου νῆες τῶν Ἀθηναίων παραγίγνονται τεσσαράκοντα· προσεβοήθησαν γὰρ τῶν τε φρουρίδων τινὲς αὐτοῖς τῶν ἐκ

3 Ναυπάκτου καὶ Χῖαι τέσσαρες. ὡς δὲ εἶδον τήν τε ἤπειρον ὁπλιτῶν περίπλεων τήν τε νῆσον, ἔν τε τῷ λιμένι οὔσας τὰς ναῦς καὶ οὐκ ἐκπλεούσας, ἀπορήσαντες ὅπη καθορμίσωνται, τότε μὲν ἐς Πρωτὴν τὴν νῆσον, ἣ οὐ πολὺ ἀπέχει ἐρῆμος οὖσα, ἔπλευσαν καὶ ηὐλίσαντο, τῇ δ' ὑστεραίᾳ παρασκευασάμενοι ὡς ἐπὶ ναυμαχίαν ἀνήγοντο, ἢν μὲν ἀντεκπλεῖν ἐθέλωσι σφίσιν

4 ἐς τὴν εὐρυχωρίαν, εἰ δὲ μή, ὡς αὐτοὶ ἐπεσπλευσούμενοι. καὶ οἱ μὲν οὔτε ἀντανήγοντο οὔτε ἃ διενοήθησαν, φάρξαι τοὺς ἔσπλους, ἔτυχον ποιήσαντες, ἡσυχάζοντες δ' ἐν τῇ γῇ τάς τε ναῦς ἐπλήρουν καὶ παρεσκευάζοντο, ἢν ἐσπλέῃ τις, ὡς ἐν

14 τῷ λιμένι ὄντι οὐ σμικρῷ ναυμαχήσοντες. οἱ δ' Ἀθηναῖοι γνόντες καθ' ἑκάτερον τὸν ἔσπλουν ὥρμησαν ἐπ' αὐτούς, καὶ τὰς μὲν πλείους καὶ μετεώρους ἤδη τῶν νεῶν καὶ ἀντιπρώρους προσπεσόντες ἐς φυγὴν κατέστησαν, καὶ ἐπιδιώκοντες ὡς διὰ βραχέος ἔτρωσαν μὲν πολλάς, πέντε δὲ ἔλαβον, καὶ μίαν τούτων αὐτοῖς ἀνδράσιν· ταῖς δὲ λοιπαῖς ἐν τῇ γῇ καταπεφευγυίαις ἐνέβαλλον. αἱ δὲ καὶ πληρούμεναι ἔτι πρὶν ἀνάγεσθαι ἐκόπτοντο· καί τινας καὶ ἀναδούμενοι

2 κενὰς εἷλκον τῶν ἀνδρῶν ἐς φυγὴν ὡρμημένων. ἃ ὁρῶντες οἱ Λακεδαιμόνιοι καὶ περιαλγοῦντες τῷ πάθει, ὅτιπερ αὐτῶν οἱ ἄνδρες ἀπελαμβάνοντο ἐν τῇ νήσῳ, παρεβοήθουν, καὶ ἐπεσβαίνοντες ἐς τὴν θάλασσαν ξὺν τοῖς ὅπλοις ἀνθεῖλκον ἐπιλαμβανόμενοι τῶν νεῶν· καὶ ἐν τούτῳ κεκωλῦσθαι ἐδόκει

3 ἕκαστος ᾧ μή τινι καὶ αὐτὸς ἔργῳ παρῆν. ἐγένετό τε ὁ θόρυβος μέγας καὶ ἀντηλλαγμένου τοῦ ἑκατέρων τρόπου περὶ τὰς ναῦς· οἵ τε γὰρ Λακεδαιμόνιοι ὑπὸ προθυμίας καὶ ἐκπλήξεως ὡς εἰπεῖν ἄλλο οὐδὲν ἢ ἐκ γῆς ἐναυμάχουν, οἵ τε Ἀθηναῖοι κρατοῦντες καὶ βουλόμενοι τῇ παρούσῃ τύχῃ

4 ὡς ἐπὶ πλεῖστον ἐπεξελθεῖν ἀπὸ νεῶν ἐπεζομάχουν. πολύν τε πόνον παρασχόντες ἀλλήλοις καὶ τραυματίσαντες διεκρίθησαν, καὶ οἱ Λακεδαιμόνιοι τὰς κενὰς ναῦς πλὴν τῶν τὸ

5 πρῶτον ληφθεισῶν διέσωσαν. καταστάντες δὲ ἑκάτεροι ἐς τὸ στρατόπεδον οἱ μὲν τροπαῖόν τε ἔστησαν καὶ νεκροὺς ἀπέδοσαν καὶ ναυαγίων ἐκράτησαν, καὶ τὴν νῆσον εὐθὺς

So for that day and part of the next the Lacedaimonians made their attack. Then they stopped; and on the third day they sent some of their ships to Asine to get wood for siege-engines. With these engines they hoped to take that part of the wall which faced the harbour: for though the wall was high there, it was the best place to land. Meanwhile the Athenian ships from Zacynthos arrived. They were now 40 in number, for they had been reinforced by some of the guard-ships from Naupactos and 4 Chian ships. The Athenians saw that the mainland and the island were full of Lacedaimonian hoplites, and that the Lacedaimonian fleet was in the harbour and not coming out to meet them: so they did not know where to anchor, and sailed off for the time being to Prote (an uninhabited island not far away), and made their camp there. On the next day they prepared themselves for a sea-battle and put out to sea: either the Lacedaimonians would be willing to come out against them into the open sea, or if not they themselves would sail into the harbour.

The Lacedaimonians did not sail out against them: nor had they in fact blocked the entrances, as they had intended. They stayed on land, showing no signs of moving, engaged only in manning their ships and making preparations to fight in the harbour (which was by no means a small one), in case any Athenians should come in. The Athenians realised this, and rushed in by both entrances to attack them. Most of the Lacedaimonian ships were already in deep water and facing the enemy: the Athenians fell on these and routed them. They pursued them as far as they could in the narrow space, and damaged many: five of them they captured, of which one was fully manned: the rest they rammed after they had fled to the shore. Others of the Lacedaimonian ships they smashed while still being manned, before they had put out to sea: others again they attached ropes to, and began to take in tow, after they had put their crews to flight.

The Lacedaimonians saw all this and were in agonies over the disaster - for now their troops on the island were being cut off. So they ran to the rescue, went out into the sea with their weapons, grabbed hold of the ships and tried to pull them back. Everyone behaved as if the battle was only really being fought at the point where he himself was in action: there was tremendous confusion. In this struggle over the ships each side was fighting in a way characteristic of their opponents. The Lacedaimonians were so alarmed, and so energetic as well, that they were in effect fighting a sea-battle from land; and the Athenians, who were winning and wanted to press home their advantage as far as possible, were fighting on foot from their ships.

Each side gave the other a stiff fight, and many were wounded. Eventually they separated, and the Lacedaimonians managed to save their unmanned ships, except those that had been captured in the beginning of the fight. Both forces then retired to their encampments. The Athenians set up a trophy, gave back the enemy dead, and took possession of the wrecks: then they immediately began to sail round the island and

περιέπλεον καὶ ἐν φυλακῇ εἶχον ὡς τῶν ἀνδρῶν ἀπειλημ-
μένων· οἱ δ' ἐν τῇ ἠπείρῳ Πελοποννήσιοι καὶ ἀπὸ πάντων
ἤδη βεβοηθηκότες ἔμενον κατὰ χώραν ἐπὶ τῇ Πύλῳ.

15 Ἐς δὲ τὴν Σπάρτην ὡς ἠγγέλθη τὰ γεγενημένα περὶ
Πύλον, ἔδοξεν αὐτοῖς ὡς ἐπὶ ξυμφορᾷ μεγάλῃ τὰ τέλη κατα-
βάντας ἐς τὸ στρατόπεδον βουλεύειν παραχρῆμα ὁρῶντας
2 ὅτι ἂν δοκῇ. καὶ ὡς εἶδον ἀδύνατον ὂν τιμωρεῖν τοῖς
ἀνδράσι καὶ κινδυνεύειν οὐκ ἐβούλοντο ἢ ὑπὸ λιμοῦ τι
παθεῖν αὐτοὺς ἢ ὑπὸ πλήθους βιασθέντας κρατηθῆναι,
ἔδοξεν αὐτοῖς πρὸς τοὺς στρατηγοὺς τῶν Ἀθηναίων, ἢν
ἐθέλωσι, σπονδὰς ποιησαμένους τὰ περὶ Πύλον ἀποστεῖλαι
ἐς τὰς Ἀθήνας πρέσβεις περὶ ξυμβάσεως καὶ τοὺς ἄνδρας
16 ὡς τάχιστα πειρᾶσθαι κομίσασθαι. δεξαμένων δὲ τῶν στρατηγῶν τὸν λόγον ἐγίγνοντο σπονδαὶ τοιαίδε, Λακεδαιμονίους
μὲν τὰς ναῦς ἐν αἷς ἐναυμάχησαν καὶ τὰς ἐν τῇ Λακωνικῇ
πάσας, ὅσαι ἦσαν μακραί, παραδοῦναι κομίσαντας ἐς Πύλον
Ἀθηναίοις, καὶ ὅπλα μὴ ἐπιφέρειν τῷ τειχίσματι μήτε κατὰ
γῆν μήτε κατὰ θάλασσαν, Ἀθηναίους δὲ τοῖς ἐν τῇ νήσῳ
ἀνδράσι σῖτον ἐᾶν τοὺς ἐν τῇ ἠπείρῳ Λακεδαιμονίους ἐκ-
πέμπειν τακτὸν καὶ μεμαγμένον, δύο χοίνικας ἑκάστῳ Ἀττικὰς
ἀλφίτων καὶ δύο κοτύλας οἴνου καὶ κρέας, θεράποντι δὲ τούτων ἡμίσεα· ταῦτα δὲ ὁρώντων τῶν Ἀθηναίων ἐσπέμπειν
καὶ πλοῖον μηδὲν ἐσπλεῖν λάθρᾳ· φυλάσσειν δὲ καὶ τὴν
νῆσον Ἀθηναίους μηδὲν ἧσσον, ὅσα μὴ ἀποβαίνοντας, καὶ
ὅπλα μὴ ἐπιφέρειν τῷ Πελοποννησίων στρατῷ μήτε κατὰ
2 γῆν μήτε κατὰ θάλασσαν. ὅτι δ' ἂν τούτων παραβαίνωσιν
ἑκάτεροι καὶ ὁτιοῦν, τότε λελύσθαι τὰς σπονδάς. ἐσπεῖσθαι
δὲ αὐτὰς μέχρι οὗ ἐπανέλθωσιν οἱ ἐκ τῶν Ἀθηνῶν Λακεδαιμονίων πρέσβεις· ἀποστεῖλαι δὲ αὐτοὺς τριήρει Ἀθηναίους
καὶ πάλιν κομίσαι. ἐλθόντων δὲ τάς τε σπονδὰς λελύσθαι
ταύτας καὶ τὰς ναῦς ἀποδοῦναι Ἀθηναίους ὁμοίας οἷασπερ
3 ἂν παραλάβωσιν. αἱ μὲν σπονδαὶ ἐπὶ τούτοις ἐγένοντο,
καὶ αἱ νῆες παρεδόθησαν οὖσαι περὶ ἑξήκοντα, καὶ οἱ πρέσβεις ἀπεστάλησαν. ἀφικόμενοι δὲ ἐς τὰς Ἀθήνας ἔλεξαν
τοιάδε.

17 ‘Ἔπεμψαν ἡμᾶς Λακεδαιμόνιοι, ὦ Ἀθηναῖοι, περὶ τῶν
ἐν τῇ νήσῳ ἀνδρῶν πράξοντας ὅτι ἂν ὑμῖν τε ὠφέλιμον ὂν
τὸ αὐτὸ πείθωμεν καὶ ἡμῖν ἐς τὴν ξυμφορὰν ὡς ἐκ τῶν
2 παρόντων κόσμον μάλιστα μέλλῃ οἴσειν. τοὺς δὲ λόγους
μακροτέρους οὐ παρὰ τὸ εἰωθὸς μηκυνοῦμεν, ἀλλ' ἐπιχώριον
ὂν ἡμῖν οὗ μὲν βραχεῖς ἀρκῶσι μὴ πολλοῖς χρῆσθαι, πλέοσι
δὲ ἐν ᾧ ἂν καιρὸς ἢ διδάσκοντάς τι τῶν προὔργου λόγοις τὸ

keep watch over it, assuming the men on it to be now cut off. The Peloponnesians on the mainland, and all the reinforcements that had already arrived from all quarters, stayed in their positions at Pylos.

When the events at Pylos were announced at Sparta, they regarded it as a major disaster, and decided that the magistrates should go to the camp, see for themselves, and decide on the spot what was best to do. The magistrates saw that nothing could be done to help the men on the island: and they did not wish to run the risk of their being starved out, or overcome by an attack with superior numbers. So they decided to make a truce at Pylos with the Athenian generals, if they were agreeable, and then to send an embassy to Athens with a view to making a permanent agreement: they wanted to get their men back as soon as they could.

The Athenian generals accepted this proposal, and a truce was made on the following terms: The Lacedaimonians should bring to Pylos and hand over to the Athenians all the ships in which they had fought, and all the warships in Laconia: they were not to make any attack, by land or by sea, against the fort. The Athenians would allow the Lacedaimonians on the mainland to send over to those on the island a fixed quantity of kneaded flour, i.e. 2 Attic choenices of barley meal, and 2 kotylai of wine, and some meat, for each hoplite: and half that amount for each servant. These rations would be sent subject to Athenian inspection; and no boat was to sail over in secret. The Athenians could guard the island as closely as they were doing before: but they would not land on it, and they would not attack the Peloponnesian army by land or sea. The slightest infringement of these conditions would mean the end of the truce. The truce was to last until the Lacedaimonian embassy returned from Athens: the Athenians were to take them there in a trireme and bring them back. When they returned the truce was to be at an end; and the Athenians were to give the Lacedaimonians back their ships in the same state and condition as they had received them. The truce was made on these terms; the ships - about 60 - were handed over; and the embassy was sent off.

When the ambassadors arrived at Athens, they spoke in these terms: "Athenians, the Lacedaimonians sent us here to reach an agreement about the men on the island. We hope to persuade you that such an agreement will be advantageous to you, and at the same time as honourable to us as we can expect in the present circumstances, after such a disaster. If we speak for some time, this is no departure from our usual custom: in our country we do not use many words when only a few will do, but we use more on those occasions when we have to point out something important and thereby get the right

3 δέον πράσσειν. λάβετε δὲ αὐτοὺς μὴ πολεμίως μηδ' ὡς ἀξύνετοι διδασκόμενοι, ὑπόμνησιν δὲ τοῦ καλῶς βουλεύσασθαι πρὸς εἰδότας ἡγησάμενοι.

4 ' Ὑμῖν γὰρ εὐτυχίαν τὴν παροῦσαν ἔξεστι καλῶς θέσθαι, ἔχουσι μὲν ὧν κρατεῖτε, προσλαβοῦσι δὲ τιμὴν καὶ δόξαν, καὶ μὴ παθεῖν ὅπερ οἱ ἀήθως τι ἀγαθὸν λαμβάνοντες τῶν ἀνθρώπων· αἰεὶ γὰρ τοῦ πλέονος ἐλπίδι ὀρέγονται διὰ τὸ 5 καὶ τὰ παρόντα ἀδοκήτως εὐτυχῆσαι. οἷς δὲ πλεῖσται μεταβολαὶ ἐπ' ἀμφότερα ξυμβεβήκασι, δίκαιοί εἰσι καὶ ἀπιστότατοι εἶναι ταῖς εὐπραγίαις· ὃ τῇ τε ὑμετέρᾳ πόλει δι' ἐμπειρίαν καὶ ἡμῖν μάλιστ' ἂν ἐκ τοῦ εἰκότος προσείη.

18 γνῶτε δὲ καὶ ἐς τὰς ἡμετέρας νῦν ξυμφορὰς ἀπιδόντες, οἵτινες ἀξίωμα μέγιστον τῶν Ἑλλήνων ἔχοντες ἥκομεν παρ' ὑμᾶς, πρότερον αὐτοὶ κυριώτεροι νομίζοντες εἶναι δοῦναι ἐφ' 2 ἃ νῦν ἀφιγμένοι ὑμᾶς αἰτούμεθα. καίτοι οὔτε δυνάμεως ἐνδείᾳ ἐπάθομεν αὐτὸ οὔτε μείζονος προσγενομένης ὑβρί-
ϲ σαντες, ἀπὸ δὲ τῶν αἰεὶ ὑπαρχόντων γνώμῃ σφαλέντες, ἐν 3 ᾧ πᾶσι τὸ αὐτὸ ὁμοίως ὑπάρχει. ὥστε οὐκ εἰκὸς ὑμᾶς διὰ τὴν παροῦσαν νῦν ῥώμην πόλεώς τε καὶ τῶν προσγεγενη-μένων καὶ τὸ τῆς τύχης οἴεσθαι αἰεὶ μεθ' ὑμῶν ἔσεσθαι.

4 σωφρόνων δὲ ἀνδρῶν οἵτινες τἀγαθὰ ἐς ἀμφίβολον ἀσφαλῶς ἔθεντο(καὶ ταῖς ξυμφοραῖς οἱ αὐτοὶ εὐξυνετώτερον ἂν προσ-φέροιντο), τόν τε πόλεμον νομίσωσι μὴ καθ' ὅσον ἄν τις αὐτοῦ μέρος βούληται μεταχειρίζειν, τούτῳ ξυνεῖναι, ἀλλ' ὡς ἂν αἱ τύχαι αὐτῶν ἡγήσωνται· καὶ ἐλάχιστ' ἂν οἱ τοιοῦτοι πταίοντες διὰ τὸ μὴ τῷ ὀρθουμένῳ αὐτοῦ πιστεύον-τες ἐπαίρεσθαι ἐν τῷ εὐτυχεῖν ἂν μάλιστα καταλύοιντο.

5 ὃ νῦν ὑμῖν, ὦ Ἀθηναῖοι, καλῶς ἔχει πρὸς ἡμᾶς πρᾶξαι, καὶ μή ποτε ὕστερον, ἢν ἄρα μὴ πειθόμενοι σφαλῆτε, ἃ πολλὰ ἐνδέχεται, νομισθῆναι τύχῃ καὶ τὰ νῦν προχωρήσαντα κρατῆσαι, ἐξὸν ἀκίνδυνον δόκησιν ἰσχύος καὶ ξυνέσεως ἐς τὸ ἔπειτα καταλιπεῖν.

19 ' Λακεδαιμόνιοι δὲ ὑμᾶς προκαλοῦνται ἐς σπονδὰς καὶ 5 διάλυσιν πολέμου, διδόντες μὲν εἰρήνην καὶ ξυμμαχίαν καὶ ἄλλην φιλίαν πολλὴν καὶ οἰκειότητα ἐς ἀλλήλους ὑπάρχειν, ἀνταιτοῦντες δὲ τοὺς ἐκ τῆς νήσου ἄνδρας, καὶ ἄμεινον ἡγούμενοι ἀμφοτέροις μὴ διακινδυνεύεσθαι, εἴτε βίᾳ δια-φύγοιεν παρατυχούσης τινὸς σωτηρίας εἴτε καὶ ἐκπολιορκη- 10 2 θέντες μᾶλλον ἂν χειρωθεῖεν. νομίζομέν τε τὰς μεγάλας

20

thing done. Please listen to what we say without hostility: when we point things out to you we appreciate that you are not stupid - take it rather as a mere reminder of what you already know to be good policy.

"We say this, because now is your chance to make the most of your present good fortune. You can keep what you have won, and gain glory and honour as well: and you can avoid the common fate of those who are unaccustomed to gaining an advantage - that is, to be bowled over by the unexpectedness of their success, and hence greedy to get more. On the other hand, men who have most experience of the way fortune changes from good to bad, and vice versa, have good grounds to be cautious when they succeed: and this is the sort of lesson, we might reasonably suppose, that experience has taught both your city and ours.

"A glance at our own misfortunes will give you further proof: we have greater prestige than any other Greek state, and before all this we regarded ourselves as more likely to grant the kind of favour which now we have come to you to ask for. Yet our misfortune came about, not through any lack of military strength, nor because an increase in power made us over-confident: no, we based our judgement on what resources we had at the time, but simply judged wrongly - an error to which any state is liable. In the same way, just because your city and empire are now in a strong position, it would not be reasonable for you to suppose that fortune will always be on your side.

"Wise men invest their gains safely for the future, and consider their advantages as uncertain - such men also take a more intelligent attitude when disaster strikes. They realise that states are involved in war to whatever extent their fortunes dictate, not only insofar as they wish to be involved in it. Such men are least likely to make mistakes, not being carried away by over-confidence resulting from success; and they would be most inclined to make peace when fortune is favouring them. This is a good opportunity for you, Athenians, to behave in such a way towards us. If you are not persuaded to do so, and run into trouble later (which is more than possible), people may think that even your present success was simply due to luck. You may, without risk, leave to posterity a reputation for both power and intelligence.

"The Lacedaimonians offer you a truce, an end to the war: they offer peace, an alliance and in general a close and friendly relationship between our two cities. In return they ask for the men on the island. They think it better for neither side to run any risks - for you risk the possibility that some chance of their being rescued may crop up, and enable them to effect an escape, and the Lacedaimonians risk the possibility of the men being besieged, forced to surrender, and captured by you.

ἔχθρας μάλιστ' ἂν διαλύεσθαι βεβαίως, οὐκ ἦν ἀνταμυνόμενός
τις καὶ ἐπικρατήσας τὰ πλείω τοῦ πολέμου κατ' ἀνάγκην
ὅρκοις ἐγκαταλαμβάνων μὴ ἀπὸ τοῦ ἴσου ξυμβῇ, ἀλλ' ἢν
παρὸν τὸ αὐτὸ δρᾶσαι πρὸς τὸ ἐπιεικὲς καὶ ἀρετῇ αὐτὸν
3 νικήσας παρὰ ἃ προσεδέχετο μετρίως ξυναλλαγῇ. ὀφείλων
γὰρ ἤδη ὁ ἐναντίος μὴ ἀνταμύνεσθαι ὡς βιασθείς, ἀλλ'
ἀνταποδοῦναι ἀρετήν, ἑτοιμότερός ἐστιν αἰσχύνῃ ἐμμένειν
4 οἷς ξυνέθετο. καὶ μᾶλλον πρὸς τοὺς μειζόνως ἐχθροὺς τοῦτο
δρῶσιν οἱ ἄνθρωποι ἢ πρὸς τοὺς τὰ μέτρια διενεχθέντας·
πεφύκασί τε τοῖς μὲν ἑκουσίως ἐνδοῦσιν ἀνθησσᾶσθαι
μεθ' ἡδονῆς, πρὸς δὲ τὰ ὑπεραυχοῦντα καὶ παρὰ γνώμην
διακινδυνεύειν.

20 ''Ἡμῖν δὲ καλῶς, εἴπερ ποτέ, ἔχει ἀμφοτέροις ἡ ξυναλλαγή,
πρίν τι ἀνήκεστον διὰ μέσου γενόμενον ἡμᾶς καταλαβεῖν, ἐν
ᾧ ἀνάγκη ἀίδιον ὑμῖν ἔχθραν πρὸς τῇ κοινῇ καὶ ἰδίαν ἔχειν,
2 ὑμᾶς δὲ στερηθῆναι ὧν νῦν προκαλούμεθα. ἔτι δ' ὄντων
ἀκρίτων καὶ ὑμῖν μὲν δόξης καὶ ἡμετέρας φιλίας προσγι-
γνομένης, ἡμῖν δὲ πρὸ αἰσχροῦ τινος ξυμφορᾶς μετρίως
κατατιθεμένης διαλλαγῶμεν, καὶ αὐτοί τε ἀντὶ πολέμου
εἰρήνην ἑλώμεθα καὶ τοῖς ἄλλοις Ἕλλησιν ἀνάπαυσιν κακῶν
ποιήσωμεν· οἳ καὶ ἐν τούτῳ ὑμᾶς αἰτιωτέρους ἡγήσονται.
πολεμοῦνται μὲν γὰρ ἀσαφῶς ὁποτέρων ἀρξάντων· κατα-
λύσεως δὲ γενομένης, ἧς νῦν ὑμεῖς τὸ πλέον κύριοί ἐστε,
3 τὴν χάριν ὑμῖν προσθήσουσιν. ἤν τε γνῶτε, Λακεδαιμονίοις
ἔξεστιν ὑμῖν φίλους γενέσθαι βεβαίως, αὐτῶν τε προκαλεσα-
4 μένων χαρισαμένοις τε μᾶλλον ἢ βιασαμένοις. καὶ ἐν τούτῳ
τὰ ἐνόντα ἀγαθὰ σκοπεῖτε ὅσα εἰκὸς εἶναι· ἡμῶν γὰρ καὶ
ὑμῶν ταὐτὰ λεγόντων τό γε ἄλλο Ἑλληνικὸν ἴστε ὅτι
ὑποδεέστερον ὂν τὰ μέγιστα τιμήσει.'

21 Οἱ μὲν οὖν Λακεδαιμόνιοι τοσαῦτα εἶπον, νομίζοντες τοὺς
'Αθηναίους ἐν τῷ πρὶν χρόνῳ σπονδῶν μὲν ἐπιθυμεῖν, σφῶν
δὲ ἐναντιουμένων κωλύεσθαι, διδομένης δὲ εἰρήνης ἀσμένους
2 δέξεσθαί τε καὶ τοὺς ἄνδρας ἀποδώσειν. οἱ δὲ τὰς μὲν
σπονδάς, ἔχοντες τοὺς ἄνδρας ἐν τῇ νήσῳ, ἤδη σφίσιν
ἐνόμιζον ἑτοίμους εἶναι, ὁπόταν βούλωνται ποιεῖσθαι πρὸς
3 αὐτούς, τοῦ δὲ πλέονος ὠρέγοντο. μάλιστα δὲ αὐτοὺς
ἐνῆγε Κλέων ὁ Κλεαινέτου, ἀνὴρ δημαγωγὸς κατ' ἐκεῖνον
τὸν χρόνον ὢν καὶ τῷ πλήθει πιθανώτατος· καὶ ἔπεισεν
ἀποκρίνασθαι ὡς χρὴ τὰ μὲν ὅπλα καὶ σφᾶς αὐτοὺς τοὺς ἐν
τῇ νήσῳ παραδόντας πρῶτον κομισθῆναι 'Αθήναζε, ἐλθόντων
δὲ ἀποδόντας Λακεδαιμονίους Νίσαιαν καὶ Πηγὰς καὶ
Τροιζῆνα καὶ 'Αχαΐαν, ἃ οὐ πολέμῳ ἔλαβον, ἀλλ' ἀπὸ τῆς

22

"We also believe that great enmity between cities cannot be effectively abolished if one city seeks revenge, and (having gained a military advantage) binds its enemy by forced oaths and an unfair treaty: but only if, when that city has such power, it nevertheless behaves reasonably, excels in generosity, and surprises its enemy by offering moderate terms. For thus the opponent will not feel that he has been forced to his knees, and hence obliged to take revenge: he will rather wish to requite generosity with generosity, and will be the more willing to abide by the treaty from a sense of honour. (This is particularly true when the two parties are bitter enemies, rather than when they only disagree on minor points.) If someone makes a voluntary concession, it is human nature to give way in return, and take pleasure in doing so: and, by contrast, if somebody is overbearing, to face dangers even against one's better judgement.

"Now, if ever, is the time for us both to be reconciled, before some other event comes between us and irremediably estranges us. If that happened, you would incur the undying enmity of Sparta in particular, as well as the dislike in which you are commonly held: and you would have no chance of the terms which we now offer. Let us be reconciled now, while the conflict is still undecided, while you can gain both honour and our friendship, and while we can avoid disgrace and disaster by moderate terms. Let us choose peace instead of war, and give the other Greeks a relief from their evils. They, indeed, will judge the responsibility in this matter to be more on your side; it is unclear which of us began the war, but it is more in your power than ours to make it end now, so that they will give you the credit for it. If you agree, you can have the firm friendship of the Lacedaimonians which they themselves offer to you, and which you can accept of your own free will rather than under compulsion. Consider the great advantages which this is likely to bring. If we and you speak with one voice, you can appreciate that the rest of Greece, being so much less powerful, will pay us both the greatest honour."

This was what the Lacedaimonians said. They thought that the Athenians had formerly wanted a treaty but had been unable to get one because the Lacedaimonians had refused; and hence that they would now gladly accept the offer of peace, and return the Lacedaimonian soldiers. But in fact the Athenians, believing that they could make peace whenever they liked (since they had the men on the island in their power), were trying to get more advantages. It was Cleon, the son of Cleaenetos, in particular who urged them in this direction, a popular leader of the time with very great influence over the common people. He persuaded them to make this reply: "First the men on the island and their weapons must be surrendered and brought to Athens: when they have arrived, the Lacedaimonians must then surrender Nisaia, Pegai, Troizene and Achaia" (these places had not been captured in war but surrendered under an earlier

23

προτέρας ξυμβάσεως Ἀθηναίων ξυγχωρησάντων κατὰ ξυμφορὰς καὶ ἐν τῷ τότε δεομένων τι μᾶλλον σπονδῶν, κομί-
22 σασθαι τοὺς ἄνδρας καὶ σπονδὰς ποιήσασθαι ὁπόσον ἂν
δοκῇ χρόνον ἀμφοτέροις. οἱ δὲ πρὸς μὲν τὴν ἀπόκρισιν
οὐδὲν ἀντεῖπον, ξυνέδρους δὲ σφίσιν ἐκέλευον ἑλέσθαι οἵτινες
2 λέγοντες καὶ ἀκούοντες περὶ ἑκάστου ξυμβήσονται κατὰ
ἡσυχίαν ὅτι ἂν πείθωσιν ἀλλήλους. Κλέων δὲ ἐνταῦθα δὴ
πολὺς ἐνέκειτο, λέγων γιγνώσκειν μὲν καὶ πρότερον οὐδὲν
ἐν νῷ ἔχοντας δίκαιον αὐτούς, σαφὲς δ' εἶναι καὶ νῦν,
οἵτινες τῷ μὲν πλήθει οὐδὲν ἐθέλουσιν εἰπεῖν, ὀλίγοις δὲ
ἀνδράσι ξύνεδροι βούλονται γίγνεσθαι· ἀλλὰ εἴ τι ὑγιὲς
3 διανοοῦνται, λέγειν ἐκέλευσεν ἅπασιν. ὁρῶντες δὲ οἱ
Λακεδαιμόνιοι οὔτε σφίσιν οἷόν τε ὂν ἐν πλήθει εἰπεῖν, εἴ
τι καὶ ὑπὸ τῆς ξυμφορᾶς ἐδόκει αὐτοῖς ξυγχωρεῖν, μὴ ἐς
τοὺς ξυμμάχους διαβληθῶσιν εἰπόντες καὶ οὐ τυχόντες, οὔτε
τοὺς Ἀθηναίους ἐπὶ μετρίοις ποιήσοντας ἃ προυκαλοῦντο,
23 ἀνεχώρησαν ἐκ τῶν Ἀθηνῶν ἄπρακτοι. ἀφικομένων δὲ
αὐτῶν διελέλυντο εὐθὺς αἱ σπονδαὶ αἱ περὶ Πύλον, καὶ τὰς
ναῦς οἱ Λακεδαιμόνιοι ἀπῄτουν, καθάπερ ξυνέκειτο· οἱ δ'
Ἀθηναῖοι ἐγκλήματα ἔχοντες ἐπιδρομήν τε τῷ τειχίσματι
παράσπονδον καὶ ἄλλα οὐκ ἀξιόλογα δοκοῦντα εἶναι οὐκ
ἀπεδίδοσαν, ἰσχυριζόμενοι ὅτι δὴ εἴρητο, ἐὰν καὶ ὁτιοῦν
παραβαθῇ, λελύσθαι τὰς σπονδάς. οἱ δὲ Λακεδαιμόνιοι
ἀντέλεγόν τε καὶ ἀδίκημα ἐπικαλέσαντες τὸ τῶν νεῶν
2 ἀπελθόντες ἐς πόλεμον καθίσταντο. καὶ τὰ περὶ Πύλον
ὑπ' ἀμφοτέρων κατὰ κράτος ἐπολεμεῖτο, Ἀθηναῖοι μὲν δυοῖν
νεοῖν ἐναντίαιν αἰεὶ τὴν νῆσον περιπλέοντες τῆς ἡμέρας
(τῆς δὲ νυκτὸς καὶ ἅπασαι περιώρμουν, πλὴν τὰ πρὸς τὸ
πέλαγος, ὁπότε ἄνεμος εἴη· καὶ ἐκ τῶν Ἀθηνῶν αὐτοῖς
εἴκοσι νῆες ἀφίκοντο ἐς τὴν φυλακήν, ὥστε αἱ πᾶσαι
ἑβδομήκοντα ἐγένοντο), Πελοποννήσιοι δὲ ἔν τε τῇ ἠπείρῳ
στρατοπεδευόμενοι καὶ προσβολὰς ποιούμενοι τῷ τείχει,
σκοποῦντες καιρὸν εἴ τις παραπέσοι ὥστε τοὺς ἄνδρας
σῶσαι.

* * *

treaty, when things were going badly for the Athenians and they had more need to make peace): "on these conditions the Lacedaimonians can get back their soldiers and make peace for as long as both sides want".

The Lacedaimonians made no full reply to this answer, but suggested that the Athenians should appoint commissioners to discuss the details of the agreement, and reach a mutual understanding at leisure. At this point Cleon became very aggressive: he said that he had always known that the Lacedaimonians had sinister intentions, and now it was only too clear - they were not prepared to say anything at all before the popular assembly, but only wanted to talk as commissioners in the presence of a very few: if they meant well, then let them talk in front of everybody. The Lacedaimonians were aware that they could not talk in the popular assembly: for suppose that they thought it sensible to make some concession in view of the disaster they had suffered, spoke to that effect, and yet still failed to reach agreement, then this might ruin their prestige in the eyes of their allies. Further, they appreciated that the Athenians were not prepared at all to make the sort of reasonable agreement they had suggested. So they left Athens without having secured any understanding.

When they got back, the truce at Pylos at once came to an end. The Lacedaimonians requested the return of their ships, according to the terms of the truce. But the Athenians accused them of having made an attack on the fort (contrary to the truce), and of other contraventions too trivial to mention; they took their stand on the wording of the truce, where it said that "the slightest infringement . . . would mean the end of the truce", and refused to give the ships back. The Lacedaimonians accused them in return of sharp practice in retaining the ships: they then went away and resumed the conflict.

Both sides now fought as hard as they could at Pylos. The Athenians had 2 ships sailing round the island in opposite directions through all the hours of daylight: at night the whole fleet anchored round the island, except on the side facing the open sea when there was a wind. 20 ships arrived from Athens to assist with the blockade, so that their fleet now totalled 70. The Peloponnesians camped on the mainland and made attacks on the wall, watching for any opportunity that might enable them to rescue the men [on the island].

*   *   *

25

26 Ἐν δὲ τῇ Πύλῳ ἔτι ἐπολιόρκουν τοὺς ἐν τῇ νήσῳ Λακεδαιμονίους οἱ Ἀθηναῖοι, καὶ τὸ ἐν τῇ ἠπείρῳ στρατόπεδον
2 τῶν Πελοποννησίων κατὰ χώραν ἔμενεν. ἐπίπονος δ' ἦν τοῖς Ἀθηναίοις ἡ φυλακὴ σίτου τε ἀπορίᾳ καὶ ὕδατος· οὐ γὰρ ἦν κρήνη ὅτι μὴ μία ἐν αὐτῇ τῇ ἀκροπόλει τῆς Πύλου καὶ αὕτη οὐ μεγάλη, ἀλλὰ διαμώμενοι τὸν κάχληκα οἱ
3 πλεῖστοι ἐπὶ τῇ θαλάσσῃ ἔπινον οἷον εἰκὸς ὕδωρ. στενοχωρίᾳ τε ἐν ὀλίγῳ στρατοπεδευομένοις ἐγίγνετο, καὶ τῶν νεῶν οὐκ ἐχουσῶν ὅρμον αἱ μὲν σῖτον ἐν τῇ γῇ ᾑροῦντο κατὰ
4 μέρος, αἱ δὲ μετέωροι ὥρμουν. ἀθυμίαν τε πλείστην ὁ χρόνος παρεῖχε παρὰ λόγον ἐπιγιγνόμενος, οὓς ᾤοντο ἡμερῶν ὀλίγων ἐκπολιορκήσειν ἐν νήσῳ τε ἐρήμῃ καὶ ὕδατι
5 ἁλμυρῷ χρωμένους. αἴτιον δὲ ἦν οἱ Λακεδαιμόνιοι προειπόντες ἐς τὴν νῆσον ἐσάγειν σῖτόν τε τὸν βουλόμενον ἀληλεμένον καὶ οἶνον καὶ τυρὸν καὶ εἴ τι ἄλλο βρῶμα, οἷ' ἂν ἐς πολιορκίαν ξυμφέρῃ, τάξαντες ἀργυρίου πολλοῦ καὶ τῶν Εἱλώτων τῷ ἐσαγαγόντι ἐλευθερίαν ὑπισχνούμενοι.
6 καὶ ἐσῆγον ἄλλοι τε παρακινδυνεύοντες καὶ μάλιστα οἱ Εἵλωτες, ἀπαίροντες ἀπὸ τῆς Πελοποννήσου ὁπόθεν τύχοιεν καὶ καταπλέοντες ἔτι νυκτὸς ἐς τὰ πρὸς τὸ πέλαγος τῆς
7 νήσου. μάλιστα δὲ ἐτήρουν ἀνέμῳ καταφέρεσθαι· ῥᾷον γὰρ τὴν φυλακὴν τῶν τριήρων ἐλάνθανον, ὁπότε πνεῦμα ἐκ πόντου εἴη· ἄπορον γὰρ ἐγίγνετο περιορμεῖν, τοῖς δὲ ἀφειδὴς ὁ κατάπλους καθειστήκει· ἐπώκελλον γὰρ τὰ πλοῖα τετιμημένα χρημάτων, καὶ οἱ ὁπλῖται περὶ τὰς κατάρσεις τῆς νήσου ἐφύλασσον. ὅσοι δὲ γαλήνῃ κινδυνεύσειαν, ἡλί-
8 σκοντο. ἐσένεον δὲ καὶ κατὰ τὸν λιμένα κολυμβηταὶ ὕφυδροι, καλῳδίῳ ἐν ἀσκοῖς ἐφέλκοντες μήκωνα μεμελιτωμένην καὶ λίνου σπέρμα κεκομμένον· ὧν τὸ πρῶτον λανθανόντων
9 φυλακαὶ ὕστερον ἐγένοντο. παντί τε τρόπῳ ἑκάτεροι ἐτεχνῶντο οἱ μὲν ἐσπέμπειν τὰ σιτία, οἱ δὲ μὴ λανθάνειν σφᾶς.

27 Ἐν δὲ ταῖς Ἀθήναις πυνθανόμενοι περὶ τῆς στρατιᾶς ὅτι ταλαιπωρεῖται καὶ σῖτος τοῖς ἐν τῇ νήσῳ ὅτι ἐσπλεῖ, ἠπόρουν καὶ ἐδεδοίκεσαν μὴ σφῶν χειμὼν τὴν φυλακὴν ἐπιλάβοι, ὁρῶντες τῶν τε ἐπιτηδείων τὴν περὶ τὴν Πελοπόννησον κομιδὴν ἀδύνατον ἐσομένην, ἅμα ἐν χωρίῳ ἐρήμῳ καὶ οὐδ' ἐν θέρει οἷοί τε ὄντες ἱκανὰ περιπέμπειν, τόν τε ἔφορμον χωρίων ἀλιμένων ὄντων οὐκ ἐσόμενον, ἀλλ' ἢ σφῶν ἀνέντων τὴν φυλακὴν περιγενήσεσθαι τοὺς ἄνδρας ἢ τοῖς πλοίοις ἃ τὸν σῖτον αὐτοῖς ἦγε χειμῶνα τηρήσαντας
2 ἐκπλεύσεσθαι. πάντων τε ἐφοβοῦντο μάλιστα τοὺς Λακε-

26

At Pylos the Athenians continued to blockade the men on the island, and the Peloponnesians stayed in their camp on the mainland. The blockade was difficult for the Athenians, for lack of food and water. For the sole source of water was the spring on the acropolis of Pylos, which was only a small one: most of the soldiers used to scrape in the shingle by the sea-shore, and drink such water as they could get there. Their troops were confined in a very narrow space, and the ships had no proper anchorage: so they were fed in relays - some of the crews in turn took their food on shore, while the others anchored in deep water. What particularly disheartened the Athenians was the unexpected length of the blockade: they had believed that they could make them surrender in a few days, since they were on an uninhabited island and had only brackish water to drink.

But this did not happen, because the Lacedaimonians had made a proclamation, promising large sums of money (and freedom to helots) to anyone who would convey to the island meal, wine, cheese and any other provisions that would help the besieged men: and some people took the risk of doing this, particularly the helots. They started from various points in the Peloponnese and sailed when it was still night to the seaward side of the island. In particular they waited for a wind to carry them onto the island: for when the wind blew from the sea, it was easier for them to escape the triremes on watch. The reason was that on those occasions the Athenians could not anchor round the island, and the helots themselves could be quite reckless in their voyage: for they had their boats valued and simply ran them aground, while the Lacedaimonian hoplites kept a lookout for them at the landing-places on the island. Those that tried it in calm weather were caught. Also divers swam under water in the harbour, pulling skins attached by a cord which contained poppy-seed mixed with honey, and pounded linseed. At first they escaped the Athenians' notice, but afterwards a watch was kept. Both parties tried every possible device, the Lacedaimonians to bring in the food, and the Athenians to catch them at it.

When the Athenians at home learnt about the hardships of their army, and how food was reaching the men on the island, they were at a loss what to do. In particular they were frightened that the season of stormy weather might put an end to the blockade. They realised that it would then be impossible to transport supplies round the Peloponnese - they were not really able to send enough even in summer - and that their troops were in an uninhabited territory: further, that they could not continue the blockade in an area which had no proper harbours, so that either they would have to give it up and allow the men to escape, or else the men would wait for stormy weather and sail off on the boats which brought them food. Most of all they were alarmed

δαιμονίους, ὅτι ἔχοντάς τι ἰσχυρὸν αὐτοὺς ἐνόμιζον οὐκέτι σφίσιν ἐπικηρυκεύεσθαι· καὶ μετεμέλοντο τὰς σπονδὰς οὐ
3 δεξάμενοι. Κλέων δὲ γνοὺς αὐτῶν τὴν ἐς αὑτὸν ὑποψίαν περὶ τῆς κωλύμης τῆς ξυμβάσεως οὐ τἀληθῆ ἔφη λέγειν τοὺς ἐξαγγέλλοντας. παραινούντων δὲ τῶν ἀφιγμένων, εἰ μὴ σφίσι πιστεύουσι, κατασκόπους τινὰς πέμψαι, ᾑρέθη
4 κατάσκοπος αὐτὸς μετὰ Θεαγένους ὑπὸ Ἀθηναίων. καὶ γνοὺς ὅτι ἀναγκασθήσεται ἢ ταὐτὰ λέγειν οἷς διέβαλλεν ἢ τἀναντία εἰπὼν ψευδὴς φανήσεσθαι, παρῄνει τοῖς Ἀθηναίοις, ὁρῶν αὐτοὺς καὶ ὡρμημένους τι τὸ πλέον τῇ γνώμῃ στρατεύειν, ὡς χρὴ κατασκόπους μὲν μὴ πέμπειν μηδὲ διαμέλλειν καιρὸν παριέντας, εἰ δὲ δοκεῖ αὐτοῖς ἀληθῆ εἶναι τὰ
5 ἀγγελλόμενα, πλεῖν ἐπὶ τοὺς ἄνδρας. καὶ ἐς Νικίαν τὸν Νικηράτου στρατηγὸν ὄντα ἀπεσήμαινεν, ἐχθρὸς ὢν καὶ ἐπιτιμῶν, ῥᾴδιον εἶναι παρασκευῇ, εἰ ἄνδρες εἶεν οἱ στρατηγοί, πλεύσαντας λαβεῖν τοὺς ἐν τῇ νήσῳ, καὶ αὐτός γ' ἄν, εἰ
28 ἦρχε, ποιῆσαι τοῦτο. ὁ δὲ Νικίας τῶν τε Ἀθηναίων τι ὑποθορυβησάντων ἐς τὸν Κλέωνα, ὅτι οὐ καὶ νῦν πλεῖ, εἰ ῥᾴδιόν γε αὐτῷ φαίνεται, καὶ ἅμα ὁρῶν αὐτὸν ἐπιτιμῶντα, ἐκέλευεν ἥντινα βούλεται δύναμιν λαβόντα τὸ ἐπὶ σφᾶς
2 εἶναι ἐπιχειρεῖν. ὁ δὲ τὸ μὲν πρῶτον οἰόμενος αὐτὸν λόγῳ μόνον ἀφιέναι ἕτοιμος ἦν, γνοὺς δὲ τῷ ὄντι παραδωσείοντα ἀνεχώρει καὶ οὐκ ἔφη αὐτὸς ἀλλ' ἐκεῖνον στρατηγεῖν, δεδιὼς ἤδη καὶ οὐκ ἂν οἰόμενός οἱ αὐτὸν τολμῆσαι ὑποχωρῆσαι.
3 αὖθις δὲ ὁ Νικίας ἐκέλευε καὶ ἐξίστατο τῆς ἐπὶ Πύλῳ ἀρχῆς καὶ μάρτυρας τοὺς Ἀθηναίους ἐποιεῖτο. οἱ δέ, οἷον ὄχλος φιλεῖ ποιεῖν, ὅσῳ μᾶλλον ὁ Κλέων ὑπέφευγε τὸν πλοῦν καὶ ἐξανεχώρει τὰ εἰρημένα, τόσῳ ἐπεκελεύοντο τῷ Νικίᾳ παρα-
4 διδόναι τὴν ἀρχὴν καὶ ἐκείνῳ ἐπεβόων πλεῖν. ὥστε οὐκ ἔχων ὅπως τῶν εἰρημένων ἔτι ἐξαπαλλαγῇ, ὑφίσταται τὸν πλοῦν, καὶ παρελθὼν οὔτε φοβεῖσθαι ἔφη Λακεδαιμονίους πλεύσεσθαί τε λαβὼν ἐκ μὲν τῆς πόλεως οὐδένα, Λημνίους δὲ καὶ Ἰμβρίους τοὺς παρόντας καὶ πελταστὰς οἳ ἦσαν ἔκ τε Αἴνου βεβοηθηκότες καὶ ἄλλοθεν τοξότας τετρακοσίους· ταῦτα δὲ ἔχων ἔφη πρὸς τοῖς ἐν Πύλῳ στρατιώταις ἐντὸς ἡμερῶν εἴκοσιν ἢ ἄξειν Λακεδαιμονίους ζῶντας ἢ αὐτοῦ
5 ἀποκτενεῖν. τοῖς δὲ Ἀθηναίοις ἐνέπεσε μέν τι καὶ γέλωτος τῇ κουφολογίᾳ αὐτοῦ, ἀσμένοις δ' ὅμως ἐγίγνετο τοῖς σώφροσι τῶν ἀνθρώπων, λογιζομένοις δυοῖν ἀγαθοῖν τοῦ ἑτέρου τεύξεσθαι, ἢ Κλέωνος ἀπαλλαγήσεσθαι, ὃ μᾶλλον ἤλπιζον, ἢ σφαλεῖσι γνώμης Λακεδαιμονίους σφίσι χειρώσεσθαι.

28

I prefer καὶ [. .] καὶ |
See Note L, pp. 104-5.|

because the Lacedaimonians no longer made overtures to them: they presumed this must be because the Lacedaimonians had some unknown source of strength, and they regretted their rejection of the treaty.

Cleon realised that he was regarded with some suspicion for having prevented an agreement, and claimed that the messengers from Pylos were lying. The messengers suggested that, if the Athenians did not believe them, they should send other observers. Theagenes and Cleon himself were chosen for this purpose: and Cleon realised that he would either have to tell the same story as the messengers whom he had just been falsely accusing, or else (if he said the opposite) be shown up as a liar. He also perceived that the Athenians were generally in favour of sending an exhibition to Pylos. So he told them not to send observers or let slip their chance by delaying, but, if they believed the report, to despatch a naval force against the Lacedaimonians. Then, pointedly referring to Nicias, the son of Niceratos, (one of the generals, and his political enemy), he said that if only the generals were real men they could easily sail with a properly-equipped force and capture the soldiers on the island. He added that he himself would do it, if he were in command.

The Athenians began to murmur against Cleon, asking him why he did not sail straightaway if he thought it so easy: and Nicias, realising that Cleon was getting at him, told him that as far as the generals were concerned Cleon might take any force he liked and try it. Cleon at first thought that Nicias' offer was only a pretence: but then he realised that Nicias was really prepared to hand over the command. He had never thought that Nicias would have the nerve to give up his place, and was now in a panic: so he tried to back out, and said that not he but Nicias was the official commander. But Nicias again told him to take command, and called the Athenians to witness that he himself was relinquishing it. The more Cleon tried to get out of sailing and to retract what he had said, the more the Athenians (as mobs often do) told Nicias to hand over the command, and roared out that Cleon should sail. So being unable to go back on what he had said, he undertook the expedition.

He came forward and said that he was not afraid of the Lacedaimonians, and would take no soldiers from Athens on the expedition, only some Lemnians and Imbrians who happened to be there, and the auxiliary light-armed troops from Ainos and . . . , and 400 archers from other places. With these forces, in addition to those already at Pylos, he promised that in 20 days he would either bring back the Lacedaimonians alive, or else kill them there. There was a certain amount of laughter among the Athenians at his boastful remarks, but the more sensible citizens were glad at what he said. For they reckoned that one or the other of two good things would happen: either they would get rid of Cleon, which was the more likely of the two: or, if they were cheated of that hope, they would get the Lacedaimonians into their power.

29

29 Καὶ πάντα διαπραξάμενος ἐν τῇ ἐκκλησίᾳ καὶ ψη-
φισαμένων Ἀθηναίων αὐτῷ τὸν πλοῦν, τῶν τε ἐν Πύλῳ
στρατηγῶν ἕνα προσελόμενος Δημοσθένη, τὴν ἀναγωγὴν
2 διὰ τάχους ἐποιεῖτο. τὸν δὲ Δημοσθένη προσέλαβε πυν-
θανόμενος τὴν ἀπόβασιν αὐτὸν ἐς τὴν νῆσον διανοεῖσθαι.
οἱ γὰρ στρατιῶται κακοπαθοῦντες τοῦ χωρίου τῇ ἀπορίᾳ καὶ
μᾶλλον πολιορκούμενοι ἢ πολιορκοῦντες ὥρμηντο διακιν-
δυνεῦσαι. καὶ αὐτῷ ἔτι ῥώμην καὶ ἡ νῆσος ἐμπρησθεῖσα
3 παρέσχεν. πρότερον μὲν γὰρ οὔσης αὐτῆς ὑλώδους ἐπὶ τὸ
πολὺ καὶ ἀτριβοῦς διὰ τὴν αἰεὶ ἐρημίαν ἐφοβεῖτο καὶ πρὸς
τῶν πολεμίων τοῦτο ἐνόμιζε μᾶλλον εἶναι· πολλῷ γὰρ ἂν
στρατοπέδῳ ἀποβάντι ἐξ ἀφανοῦς χωρίου προσβάλλοντας
αὐτοὺς βλάπτειν. σφίσι μὲν γὰρ τὰς ἐκείνων ἁμαρτίας
καὶ παρασκευὴν ὑπὸ τῆς ὕλης οὐκ ἂν ὁμοίως δῆλα εἶναι,
τοῦ δὲ αὐτῶν στρατοπέδου καταφανῆ ἂν εἶναι πάντα τὰ
ἁμαρτήματα, ὥστε προσπίπτειν ἂν αὐτοὺς ἀπροσδοκήτως
ᾗ βούλοιντο· ἐπ᾽ ἐκείνοις γὰρ εἶναι ἂν τὴν ἐπιχείρησιν.
4 εἰ δ᾽ αὖ ἐς δασὺ χωρίον βιάζοιτο ὁμόσε ἰέναι, τοὺς ἐλάσσους, ἐμπείρους δὲ τῆς χώρας, κρείσσους ἐνόμιζε τῶν πλεόνων
ἀπείρων· λανθάνειν τε ἂν τὸ ἑαυτῶν στρατόπεδον πολὺ ὂν
διαφθειρόμενον, οὐκ οὔσης τῆς προσόψεως ᾗ χρῆν ἀλλήλοις
30 ἐπιβοηθεῖν. ἀπὸ δὲ τοῦ Αἰτωλικοῦ πάθους, ὃ διὰ τὴν
2 ὕλην μέρος τι ἐγένετο, οὐχ ἥκιστα αὐτὸν ταῦτα ἐσῄει. τῶν
δὲ στρατιωτῶν ἀναγκασθέντων διὰ τὴν στενοχωρίαν τῆς
νήσου τοῖς ἐσχάτοις προσίσχοντας ἀριστοποιεῖσθαι διὰ
προφυλακῆς καὶ ἐμπρήσαντός τινος κατὰ μικρὸν τῆς ὕλης
ἄκοντος καὶ ἀπὸ τούτου πνεύματος ἐπιγενομένου τὸ πολὺ
3 αὐτῆς ἔλαθε κατακαυθέν. οὕτω δὴ τούς τε Λακεδαιμονίους
μᾶλλον κατιδὼν πλείους ὄντας, ὑπονοῶν πρότερον ἐλάσσοσι
τὸν σῖτον αὐτοῦ ἐσπέμπειν, τήν τε νῆσον εὐαποβατωτέραν
οὖσαν, τότε ὡς ἐπ᾽ ἀξιόχρεων τοὺς Ἀθηναίους μᾶλλον
σπουδὴν ποιεῖσθαι τὴν ἐπιχείρησιν παρεσκευάζετο, στρατιάν
τε μεταπέμπων ἐκ τῶν ἐγγὺς ξυμμάχων καὶ τὰ ἄλλα
ἑτοιμάζων.

4 Κλέων δὲ ἐκείνῳ τε προπέμψας ἄγγελον ὡς ἥξων καὶ
ἔχων στρατιὰν ἣν ᾐτήσατο, ἀφικνεῖται ἐς Πύλον. καὶ ἅμα
γενόμενοι πέμπουσι πρῶτον ἐς τὸ ἐν τῇ ἠπείρῳ στρατόπεδον
κήρυκα, προκαλούμενοι, εἰ βούλοιντο, ἄνευ κινδύνου τοὺς ἐν
τῇ νήσῳ ἄνδρας σφίσι τά τε ὅπλα καὶ σφᾶς αὐτοὺς κελεύειν
παραδοῦναι, ἐφ᾽ ᾧ φυλακῇ τῇ μετρίᾳ τηρήσονται, ἕως ἄν τι
31 περὶ τοῦ πλέονος ξυμβαθῇ. οὐ προσδεξαμένων δὲ αὐτῶν

So Cleon completed all the official business in the assembly, and the Athenians voted that he should conduct the expedition. He chose one of the generals at Pylos, Demosthenes, as his colleague and arranged to sail as soon as possible. He picked Demosthenes, because he had learned that Demosthenes was intending to make the landing on the island himself. The soldiers at Pylos were suffering a good deal from lack of supplies, and were in the position of being blockaded rather than blockading, and so they were eager to risk the attempt.

Demosthenes had been further encouraged by a fire on the island. Hitherto, it had been mostly covered with thickets, and there were no paths on it because it had never been inhabited; these facts had discouraged him, for he considered them to favour the enemy - if he landed with a whole army of troops, the enemy could attack him from a concealed position and do a good deal of damage. Similarly, the enemy's mistakes and preparations would not be visible because of the thickets, whereas all the mistakes made by his own army would easily be seen, and the enemy could attack it unexpectedly from any point they wished: they would have the initiative. Again, if they had to advance at close quarters into the undergrowth, Demosthenes reckoned that a smaller number of men who knew the terrain would be better than a larger number who did not. His own large army would be destroyed unobserved, for they would not be able to see just where reinforcements were needed. He was led to consider these points by the disaster in Aetolia in particular, which was partly due to the wooded terrain.

What had happened was this: the Athenian soldiers were compelled, for shortage of space, to land on the extremities of the island and take their meals there, posting an advance guard. One of them unintentionally set fire to a portion of the thickets; after that a wind came on, and before anyone realised it most of the thickets were burned down. In this way Demosthenes, who had hitherto suspected that there were fewer Lacedaimonians on the island than the official number for whom they were sending supplies, was now able to see that there were more than he had thought. He also saw that the island was now less impenetrable to a sea-borne attack. So it seemed to him really worth the Athenians' while to undertake the enterprise with enthusiasm; and he made the preparations for it, dispatching messengers asking for reinforcements to the allies who were nearby, and making everything else ready.

Cleon had sent a messenger to him to announce his arrival, and now reached Pylos with the force he had originally requested. When he and Demosthenes met, they began by sending a herald to the Peloponnesian camp on the mainland, inviting them, if they agreed, to take no more risks but to tell the men on the island to surrender themselves and their arms to the Athenians: the men would be kept in honourable custody until some more general agreement was made. The Lacedaimonians rejected this offer: so

μίαν μὲν ἡμέραν ἐπέσχον, τῇ δ' ὑστεραίᾳ ἀνηγάγοντο μὲν νυκτὸς ἐπ' ὀλίγας ναῦς τοὺς ὁπλίτας πάντας ἐπιβιβάσαντες, πρὸ δὲ τῆς ἔω ὀλίγον ἀπέβαινον τῆς νήσου ἑκατέρωθεν, ἔκ τε τοῦ πελάγους καὶ πρὸς τοῦ λιμένος, ὀκτακόσιοι μάλιστα ὄντες ὁπλῖται, καὶ ἐχώρουν δρόμῳ ἐπὶ τὸ πρῶτον φυλα-
2 κτήριον τῆς νήσου. ὧδε γὰρ διετετάχατο· ἐν ταύτῃ μὲν τῇ πρώτῃ φυλακῇ ὡς τριάκοντα ἦσαν ὁπλῖται, μέσον δὲ καὶ ὁμαλώτατόν τε καὶ περὶ τὸ ὕδωρ οἱ πλεῖστοι αὐτῶν καὶ Ἐπιτάδας ὁ ἄρχων εἶχε, μέρος δέ τι οὐ πολὺ αὐτὸ τὸ ἔσχατον ἐφύλασσε τῆς νήσου τὸ πρὸς τὴν Πύλον, ὃ ἦν ἔκ τε θαλάσσης ἀπόκρημνον καὶ ἐκ τῆς γῆς ἥκιστα ἐπίμαχον· καὶ γάρ τι καὶ ἔρυμα αὐτόθι ἦν παλαιὸν λίθων λογάδην πεποιημένον, ὃ ἐνόμιζον σφίσιν ὠφέλιμον ἂν εἶναι, εἰ καταλαμβάνοι ἀναχώρησις βιαιοτέρα. οὕτω μὲν τεταγμένοι ἦσαν.

32 Οἱ δὲ Ἀθηναῖοι τοὺς μὲν πρώτους φύλακας, οἷς ἐπέδρα-μον, εὐθὺς διαφθείρουσιν ἔν τε ταῖς εὐναῖς ἔτι καὶ ἀναλαμ-βάνοντας τὰ ὅπλα, λαθόντες τὴν ἀπόβασιν, οἰομένων αὐτῶν
2 τὰς ναῦς κατὰ τὸ ἔθος ἐς ἔφορμον τῆς νυκτὸς πλεῖν. ἅμα δὲ ἕῳ γιγνομένῃ καὶ ὁ ἄλλος στρατὸς ἀπέβαινεν, ἐκ μὲν νεῶν ἑβδομήκοντα καὶ ὀλίγῳ πλεόνων πάντες πλὴν θα-λαμιῶν, ὡς ἕκαστοι ἐσκευασμένοι, τοξόται δὲ ὀκτακόσιοι καὶ πελτασταὶ οὐκ ἐλάσσους τούτων, Μεσσηνίων τε οἱ βεβοηθηκότες καὶ οἱ ἄλλοι ὅσοι περὶ Πύλον κατεῖχον πάντες
3 πλὴν τῶν ἐπὶ τοῦ τείχους φυλάκων. Δημοσθένους δὲ τάξαν-τος διέστησαν κατὰ διακοσίους τε καὶ πλείους, ἔστι δ' ἧ ἐλάσσους, τῶν χωρίων τὰ μετεωρότατα λαβόντες, ὅπως ὅτι πλείστη ἀπορία ἦ τοῖς πολεμίοις πανταχόθεν κεκυκλω-μένοις καὶ μὴ ἔχωσι πρὸς ὅτι ἀντιτάξωνται, ἀλλ' ἀμφίβολοι γίγνωνται τῷ πλήθει, εἰ μὲν τοῖς πρόσθεν ἐπίοιεν, ὑπὸ τῶν κατόπιν βαλλόμενοι, εἰ δὲ τοῖς πλαγίοις, ὑπὸ τῶν ἑκατέ-
4 ρωθεν παρατεταγμένων. κατὰ νώτου τε αἰεὶ ἔμελλον αὐτοῖς, ἧ χωρήσειαν, οἱ πολέμιοι ἔσεσθαι ψιλοὶ καὶ οἱ ἀπορώτατοι, τοξεύμασι καὶ ἀκοντίοις καὶ λίθοις καὶ σφενδόναις ἐκ πολλοῦ ἔχοντες ἀλκήν, οἷς μηδὲ ἐπελθεῖν οἷόν τε ἦν· φεύγοντές τε γὰρ ἐκράτουν καὶ ἀναχωροῦσιν ἐπέκειντο.

Τοιαύτῃ μὲν γνώμῃ ὁ Δημοσθένης τό τε πρῶτον τὴν
33 ἀπόβασιν ἐπενόει καὶ ἐν τῷ ἔργῳ ἔταξεν· οἱ δὲ περὶ τὸν Ἐπιτάδαν καὶ ὅπερ ἦν πλεῖστον τῶν ἐν τῇ νήσῳ, ὡς εἶδον τό τε πρῶτον φυλακτήριον διεφθαρμένον καὶ στρατὸν σφίσιν ἐπιόντα, ξυνετάξαντο καὶ τοῖς ὁπλίταις τῶν Ἀθηναίων ἐπῇσαν, βουλόμενοι ἐς χεῖρας ἐλθεῖν· ἐξ ἐναντίας γὰρ

the Athenians waited for one day, and on the next they put out to sea, having placed all their hoplites on board a few ships at night. A little before dawn they landed this force, about 800 hoplites, on both sides of the island - on the seaward side and on the side facing the harbour - and ran to attack the first guardpost on the island.

Now these were the Lacedaimonian dispositions: in this first guardpost there were about 30 hoplites: most of their troops, together with Epitadas the commander, were in the middle of the island, where the ground was most level, around the water-supply: and a small number of them guarded the end of the island next to Pylos, where the cliffs were sheer on the sea side, and which was the strongest point of all on the land-ward side. Moreover, there was an old fortification there made of stones roughly put together, which they thought would be useful to them if they were compelled to retreat. Such was the disposition of the Lacedaimonian troops.

The Athenians rushed upon the men of the first guardpost and killed them while they were still in their beds and in process of arming themselves: for the Lacedaimon-ians had not observed the landing, but thought that the ships were just sailing to their night-time anchorages as usual. At dawn the rest of the Athenian force landed. This consisted of the crews of rather more than 70 ships (except for the lowest bank of rowers), with whatever equipment each happened to have: also 800 archers and as many or more light-armed troops: the Messenian reinforcements: and all those troops who were stationed around Pylos, except for those who were guarding the walls.

Demosthenes had divided them into groups of about 200 - sometimes more, sometimes less: and they seized the highest points of the terrain, in order to surround the enemy and thus make things as difficult as possible for them. In this way the Lacedaimonians would not know whom to face first, but would be exposed to fire from superior numbers on all sides: if they attacked the troops immediately in front of them, they would be hit by those behind, and if they attacked those on one quarter, they would be hit by those on the opposite quarter. Whichever way they went, the Athenian light-armed troops could always get behind them: and these troops were the Lacedaimonians' most difficult opponents, since they could fight effectively at a distance with arrows, javelins, stones and slings. The Lacedaimonians would not even get near them: the troops would overcome them by running away and then again by harrying the Lacedaimonians when they retreated in their turn. This was the plan which Demosthenes originally had for the assault, and this is how in fact he organised it when it came to the point.

The main body of the Lacedaimonians on the island, the ones under Epitadas' direct control, saw the first guardpost destroyed and the Athenian army approaching them. So they drew up their battle-line and went for the Athenian hoplites, intending to come to close quarters with them. The Athenian hoplites were right opposite the

οὗτοι καθειστήκεσαν, ἐκ πλαγίου δὲ οἱ ψιλοὶ καὶ κατὰ νώτου.

2 τοῖς μὲν οὖν ὁπλίταις οὐκ ἐδυνήθησαν προσμεῖξαι οὐδὲ τῇ σφετέρᾳ ἐμπειρίᾳ χρήσασθαι· οἱ γὰρ ψιλοὶ ἑκατέρωθεν βάλλοντες εἶργον, καὶ ἅμα ἐκεῖνοι οὐκ ἀντεπῇσαν, ἀλλ᾽ ἡσύχαζον· τοὺς δὲ ψιλούς, ᾗ μάλιστα αὐτοῖς ἐπιθέοντες προσκέοιντο, ἔτρεπον, καὶ οἱ ὑποστρέφοντες ἡμύνοντο, ἄνθρωποι κούφως τε ἐσκευασμένοι καὶ προλαμβάνοντες ῥᾳδίως τῆς φυγῆς χωρίων τε χαλεπότητι καὶ ὑπὸ τῆς πρὶν ἐρημίας τραχέων ὄντων, ἐν οἷς οἱ Λακεδαιμόνιοι οὐκ ἐδύναντο διώκειν

34 ὅπλα ἔχοντες. χρόνον μὲν οὖν τινὰ ὀλίγον οὕτω πρὸς ἀλλήλους ἠκροβολίσαντο· τῶν δὲ Λακεδαιμονίων οὐκέτι ὀξέως ἐπεκθεῖν ᾗ προσπίπτοιεν δυναμένων, γνόντες αὐτοὺς οἱ ψιλοὶ βραδυτέρους ἤδη ὄντας τῷ ἀμύνασθαι, καὶ αὐτοὶ τῇ τε ὄψει τοῦ θαρσεῖν τὸ πλεῖστον εἰληφότες πολλαπλάσιοι φαινόμενοι καὶ ξυνειθισμένοι μᾶλλον μηκέτι δεινοὺς αὐτοὺς ὁμοίως σφίσι φαίνεσθαι, ὅτι οὐκ εὐθὺς ἄξια τῆς προσδοκίας ἐπεπόνθεσαν, ὥσπερ ὅτε πρῶτον ἀπέβαινον τῇ γνώμῃ δεδουλωμένοι ὡς ἐπὶ Λακεδαιμονίους, καταφρονήσαντες καὶ ἐμβοήσαντες ἀθρόοι ὥρμησαν ἐπ᾽ αὐτοὺς καὶ ἔβαλλον λίθοις τε καὶ τοξεύμασι καὶ ἀκοντίοις, ὡς ἕκαστός

2 τι πρόχειρον εἶχεν. γενομένης δὲ τῆς βοῆς ἅμα τῇ ἐπιδρομῇ ἔκπληξίς τε ἐνέπεσεν ἀνθρώποις ἀήθεσι τοιαύτης μάχης καὶ ὁ κονιορτὸς τῆς ὕλης νεωστὶ κεκαυμένης ἐχώρει πολὺς ἄνω, ἄπορόν τε ἦν ἰδεῖν τὸ πρὸ αὐτοῦ ὑπὸ τῶν τοξευμάτων καὶ λίθων ἀπὸ πολλῶν ἀνθρώπων μετὰ τοῦ

3 κονιορτοῦ ἅμα φερομένων. τό τε ἔργον ἐνταῦθα χαλεπὸν τοῖς Λακεδαιμονίοις καθίστατο· οὔτε γὰρ οἱ πῖλοι ἔστεγον τὰ τοξεύματα, δοράτιά τε ἐναπεκέκλαστο βαλλομένων, εἶχόν τε οὐδὲν σφίσιν αὐτοῖς χρήσασθαι ἀποκεκλῃμένοι μὲν τῇ ὄψει τοῦ προορᾶν, ὑπὸ δὲ τῆς μείζονος βοῆς τῶν πολεμίων τὰ ἐν αὐτοῖς παραγγελλόμενα οὐκ ἐσακούοντες, κινδύνου τε πανταχόθεν περιεστῶτος καὶ οὐκ ἔχοντες ἐλπίδα καθ᾽ ὅτι

35 χρὴ ἀμυνομένους σωθῆναι. τέλος δὲ τραυματιζομένων ἤδη πολλῶν διὰ τὸ αἰεὶ ἐν τῷ αὐτῷ ἀναστρέφεσθαι, ξυγκλῄσαντες ἐχώρησαν ἐς τὸ ἔσχατον ἔρυμα τῆς νήσου, ὃ οὐ

2 πολὺ ἀπεῖχε, καὶ τοὺς ἑαυτῶν φύλακας. ὡς δὲ ἐνέδοσαν, ἐνταῦθα ἤδη πολλῷ ἔτι πλέονι βοῇ τεθαρσηκότες οἱ ψιλοὶ ἐπέκειντο, καὶ τῶν Λακεδαιμονίων ὅσοι μὲν ὑποχωροῦντες ἐγκατελαμβάνοντο, ἀπέθνῃσκον, οἱ δὲ πολλοὶ διαφυγόντες ἐς τὸ ἔρυμα μετὰ τῶν ταύτῃ φυλάκων ἐτάξαντο παρὰ πᾶν ὡς

3 ἀμυνούμενοι ᾗπερ ἦν ἐπίμαχον. καὶ οἱ Ἀθηναῖοι ἐπισπόμενοι περίοδον μὲν αὐτῶν καὶ κύκλωσιν χωρίου ἰσχύι οὐκ εἶχον,

Lacedaimonians, and the light-armed troops on their flanks and behind them. But the Lacedaimonians were unable to take advantage of their military efficiency by getting to grips with the hoplites: for the light-armed troops shot at them from both flanks and kept them off, and the hoplites did not advance to meet them but stayed where they were. Wherever the light-armed troops came close to attack the Lacedaimonians, the Lacedaimonians made them retreat: but then the troops wheeled round again and fought back: their equipment was light, and they had the advantage in making their escape because of the difficulty of the terrain (which was very rough because it had not been inhabited). On such ground the Lacedaimonians could not well pursue them, because of their heavy equipment.

For a short time, then, they fought each other at a distance in this way: and in a while the Lacedaimonians were no longer able to rush out at their attackers so quickly. The light-armed Athenians noticed that their resistance was getting more sluggish: and they themselves had acquired a high degree of confidence, for they saw how superior their numbers were, and familiarity with the Lacedaimonians made them appear much less terrible than before. When they first made the landing they had been frightened of meeting the Lacedaimonians in battle, but their own losses had been much less than they had expected. So now they began to be contemptuous of them; they raised a shout and rushed on them in a body, attacking them with stones, arrows, javelins and whatever each of them had to hand. What with the shouting and the sudden assault, the Lacedaimonians, who were unaccustomed to this sort of battle, became dismayed. Great clouds of dust arose high in the air from the thickets that had just been burned down, and there were vast numbers of Athenian arrows and stones flying at them in the dust-clouds: so that the Lacedaimonians could not get a clear view of what was in front of them.

At this point the battle became hard for the Lacedaimonians. For their felt caps did not protect them against the arrows, and javelins that hit them broke off and stayed in their bodies: they were unable to see in front of them, and unable to hear their words of command because of the louder cries of the enemy. Hence they had no way of saving the situation; they were surrounded by danger on every side, and had no effective method of defending themselves. Many of them were being wounded because they were always moving about on the same terrain; and finally they closed their ranks and went to the fort where their own guardpost was at the end of the island, which was not far off.

As they retreated, the light-armed Athenians became even more confident and pressed hard on them with still louder shouts. Those Lacedaimonians that were caught by them during the retreat were killed: but most of them got safely to the fort, and organised their defence there together with the men of the guardpost, at every point where the position was assailable. The Athenians followed, but because of the strength

προσιόντες δὲ ἐξ ἐναντίας ὤσασθαι ἐπειρῶντο. καὶ χρόνον
μὲν πολὺν καὶ τῆς ἡμέρας τὸ πλεῖστον ταλαιπωρούμενοι
ἀμφότεροι ὑπό τε τῆς μάχης καὶ δίψης καὶ ἡλίου ἀντεῖχον,
πειρώμενοι οἱ μὲν ἐξελάσασθαι ἐκ τοῦ μετεώρου, οἱ δὲ μὴ
ἐνδοῦναι· ῥᾷον δ' οἱ Λακεδαιμόνιοι ἡμύνοντο ἢ ἐν τῷ πρίν,
οὐκ οὔσης σφῶν τῆς κυκλώσεως ἐς τὰ πλάγια.

36   Ἐπειδὴ δὲ ἀπέραντον ἦν, προσελθὼν ὁ τῶν Μεσσηνίων
στρατηγὸς Κλέωνι καὶ Δημοσθένει ἄλλως ἔφη πονεῖν σφᾶς·
εἰ δὲ βούλονται ἑαυτῷ δοῦναι τῶν τοξοτῶν μέρος τι καὶ τῶν
ψιλῶν περιιέναι κατὰ νώτου αὐτοῖς ὁδῷ ᾗ ἂν αὐτὸς εὕρῃ,
2 δοκεῖν βιάσεσθαι τὴν ἔφοδον. λαβὼν δὲ ἃ ᾐτήσατο, ἐκ
τοῦ ἀφανοῦς ὁρμήσας ὥστε μὴ ἰδεῖν ἐκείνους, κατὰ τὸ αἰεὶ
παρεῖκον τοῦ κρημνώδους τῆς νήσου προσβαίνων, καὶ ᾗ οἱ
Λακεδαιμόνιοι χωρίου ἰσχύι πιστεύσαντες οὐκ ἐφύλασσον,
χαλεπῶς τε καὶ μόλις περιελθὼν ἔλαθε, καὶ ἐπὶ τοῦ μετεώρου
ἐξαπίνης ἀναφανεὶς κατὰ νώτου αὐτῶν τοὺς μὲν τῷ ἀδοκήτῳ
ἐξέπληξε, τοὺς δὲ ἃ προσεδέχοντο ἰδόντας πολλῷ μᾶλλον
3 ἐπέρρωσεν. καὶ οἱ Λακεδαιμόνιοι βαλλόμενοί τε ἀμφοτέρωθεν ἤδη καὶ γιγνόμενοι ἐν τῷ αὐτῷ ξυμπτώματι, ὡς
μικρὸν μεγάλῳ εἰκάσαι, τῷ ἐν Θερμοπύλαις, ἐκεῖνοί τε γὰρ
τῇ ἀτραπῷ περιελθόντων τῶν Περσῶν διεφθάρησαν, οὗτοί
τε ἀμφίβολοι ἤδη ὄντες οὐκέτι ἀντεῖχον, ἀλλὰ πολλοῖς τε
ὀλίγοι μαχόμενοι καὶ ἀσθενείᾳ σωμάτων διὰ τὴν σιτοδείαν
ὑπεχώρουν, καὶ οἱ Ἀθηναῖοι ἐκράτουν ἤδη τῶν ἐφόδων.

37   Γνοὺς δὲ ὁ Κλέων καὶ ὁ Δημοσθένης [ὅτι], εἰ καὶ ὁπο-
σονοῦν μᾶλλον ἐνδώσουσι, διαφθαρησομένους αὐτοὺς ὑπὸ
τῆς σφετέρας στρατιᾶς, ἔπαυσαν τὴν μάχην καὶ τοὺς ἑαυτῶν
ἀπεῖρξαν, βουλόμενοι ἀγαγεῖν αὐτοὺς Ἀθηναίοις ζῶντας, εἴ
πως τοῦ κηρύγματος ἀκούσαντες ἐπικλασθεῖεν τῇ γνώμῃ
τὰ ὅπλα παραδοῦναι καὶ ἡσσηθεῖεν τοῦ παρόντος δεινοῦ.
2 ἐκήρυξάν τε, εἰ βούλονται, τὰ ὅπλα παραδοῦναι καὶ σφᾶς
αὐτοὺς Ἀθηναίοις ὥστε βουλεῦσαι ὅτι ἂν ἐκείνοις δοκῇ.

38 οἱ δὲ ἀκούσαντες παρῆκαν τὰς ἀσπίδας οἱ πλεῖστοι καὶ τὰς
χεῖρας ἀνέσεισαν, δηλοῦντες προσίεσθαι τὰ κεκηρυγμένα.
μετὰ δὲ ταῦτα γενομένης τῆς ἀνοκωχῆς ξυνῆλθον ἐς λόγους
ὅ τε Κλέων καὶ ὁ Δημοσθένης καὶ ἐκείνων Στύφων ὁ
Φάρακος, τῶν πρότερον ἀρχόντων τοῦ μὲν πρώτου τεθνη-
κότος Ἐπιτάδου, τοῦ δὲ μετ' αὐτὸν Ἱππαγρέτου ἐφῃρημένου
ἐν τοῖς νεκροῖς ἔτι ζῶντος κειμένου ὡς τεθνεῶτος, αὐτὸς

of the position they could not encircle it and surround the Lacedaimonians: so they made a frontal attack and tried to force them back.

For a long time - most of that day, indeed - both sides suffered considerably from the fighting, from thirst, and from the heat of the sun: but they stuck it out, the Athenians trying to drive the Lacedaimonians off the high ground, and the Lacedaimonians determined not to give way. The Lacedaimonians defended themselves with more ease than before, since the Athenians could not now get round the flanks of their position. When it seemed as if it would go on for ever, the commander of the Messenians came up and told Cleon and Demosthenes that they were wasting their labour. He asked them to give him some archers and light-armed troops, and he would go round behind the Lacedaimonians by any path he could find that looked as if it might enable them to force the approach.

They granted his request, and he started off from a point invisible to the Lacedaimonians, so that they should not observe the manoeuvre. He made his way along this precipitous part of the island wherever the ground gave him a footing, and wherever the Lacedaimonians had set no guards because of the natural strength of the position. Slowly and with difficulty he managed to get round them unobserved, and suddenly appeared on the high ground behind them. The Lacedaimonians were dismayed by this unexpected event, and the Athenians were heartened when they saw them as they had expected.

The Lacedaimonians were now under fire from both sides, and were in the same wretched position (to compare small things with great) as those at Thermopylae, who had perished because the Persians managed to encircle them by using the path. Caught between two fires, the Lacedaimonians could no longer keep the Athenians back: they were only a few against many, and lack of food had diminished their physical strength. They yielded ground; and now the Athenians were already beginning to gain control of the approaches.

Cleon and Demosthenes realised that if the Lacedaimonians retreated even a little further they would be totally destroyed by the Athenian army. So they stopped the fighting and kept their own men back: for they wanted to bring them to Athens alive, and thought that if they heard an offer of terms from a herald their spirit might be broken, and they might be induced by their desperate position to lay down their arms. Accordingly, they proclaimed to them that, if they wished, they could surrender their weapons and themselves to the Athenians, who would decide what to do as they thought best. When the Lacedaimonians heard this, most of them put down their shields and waved their hands to show that they agreed to the offer. There was then a cease-fire, and a parley between Cleon and Demosthenes for the Athenians, and for the Lacedaimonians Styphon the son of Pharax. The original commander, Epitadas, was

τρίτος ἐφῃρημένος ἄρχειν κατὰ νόμον, εἴ τι ἐκεῖνοι πάσχοιεν. 2 ἔλεγε δὲ ὁ Στύφων καὶ οἱ μετ᾽ αὐτοῦ ὅτι βούλονται διακηρυκεύσασθαι πρὸς τοὺς ἐν τῇ ἠπείρῳ Λακεδαιμονίους ὅτι χρὴ 3 σφᾶς ποιεῖν. καὶ ἐκείνων μὲν οὐδένα ἀφέντων, αὐτῶν δὲ τῶν Ἀθηναίων καλούντων ἐκ τῆς ἠπείρου κήρυκας καὶ γενομένων ἐπερωτήσεων δὶς ἢ τρίς, ὁ τελευταῖος διαπλεύσας αὐτοῖς ἀπὸ τῶν ἐκ τῆς ἠπείρου Λακεδαιμονίων ἀνὴρ ἀπήγγειλεν ὅτι [οἱ] ᾽ Λακεδαιμόνιοι κελεύουσιν ὑμᾶς αὐτοὺς περὶ ὑμῶν αὐτῶν βουλεύεσθαι μηδὲν αἰσχρὸν ποιοῦντας᾽· οἱ δὲ καθ᾽ ἑαυτοὺς βουλευσάμενοι τὰ ὅπλα παρέδοσαν καὶ σφᾶς 4 αὐτούς. καὶ ταύτην μὲν τὴν ἡμέραν καὶ τὴν ἐπιοῦσαν νύκτα ἐν φυλακῇ εἶχον αὐτοὺς οἱ Ἀθηναῖοι· τῇ δ᾽ ὑστεραίᾳ οἱ μὲν Ἀθηναῖοι τροπαῖον στήσαντες ἐν τῇ νήσῳ τἄλλα διεσκευάζοντο ὡς ἐς πλοῦν, καὶ τοὺς ἄνδρας τοῖς τριηράρχοις διεδίδοσαν ἐς φυλακήν, οἱ δὲ Λακεδαιμόνιοι κήρυκα πέμ- 5 ψαντες τοὺς νεκροὺς διεκομίσαντο. ἀπέθανον δ᾽ ἐν τῇ νήσῳ καὶ ζῶντες ἐλήφθησαν τοσοίδε· εἴκοσι μὲν ὁπλῖται διέβησαν καὶ τετρακόσιοι οἱ πάντες· τούτων ζῶντες ἐκομίσθησαν ὀκτὼ ἀποδέοντες τριακόσιοι, οἱ δὲ ἄλλοι ἀπέθανον. καὶ Σπαρτιᾶται τούτων ἦσαν τῶν ζώντων περὶ εἴκοσι καὶ ἑκατόν. Ἀθηναίων δὲ οὐ πολλοὶ διεφθάρησαν· ἡ γὰρ μάχη οὐ σταδαία ἦν.

39 Χρόνος δὲ ὁ ξύμπας ἐγένετο ὅσον οἱ ἄνδρες [οἱ] ἐν τῇ νήσῳ ἐπολιορκήθησαν, ἀπὸ τῆς ναυμαχίας μέχρι τῆς ἐν τῇ 2 νήσῳ μάχης, ἑβδομήκοντα ἡμέραι καὶ δύο. τούτων περὶ εἴκοσιν ἡμέρας, ἐν αἷς οἱ πρέσβεις περὶ τῶν σπονδῶν ἀπῇσαν, ἐσιτοδοτοῦντο, τὰς δὲ ἄλλας τοῖς ἐσπλέουσι λάθρα διετρέφοντο. καὶ ἦν σῖτός τις ἐν τῇ νήσῳ καὶ ἄλλα βρώματα ἐγκατελήφθη· ὁ γὰρ ἄρχων Ἐπιτάδας ἐνδεεστέρως 3 ἑκάστῳ παρεῖχεν ἢ πρὸς τὴν ἐξουσίαν. οἱ μὲν δὴ Ἀθηναῖοι καὶ οἱ Πελοποννήσιοι ἀνεχώρησαν τῷ στρατῷ ἐκ τῆς Πύλου ἑκάτεροι ἐπ᾽ οἴκου, καὶ τοῦ Κλέωνος καίπερ μανιώδης οὖσα ἡ ὑπόσχεσις ἀπέβη· ἐντὸς γὰρ εἴκοσιν ἡμερῶν ἤγαγε τοὺς 40 ἄνδρας, ὥσπερ ὑπέστη. παρὰ γνώμην τε δὴ μάλιστα τῶν κατὰ τὸν πόλεμον τοῦτο τοῖς Ἕλλησιν ἐγένετο· τοὺς γὰρ Λακεδαιμονίους οὔτε λιμῷ οὔτ᾽ ἀνάγκῃ οὐδεμιᾷ ἠξίουν τὰ ὅπλα παραδοῦναι, ἀλλὰ ἔχοντας καὶ μαχομένους ὡς ἐδύναντο 2 ἀποθνήσκειν. ἀπιστοῦντές τε μὴ εἶναι τοὺς παραδόντας τοῖς τεθνεῶσιν ὁμοίους, καί τινος ἐρομένου ποτὲ ὕστερον τῶν Ἀθηναίων ξυμμάχων δι᾽ ἀχθηδόνα ἕνα τῶν ἐκ τῆς νήσου αἰχμαλώτων εἰ οἱ τεθνεῶτες αὐτῶν καλοὶ κἀγαθοί, ἀπεκρίνατο αὐτῷ πολλοῦ ἂν ἄξιον εἶναι τὸν ἄτρακτον, λέγων τὸν

dead: and the man chosen as second-in-command, Hippagretas, was (though still alive) lying apparently dead among the corpses: and Styphon had been chosen as the third commander, in accordance with Spartan convention, in case something happened to the first two.

Styphon and his comrades replied that they wished first to communicate with the Lacedaimonians on the mainland, to ask what they ought to do. The Athenians would not permit any Lacedaimonian to go, but themselves requested heralds from the mainland. After two or three consultations, the herald who came over last from the Lacedaimonians on the mainland said: "The Lacedaimonians order you to make your own decision about yourselves, but to do nothing dishonourable". They discussed the matter with each other, and then surrendered their arms and themselves.

For the rest of that day and the following night the Athenians kept them under guard. On the next day the Athenians set up a trophy on the island, made preparations to sail, and handed the men under guard over to the trireme-commanders. The Lacedaimonians sent a herald and took back their dead. The numbers of men killed and taken alive on the island were as follows: 420 hoplites in all crossed over, of whom 292 were brought alive to Athens; the others were all killed. Of these 292 who remained alive, about 120 were Spartiates. Not many Athenians were killed, for there had been no set battle.

The whole time during which the men had been blockaded on the island, from the sea-battle up to the battle on the island, was 72 days. For about 20 of these days, after the ambassadors had gone to Athens about the truce, the Lacedaimonians were given food: for the rest they were kept alive by boats coming in secretly. Some corn and other foodstuffs were captured on the island: for Epitadas the commander rationed each man more sparingly than his supplies compelled him to. The Athenian and the Peloponnesian forces went away from Pylos, each to their own country. Cleon's promise, though lunatic, was fulfilled: he brought the Lacedaimonians to Athens within 20 days, as he had undertaken.

For the Greeks in general, this was perhaps the most unexpected event of the war: they did not believe that Lacedaimonians would surrender either because of hunger or anything else, but that they would die fighting with their weapons as best they could. They thought that those who had surrendered must be of a different character from those who had died. On a later occasion, one of the Athenian allies insultingly asked one of the prisoners from the island "Those of you that *died* were brave men, were they?" The prisoner answered "Spindles" [i.e. arrows] "would be worth a lot, if they could

οἰστόν, εἰ τοὺς ἀγαθοὺς διεγίγνωσκε, δήλωσιν ποιούμενος ὅτι ὁ ἐντυγχάνων τοῖς τε λίθοις καὶ τοξεύμασι διεφθείρετο.

41 Κομισθέντων δὲ τῶν ἀνδρῶν οἱ Ἀθηναῖοι ἐβούλευσαν δεσμοῖς μὲν αὐτοὺς φυλάσσειν μέχρι οὗ τι ξυμβῶσιν, ἢν δ' οἱ Πελοποννήσιοι πρὸ τούτου ἐς τὴν γῆν ἐσβάλωσιν,
2 ἐξαγαγόντες ἀποκτεῖναι. τῆς δὲ Πύλου φυλακὴν κατεστήσαντο, καὶ οἱ ἐκ τῆς Ναυπάκτου Μεσσήνιοι ὡς ἐς πατρίδα ταύτην (ἔστι γὰρ ἡ Πύλος τῆς Μεσσηνίδος ποτὲ οὔσης γῆς) πέμψαντες σφῶν αὐτῶν τοὺς ἐπιτηδειοτάτους ἐλῄζοντό τε
3 τὴν Λακωνικὴν καὶ πλεῖστα ἔβλαπτον ὁμόφωνοι ὄντες. οἱ δὲ Λακεδαιμόνιοι ἀμαθεῖς ὄντες ἐν τῷ πρὶν χρόνῳ λῃστείας καὶ τοῦ τοιούτου πολέμου, τῶν τε Εἱλώτων αὐτομολούντων καὶ φοβούμενοι μὴ καὶ ἐπὶ μακρότερον σφίσι τι νεωτερισθῇ τῶν κατὰ τὴν χώραν, οὐ ῥᾳδίως ἔφερον, ἀλλὰ καίπερ οὐ βουλόμενοι ἔνδηλοι εἶναι τοῖς Ἀθηναίοις ἐπρεσβεύοντο παρ' αὐτοὺς καὶ ἐπειρῶντο τήν τε Πύλον καὶ τοὺς ἄνδρας κομί-
4 ζεσθαι. οἱ δὲ μειζόνων τε ὠρέγοντο καὶ πολλάκις φοιτώντων αὐτοὺς ἀπράκτους ἀπέπεμπον. ταῦτα μὲν τὰ περὶ Πύλον γενόμενα.

distinguish the brave from the cowardly". He implied that it was a matter of chance who had been killed by the stones and arrows.

When the men were brought to Athens, the Athenians decided to keep them in prison until some agreement was reached, but to take them out and kill them if before then the Lacedaimonians invaded Attica. They established a garrison for Pylos: and the Messenians from Naupactos, who regarded the place as part of their homeland (Pylos is in what was once Messenia), sent some of their most suitable troops. These ravaged Laconian territory, and did a great deal of damage, since they spoke with the same dialect as the inhabitants. The Lacedaimonians had hitherto been unaccustomed to raids and warfare of this kind: and helots deserted to Pylos, so that the Lacedaimonians were frightened that there might be some considerable uprising in their country. They suffered a good deal; and although they did not wish the Athenians to realise their difficulties, they continued to send embassies to Athens, and tried to recover Pylos and the prisoners. But the Athenians were intent on further gains, and although the Lacedaimonians sent many embassies they dismissed them without reaching any agreement. Such were the events at Pylos.

SUPPLEMENTARY TEXTS

τάδε δὲ ἔδοξε Λακεδαιμονίοις καὶ τοῖς ἄλλοις ξυμμάχοις ἐὰν σπονδὰς ποιῶνται οἱ Ἀθηναῖοι, ἐπὶ τῆς αὐτῶν μένειν ἑκατέρους ἔχοντας ἅπερ νῦν ἔχομεν, τοὺς μὲν ἐν τῷ Κορυφασίῳ ἐντὸς τῆς Βουφράδος καὶ τοῦ Τομέως μένοντας, τοὺς δὲ ἐν Κυθήροις μὴ ἐπιμισγομένους ἐς τὴν ξυμμαχίαν, μήτε ἡμᾶς πρὸς αὐτοὺς μήτε αὐτοὺς πρὸς ἡμᾶς, τοὺς δ᾽ ἐν Νισαίᾳ καὶ Μινῴᾳ μὴ ὑπερβαίνοντας τὴν ὁδὸν τὴν ἀπὸ τῶν πυλῶν τῶν παρὰ τοῦ Νίσου ἐπὶ τὸ Ποσειδώνιον, ἀπὸ δὲ τοῦ Ποσειδωνίου εὐθὺς ἐπὶ τὴν γέφυραν τὴν ἐς Μινῴαν (μηδὲ Μεγαρέας καὶ τοὺς ξυμμάχους ὑπερβαίνειν τὴν ὁδὸν ταύτην) καὶ τὴν νῆσον, ἥνπερ ἔλαβον οἱ Ἀθηναῖοι, ἔχοντας, μηδὲ ἐπιμισγομένους μηδετέρους μηδετέρωσε, καὶ τὰ ἐν Τροιζῆνι, ὅσαπερ νῦν ἔχουσι, καθ᾽ ἃ ξυνέθεντο πρὸς Ἀθηναίους·

Thuc. IV, 118.4

If the Athenians are willing to make a treaty, the Lacedaimonians and their other allies agree to the following: Each side to stay on its own territory, holding what it now holds, i.e., the Athenians in Koryphasion to stay within Bouphras and Tomeus; those on Cythera not to communicate with a view to any alliance, neither we with them nor they with us; those in Nisaia and Minoa not to go further than the road leading from the gates of the temple of Nisos to the temple of Poseidon, and from there straight on to the bridge to Minoa, and the Megarians and their allies not to cross this road: the Athenians to keep the island they have taken: neither side to communicate with the other: in the territory of Troizene each side to keep what it now holds, as the Athenians have agreed.

Λακεδαιμόνιοι δὲ πυνθανόμενοι περὶ τὸν Ἑλλήσποντον ὑπάρχειν ἀπάσας τὰς τῶν Ἀθηναίων δυνάμεις ἐστράτευσαν ἐπὶ Πύλον, ἣν Μεσσήνιοι φρουρᾷ κατεῖχον, κατὰ μὲν θάλατταν ἕνδεκα ναυσίν, ὧν ἦσαν αἱ μὲν ἀπὸ Σικελίας πέντε, ἓξ δὲ ἐκ τῶν πολιτῶν πεπληρωμέναι. πεζῇ δὲ παρήγαγον ἱκανὴν δύναμιν, καὶ περιστρατοπεδεύσαντες τὸ φρούριον ἐπολιόρκουν ἅμα καὶ κατὰ γῆν καὶ κατὰ θάλατταν. ἃ δὴ πυθόμενος ὁ τῶν Ἀθηναίων δῆμος ἐξαπέστειλε τοῖς πολιορκουμένοις εἰς βοήθειαν ναῦς τριάκοντα καὶ στρατηγὸν Ἄνυτον τὸν Ἀνθεμίωνος. οὗτος μὲν οὖν ἐκπλεύσας καὶ διά τινας χειμῶνας οὐ δυνηθεὶς τὸν Μαλέαν κάμψαι, ἀνέπλευσεν εἰς Ἀθήνας ....οἱ δ᾽ ἐν τῇ Πύλῳ Μεσσήνιοι μέχρι μέν τινος ἀντεῖχον, προσδοκῶντες παρὰ τῶν Ἀθηναίων βοήθειαν. ὡς δ᾽ οἱ μὲν πολέμιοι τὰς προσβολὰς ἐκ διαδοχῆς ἐποιοῦντο, τῶν δὲ ἰδίων οἱ μὲν ἐκ τῶν τραυμάτων ἀπέθνῃσκον, οἱ δ᾽ ἐκ τῆς σιτοδείας κακῶς ἀπήλλαττον, ὑπόσπονδοι τὸν τόπον ἐξέλιπον.

τῷ δ᾽ αὐτῷ χρόνῳ καὶ Λακεδαιμόνιοι τοὺς εἰς τὸ Κορυφάσιον τῶν Εἱλώτων ἀφεστῶτας ἐκ Μαλέας ὑποσπόνδους ἀφῆκαν.

44

Diodorus XIII, 64.5

When the Lacedaimonians learned that all the Athenian forces were in the Hellespont region, they made an expedition against Pylos, which the Messenians held with a garrison. On the sea they had eleven ships, of which five came from Sicily, and six were manned by their own citizens; on land, they brought a sufficiently large force. They invested the fortress and besieged it by land and sea at the same time. When the Athenian people learned of this, they sent out thirty ships under the command of Anytus son of Anthemion, to help the besieged. So he sailed off; but he was unable to round Cape Malea because of storms, and sailed back to Athens . . . The Messenians in Pylos held out for a time, expecting aid from the Athenians. But the enemy kept launching successive attacks; and of their own men some were dying of wounds, and others in a bad way from lack of food. So they made a truce and abandoned the place.

Xenophon Hell. 1 ii. 18

At the same time also the Lacedaimonians allowed the Helots who had deserted from Malea to Koryphasion to depart under truce.

45

HISTORICAL NOTES

I. PYLOS

A. THE ARRIVAL AND THE GEOGRAPHY

The Storm and the Landing

ὡς ἐγένοντο πλέοντες κατὰ τὴν Λακωνικὴν ..., ὁ μὲν Εὐρυμέδων καὶ
Σοφοκλῆς ἠπείγοντο ἐς τὴν Κέρκυραν, ὁ δὲ Δημοσθένης ἐκέλευε ...
ἀντιλεγόντων δὲ κατὰ τύχην χειμών ... κατήνεγκε τὰς ναῦς ἐς τὴν Πύλον.
(3. 1)

At what point round the Peloponnese did this storm occur? Not, surely, at some
point off 'Laconian territory' in a narrow sense of the phrase, i.e., excluding Messenia.
For the end of this territory is at least fifty sea-miles from Pylos (more if the Athenians
hugged the coast instead of sailing straight across the Messenian Gulf), and they would
have taken shelter well before that. (Certainly they would not have tried to weather
Cape Akritas. There are places tolerably sheltered from north-westerly gales along the
comparatively deserted Messenian coast up to and including Methone.) So Thucydides
here uses Λακωνική to include Messenia.[1]

We are dealing here with an area where summer storms nearly always come from
the north-west, varying occasionally to WNW or NNW. If, as is highly probable, the gale
was a north-westerly one, the ships must have been to the north or north-west of Pylos
at this point: for it is not plausible that triremes caught by a storm could have continued
into it; they would rather have run before it, if at all possible. This view also allows us to
take κατήνεγκε as 'carried the ships to' Pylos, rather than (more loosely) as 'forced the
ships to put in at' Pylos. This is the better and more natural meaning (cf. Thucydides
I.137.2, where Themistocles is carried by a storm to Naxos). From this it follows that
the ships were somewhere between Pylos and the Messenian or Laconian frontier to the
north.

---

1. The point is worth establishing, because it is always *possible* that Thucydides might be using
Λακωνική as a regional or geographic term rather than a political one. But elsewhere it is
normally political: most obviously in ἐς Μεθώνην τῆς Λακωνικῆς (Bk. II, 25.1: see Gomme's
note on I, 10.2, in Vol. I, p. 112), which refers to Methone in the south-west Peloponnese, but
also in our own Bk. IV where he describes Pylos as ἐν τῇ Μεσσηνίᾳ ποτὲ οὔσῃ γῇ (3.2) and
τῆς Μεσσηνίδος ποτὲ οὔσης γῆς (41.2) - the ποτὲ makes Thucydides' position clear.
    This has to be borne in mind when considering the functions of the garrison of Pylos (Note
R): the Messenians ἐλῄζοντο τὴν Λακωνικὴν (41.2), and this will include Messenia as well as
(in the geographical sense) 'Laconia'.

47

A *prima facie* objection to this is that the discussion of whether to put in at Pylos before going on to Corcyra *ought* to have taken place before the ships passed Pylos. But Thucydides does not say that it did: and it would have been quite in order for Demosthenes to continue arguing the point so long as the ships were somewhere in the Pylos area. Moreover, while Demosthenes was arguing the point, the generals were in fact pressing on (i.e., having passed Pylos) to Corcyra: ἠπείγοντο ἐς τὴν Κέρκυραν. Editors often take this imperfect in the sense of "were in favour of pressing on"; this is required, however, only by the pre-determined view that Pylos had not already been passed; and it is in itself plausible only if we take the parallel imperfect, ἐκέλευε, in the sense of "was in favour of ordering" - that is, not "was telling the generals", as it is usually (and rightly) translated, but "was in favour of orders being given to the troops". All this seems unnecessary and improbable. It is perfectly legitimate, both from the textual and topographic viewpoints, to assume that Pylos had already been passed and that the north-westerly gale drove them back to it.

Where did the Athenians actually land? Almost certainly on what is now the sand-bar at the north end of the bay near to Pylos itself (marked on map B): this is one of the few places where there is both shelter and a shallow beach (see p. 96). This fits well with the initial Athenian fortification (4.1). On hostile (even if uninhabited) territory, the Athenians would have been unlikely to stray far from their ships: and the soldiers would hardly have felt inclined on their own initiative to fortify Pylos if, for instance, the ships were lying five or so miles away at the southern end of the bay (αὐτοῖς τοῖς στρατιώταις - - - - ὁρμὴ ἐνέπεσε - - - ἐκτειχίσαι τὸ χωρίον, 4.1).

The advantages of Pylos (3.2-3)

All these are readily intelligible as set out by Thucydides, and not in dispute, except for the two that follow.

ἐρημία

This is of importance in relation to the function of the garrison (see Note R). Gomme says:[2] " . . . the valley of the Pamisos is one of the richest districts in Greece. ἐρῆμος therefore must again be used in the sense of 'unguarded', 'with no armed force to defend it', as in iii.106.1. This gives the connexion of thought with the next sentence, ἀπέχει γὰρ, κτλ: the hoplites of Sparta are a long way away, and this is an additional advantage. See also ὁμοφώνους, §3 below (there were inhabitants there) and πλεῖστ᾽ ἂν βλάπτειν - for they would do little harm by ravaging uninhabited land". But: ἐρῆμος rarely (if ever) actually *means* 'undefended' or 'unguarded', except with reference to

___
2.   p. 439.

48

law-suits. It means 'deserted', 'bereft' or 'abandoned'. In a context which shows clearly that it can only be defenders or armed men of which a place is bereft, ἐρῆμος may indeed come to have the implication of, or boil down to meaning, 'undefended'. But this is not such a context. Throughout this part of Bk. IV Thucydides uses ἐρῆμος and ἐρημία in its usual sense (e.g. 8.6, 27.1, and 29.3). More importantly, the passage in 27.1 specifically makes the point that Pylos is in a deserted or uninhabited area (ἐν χωρίῳ ἐρήμῳ). So it is hard to believe that ἐρῆμος does not mean the same in this passage: and virtually impossible to believe that it *could* not mean the same.

The Pamisos valley is irrelevant, since ἐπὶ πολὺ τῆς χώρας need not extend so far as the Pamisos (more than 30 miles away as the crow flies). So too with ὁμοφώνους and πλεῖστ' ἄν βλάπτειν. Probably the garrison did most of their work by sea (see Note R): it is not clear how far their activities extended, but there is no reason at all to believe that they were confined to the hinterland of Pylos.

There are at least three other possibilities which give sense to γάρ, besides Gomme's:

(a) As Mills says[3] "the place was uninhabited because (1) it was a long way from Sparta, and (2) it was in the Messenian country, which had lost a large part of its population".

(b) γάρ need not refer solely to ἐρῆμον (why should it?), but to the earlier ἠξίου τειχίσεσθαι "he thought it a good place to fortify . . . because it was a long way from Sparta". Here the point is similar to Gomme's ("the hoplites of Sparta are a long way away"), but nothing follows about the sense of ἐρῆμος. Demosthenes thought, perhaps, that it was a good place to fortify because (owing to the distance) the Spartans could not react quickly enough to stop the fortification, or because it would extend Spartan resources to maintain an attack upon it.

(c) γάρ might well mean something much more indefinite, e.g. "all this is relevant, for (in case the reader does not know) Pylos . . . " and then follows a general description (including the fact that the Spartans called it Koryphasion, which connects with nothing specific in what has gone before). This sounds vague: but γάρ is used in a far more elusive way than the English 'for', and I personally prefer this interpretation. Compare the γάρ of 8.6, introducing the basic facts about Sphacteria. We must then translate ἐρῆμον as 'deserted', giving Demosthenes the advantages mentioned in (b) above.

This ἐρημία connects with certain very cloudy (and not here to be fully examined) elements in Spartan-Messenian history. It appears at least from Pausanias[5] that after the Second Messenian War the Messenians in the Pylos area fled by sea: that the Spartans

---

3. Mills *ad loc.*
4. Also those mentioned in the main text: but it is difficult to say how far Demosthenes appreciated such points.
5. *Messenia* VIII.3, XXIII.1, XXIV.4, XXVII.8, and elsewhere. See also Herodotus viii, 73, 2.

made helots of the Messenians further east, and 'divided up' their lands (διελάγχανον): that Asine, though remaining neutral in the Second Messenian War, had previously been settled by Dryopes with the help of Sparta: and that after the war the Spartans put Methone in the hands of Nauplians who had been driven out by the Argives.

This picture, however vague and historically uncertain, makes perfectly good sense of the ἐρημία in terms of the Pylos campaign. In the extreme south of this western peninsula of the Peloponnese, we have an area occupied by pro-Spartan cities (Methone and Asine, to the latter of which the Spartans went for supplies of timber). To the east we have the Pamisos valley, where the Messenian helots worked for Sparta. But the whole area west of Mts. Aegaleon and Lykodemon, which includes the coastline southwards from Kyparissia to the barren shore just north of Methone, may well have been ἐρῆμος: more than enough to justify the phrase ἐπὶ πολὺ τῆς χώρας.

Despite the fertility of many parts of the area (particularly around Pylos itself), it seems that the Spartans were unwilling or unable to incorporate it into the Lacedaemonian state as fully as they had incorporated central Messenia. Spartan man-power was already over-extended; and the mountain barrier from Aegaleon southwards makes access to the area difficult. There were no doubt helots here and there, or even groups of semi-free Messenians: the former will include those who risked their lives to feed the Spartans on Sphacteria, the latter perhaps the crews of the two privateers who 'happened to be there' (ἔτυχον παραγενόμενοι, 9.1) when Demosthenes was defending Pylos.

In the light of this general picture, Demosthenes' choice seems to have been excellent: and the picture must be borne in mind when considering the success of the garrison after the final Athenian victory.

Gomme[6] claims that Demosthenes' choice of Pylos must "have been made after consultation with Messenians, not from personal knowledge of the Lakonian coastline": and in reference to the Messenian privateers in 9.1, "that the Messenians had arrived by arrangement with Demosthenes is obvious, and is implied by 3.3". This is far too · strong. For (i) as Thucydides makes clear in 3.3, the two chief criteria of merit for Pylos were the existence of a harbour, and the fact that it was in Messenian territory. Both these were common knowledge; and it would also be known that no other place satisfied both conditions. So there was no need for consultation, though no doubt Demosthenes did consult, with the Messenian expatriates. (ii) No serious 'arrangement' can have been made with the Messenians (certainly none is implied in 3.3), since it had not at that stage been decided to fortify Pylos at all. No doubt as soon as the decision was made, news was spread to the Messenians, including requests

___
6.   p. 488.

50

by Demosthenes for assistance: but that is all. Indeed ἔτυχον in οἳ ἔτυχον παραγενόμενοι, of the Messenians in 9.1, implies a definite lack of any arrangement.

Wood on Pylos and Sphacteria

Problems here are interconnected and may be dealt with most conveniently together: though they relate to various stages of the campaign, in particular to 3.2, 8.6, 13.1, 29.2-30.3, and the fighting on Sphacteria.

From evidence outside Thucydides we do not know, and may never know for certain despite sophisticated research-techniques involving pollen-counts, etc., just how much wood or undergrowth existed in 425 on Pylos, Sphacteria or elsewhere in the area. But the Thucydidean evidence is sufficient to give us a fairly clear picture.

In 3.2 Demosthenes pointed out to the generals that there was plenty of wood (πολλὴν εὐπορίαν ξύλων). Gomme comments:[7] "There is plenty of stone about now, but no timber in the near neighbourhood. And the Spartans, commanding the whole area round Pylos, had to send to Asine for it (13.1)", implying the existence of an inconsistency or a problem. We might be tempted to argue that there was (in 425) wood on Pylos itself - in fact there are some fair-sized trees on Pylos today - but nowhere else in the area nearer than Asine. But this is implausible: there are many places in the immediate vicinity more suitable for the growth of trees than the exposed heights of Pylos.

Thucydides describes Sphacteria with the words ὕλη, ὑλώδης and δασύς. These need only imply brushwood or undergrowth. But it is plain from his account of the changes produced by the fire that this 'undergrowth' must have been tall enough to conceal men. In particular (29.3), it was enough to conceal the Spartan παρασκευὴν. It was therefore sufficient to provide 'wood' on a small scale, e.g. for scaling-ladders. We can hardly believe that the Spartans went all the way to Asine for this sort of 'wood', when it was available on Sphacteria (and doubtless elsewhere in the nearer vicinity).

This brings out the interesting point that the ξύλα ἐς μηχανὰς (13.1) must have been on quite a large scale: something more in the nature of siege-towers than simple scaling-ladders is implied. The transport, as well as the provision, of such ξύλα would no doubt have been easier by ship from Asine. This casts a (faint) light on the Athenian wall κατὰ τὸν λιμένα (13.1) which the Spartans were proposing to ἑλεῖν μηχαναῖς: it must have been sufficiently high to justify μηχαναῖς more complicated, or at least larger, than (say) six-foot ladders - for which perhaps the word μηχαναῖς is anyway hardly appropriate.

---

7.   p. 439.

51

Demosthenes' εὐπορίαν ξύλων is a different matter, because the Athenians had no need of siege-engines. There was ξύλον, but we need not believe that there was any large-scale timber. Demosthenes is here contrasting the thicketed and bushy - in a sense, 'wooded' - nature of Pylos with that of more barren promontories (e.g. perhaps Methone in the north-east Peloponnese, captured by Athens in 424). The Athenians would have had plenty of uses for wood apart from making siege-engines; as for instance Demosthenes' own construction of a palisade for his triremes (9.1).

Thucydides and the length of Sphacteria

In 8.6 Thucydides gives us a detailed description of Sphacteria, which (in the text as we have it) includes a number of errors. First, there is something wrong with what he says about the ἔσπλους: and secondly, the length of the island is given as 'about 15 stades', when in fact it is about 24 or 25. Now in Note F I shall argue that what he says about the ἔσπλους is wrong in only one respect - the *position* of them, not their dimensions, nor anything about the Spartan plan. Moreover, it is plain that Thucydides' description is, even if erroneous, highly detailed. Whether or not he had been to Pylos, he *claims* accurate knowledge.

The fact that Thucydides (in the present MSS reading) is wrong about the length, according to Gomme, "in itself is not surprising, in a hilly place, with no accurate survey."[8] This will hardly do. Whether his sources were Athenian or Spartan (almost certainly both[9]), they would have had good reason to be tolerably accurate on the point. The Spartans were actually on the island, and had considered its topography carefully in order to defend themselves: the Athenians rowed round and observed it constantly for several weeks. A mistake which practically halves the length of a piece of terrain probably more closely inspected than almost any other in the war is not plausible.

The (undeniable) mistake about the ἔσπλους, as we shall see in Note F, is one which arises from a false induction (albeit a natural one) by Thucydides, not from direct topographical ignorance or misinformation. We should therefore not expect from him a straightforward topographical mistake about the length. His use of περὶ and μάλιστα in the phrase περὶ πέντε καὶ δέκα σταδίους μάλιστα is further evidence, not of general vagueness, but of the caution of one who is certain of his basic facts. It is as if one were to write "about 15 stades, in round figures" - showing certainty that it was not 5 or 25, but being careful to say that it was not necessarily *exactly* 15 stades.

In view of all this it seems that we are bound to accept Burrows' obvious and easy emendation, from ΔΠ or ιέ (15) to ΔΔΠ or κέ (25). For those who are fussy enough

8.   p. 484.
9.   See refs. in Gomme, p. 485.

52

to insist that the correct figure is 24 rather than 25, it is worth remembering that the question of whether to count the rocks and islets at the south end of Sphacteria as part of the island itself seems an open one: if we do, 25 is in fact better than 24.

B. ATHENIAN FORTIFICATIONS

The problems here are very complicated, and have been much discussed.[1] I shall deal in turn with the northern sector, the south-east, and the west or south-west fortifications. (See Map C.)

The northern wall

This is comparatively easy to establish, and we do not need to do much more than echo Pritchett[2] and Burrows[3], who place the defence-line as marked on our map (N-O). The evidence for this is overwhelming. It is perhaps worth adding that if, as we shall argue (see Note F), the Spartans had in mind to block the entrance to Voidokoilia, then the northern end of Pylos must have been Spartan-held territory and not defended by the Athenians.

The placing of the defence-line in the north-east sector (above the Cave of Nestor) is sufficiently well-documented in the references given above. But we need also to observe that natural defences alone would not suffice. There are several points to the north-west at which it is possible, either to work one's way round (some 200 feet below the summit) to the western side of the promontory, or to climb up to the summit itself. Some of these approaches require stiff climbing: but others do not. (There is today an easy path which leads along the whole west side of the promontory, round the north-west corner, and descends gently to the little cape overlooking Voidokoilia and/or to the sandhills surrounding the bay.) These approach-points would have required some defence, though not very much: in particular, with the northern end of the promontory in Spartan hands, the Athenians would have needed to make sure that the Spartans could not have worked their way round to the west. A possible defence-point is marked P on the map.

The south-east

The north-south cliff-line on the east side of Pylos certainly οὐδὲν ἔδει τείχους (4.3). This is not to say that determined men might not have made their way up at certain points (perhaps by night), particularly at point Q on the map: but the approach is so steep that the Athenians could easily have guarded it without a wall. The position changes, however, as we approach the south-east corner. Here the cliff falls fairly sharply, and allows easy access. Most commentators have seen that there must be a wall here, and referred to Thucydides' τὸ κατὰ τὸν λιμένα τεῖχος (13.1).[4] But the problem is much more complex, and we shall have to look closely at evidence from later in the campaign.

---

1.   See references to the literature in the Appendix.
2.   p. 20.
3.   Burrows (1898).   4.   Pritchett, p. 21.

54

The Spartan plan

13.1: ἐλπίζοντες τὸ κατὰ τὸν λιμένα τεῖχος ὕψος μὲν ἔχειν, ἀποβάσεως δὲ μάλιστα οὔσης ἐλεῖν μηχαναῖς. The problem raised by this passage is as follows. Pritchett's evidence shows that Pylos was approachable by land on a broad front, i.e. the whole of the east side. But if the passage implies that the Spartans could only arrange for troops to assault that part of the wall which faces the harbour (κατὰ τὸν λιμένα) by landing them *by sea*, then this is *prima facie* inconsistent with Pritchett's picture: for, it seems, the Spartans could have reached any wall which the Athenians built along the south-east corner of Pylos *by land*. This would be true, not only if the whole Osmyn Aga lagoon was dry, but even if the southern sand-bar or a narrow passage along the base of the eastern cliff was dry.

Pritchett's way out of this[5] is to claim that ἀπόβασις does not have to mean the disembarkation of men, only of materials: and that Thucydides is simply saying that the timber for the siege-engines was to be landed there, where there was in fact a landing-place. "This was a matter of logistics." But this will hardly do. ἀπόβασις may well bear Pritchett's sense: and we can certainly translate 'there was a landing-place'. But the context makes it quite clear that Thucydides is not giving us this (somewhat gratuitous) information about where the Spartans were going to land their siege-engine materials. 13.1 occurs immediately after a long passage describing the difficulties of landing experienced by Brasidas and the other Spartans: then he says that they hoped with the siege-engines to assault the wall near the harbour "where, though the fortifications were high" (*sc.* higher than the ones at Brasidas' landing-place) "there was a good landing", or "the landing was easier" (*sc.*, surely, also than the Brasidas one). However the Greek be interpreted, there is no point in mentioning the height of the fortifications except by contrast with the greater ease of landing *against opposition.*

If we accept the notion of disembarking troops and the accessibility by land of the south-east part of Pylos - and it seems that we must accept both of these - then we must see what arrangement of Athenian fortifications could satisfy these conditions.

The sheer cliff which runs along most of the east side is more or less impregnable: the problem concerns the fortifications at the south-east corner. Now for ships to be necessary, the point of the ἀπόβασις must be to the *west* of some Athenian wall: for if it were to the east, it could have been reached by land. Assume then, to begin with, a wall placed as marked L-M on the map, and that the point of the intended ἀπόβασις was somewhere to the west of that, *on a sandy or shingle beach.* But now we must assume *another* wall, which is the one referred to by Thucydides as being 'higher', and the one which the siege-engines (when landed) would assault. This wall cannot, however,

---

5.   p. 24.

55

be simply continuous with the wall outside which Demosthenes led his troops to deal with Brasidas' landing (9.2): if it were, the Spartans of the ἀπόβασις plan now under discussion would not have had to assault a *higher* wall (i.e. a wall higher than the one behind Brasidas' landing) at all - they could have worked their way round west and north until they came to the Brasidas wall (marked R-S). This second wall, then, must have run directly to the sea at some point.

Within these logical limits, various locations for this wall are topographically possible. It might have run in a south-westerly direction, to any point west of G on our sketch. However, two considerations seem to favour the location we have marked:-

(a)   There is a weak but not negligible argument from the phrase κατὰ τὸν λιμένα. If we take κατὰ to have the exact sense of 'opposite', or 'facing', then the location must have been something like that marked on the sketch (L-G): other locations would face either the Sikia channel and Sphacteria, or the mainland. Thucydides may only draw a simple distinction between walls facing the open sea (where Brasidas landed) and other walls, some of which latter he might generally describe as 'on the harbour side' simply in virtue of the fact that they were not facing the open sea. But I am inclined to take him literally, and place the wall as marked.

(b)   More weighty is the point that it would have been purposeless to carry the wall further west than G. As soon as we attend to the logic of the situation, it becomes clear that the Athenians intended the walls LM and LG to enclose a landing-ground for triremes. Further west than G, however, it is impossible for triremes to land owing to the steepness of the ground facing the Sikia channel (see p. 60 below). G to M includes the only possible ground. The Athenians were in a hurry when they built the walls, and a wall to any point further west than G would have served no purpose and taken longer. It may be added that the line LG, like LM, is assisted by the rock-formation (see p. 60 below), which affords some natural protection.

The point of the ἀπόβασις must be

(a)   to the west of the furthest point east at which the Athenians could have built a wall effectively preventing the land-based Spartans from getting into Pylos;

(b)   at a place more easy for disembarkation than Brasidas';

(c)   at a place above which the Athenians could have built the 'higher' wall which the siege-engines could assault, so as to contain the projected ἀπόβασις;

(d)   such that the Athenian fleet (and perhaps also Demosthenes' triremes) could have used it as a στρατόπεδον, however inadequate. For (see p. 58 below) the στρατόπεδον must have been within the eastern fortifications; and there is nowhere else on Pylos where (comparative) ease of landing is possible. Point T on our map satisfies all these conditions.

Demosthenes' triremes

9.1 καὶ τὰς τριήρεις . . . ἀνασπάσας ὑπὸ τὸ τείχισμα προσεσταύρωσε κτλ.

ὑπὸ τὸ τείχισμα might mean (i) up to under the fortifications (but not within them), or (ii) up to under (the shelter of) the fortifications (and hence inside them). ὑπὸ can bear either sense, and we must rely on the general context for our choice. However, there is an important ambiguity here. We have argued above that the Spartan plan (for attacking the fortifications where there was an easier ἀπόβασις) only makes sense if we assume two logically distinct categories of fortification: (1) walls to keep the land-based Spartans out, and (2) walls to protect Pylos from an attack by sea. Now if, as we shall argue, Demosthenes dragged up the triremes at some such point as T in the sketch, are we to say that this is ὑπὸ τὸ τείχισμα in sense (ii): that is, under the shelter of the fortifications? It is under the shelter of the category (1) wall, L-M, but not under the shelter of the category (2) wall, L-G. We shall leave this particular point until its relevance becomes plainer.

We may read προεσταύρωσε or προσεσταύρωσε.

(a)   προεσπαύρωσε must mean 'put a palisade in front of them', as in Bk. VI, 75, 1 (τὴν θάλασσαν προυσταύρωσαν).

(b)   προσεσταύρωσε is a ἅπαξ λεγόμενον, and open to various interpretations:-

    (i)   as for προεσταύρωσε, 'put a palisade in front of them'.

    (ii)   taking προς as 'in addition', 'put a palisade (in front of them) as well', sc. as well as the stone walls.

    (iii)   taking προς as 'in addition' again, 'included them also within the palisade': on the analogy of προστειχίζω (Bk. VI, 3. offers a parallel).

    (iv)   taking προς as 'in addition' again, 'included them as part of the palisade'.

57

(b) (iii) and (iv) are extremely improbable, because we have no reason to believe that there was a palisade to include them, either 'within' or 'as part of'. σταυρός cannot refer generally to walls or fortifications: it means a wooden pale or stake. The area T, within the walls L-G and L-M, is the only part of the Pylos coastline in which the Athenians could have driven stakes: there is no question of their making this palisade for any other purpose than to protect the triremes. (b) (iv) is particularly unlikely, since Demosthenes would hardly have used three valuable triremes as a palisade.

(b) (ii), 'put a palisade in front of them as well', looks at first sight as if it can be ruled out also. For 'in addition' can only mean 'in addition to the other fortifications' (presumably of stone): so we have the picture of the triremes *behind* the stone fortifications, with a palisade in front of them. But if the Spartans penetrated the stone fortifications, the Athenian position was lost in any case: a palisade for the triremes would have been pointless.

However, the remarks above on ὑπὸ τὸ τείχισμα may already have shown that the argument for ruling out (b) (ii) is only valid on one interpretation: that is, if we assume that the triremes were behind not only category (1) walls but also category (2), i.e. not at T on the map but at some point within the category (2) wall L-G. Then, indeed, there would be no point in an additional palisade. But if we take Thucydides to be referring only to the category (1) wall, and some such point as T to be a possible candidate, the arguments do not apply. *For Demosthenes was protecting them against a sea-borne attack.* He was afraid (since the Peloponnesians had superiority at sea at this phase) that the Peloponnesian ships would conduct a quick cutting-out expedition to destroy them. Against such an attack a palisade would be a very sensible defence. We may thus allow (a), (b) (i) or (b) (ii).

It would have been virtually impossible for the triremes to have been dragged up to any point much higher than T on the map, in the south-east corner. The line of cliffs on the east side begins to break up at point L, and descends in a broken but generally fan-like formation which, as approached from the shore, nevertheless rapidly becomes too steep for any triremes to have been dragged far up it.

14.5 τὸ στρατόπεδον.

Gomme talks of the Athenian 'base', and 'their landing-ground (or τὸ στρατόπεδον, 14.5)' [6], and quotes Steup's translation 'feste Stellung'. But στρατόπεδον means only a place in which an army encamps, and these editors' difficulties are imaginary. First, the Spartan camp (see Note I) was almost certainly at or near the modern Gialova, at the north of Navarino Bay. The Athenian camp was of course on Pylos. We may ask where

---

6.   p. 485.

the Athenian fleet beached their ships: but this is a different question, and not hard to answer. Like Demosthenes' triremes, the Athenian beached ships must have been behind category (1) walls, or else the land-based Spartans could have captured them. The obvious candidate for the location is the south-east corner of Pylos: not, as Gomme says, because it was only approachable by sea, but because it was within the line of fortifications, and the best place for a landing-ground that was available.

Gomme also makes great play with the 'defect' in Thucydides' narrative: "in essentials, after the battle in the bay . . . the position of the Athenian fleet was the same, the island and the mainland still occupied by the Spartans and denied to the Athenians, with the exception of the south-east corner of Pylos promontory . . . this would be a very inadequate base . . . Thucydides emphasizes the inadequacy (26. 2-3, 30.2); but what he fails to do is to point out at least some change in this respect brought about by the naval victory of the Athenians . . . " [7] But the change is obvious enough. Before the battle, the Athenian fleet could not lie at anchor μετέωροι, nor beach their ships: for the Peloponnesian ships would have destroyed them in just the same way as they would have destroyed Demosthenes' triremes. After the battle, the Peloponnesian fleet was out of action; the λιμήν was available for anchoring μετέωροι, and the south-east corner for beaching.

More worrying, at first sight, than Gomme's criticism is the τῶν νεῶν οὐκ ἐχουσῶν ὅρμον in 26.3. Yet here Thucydides uses ὅρμον quite specifically: he means a proper anchorage as opposed to a place where the ships could be beached. The next part of the sentence makes it quite plain: "since the ships had no *proper place of anchorage*, some of the (crews of the) ships took their meals on the land, in turns, whilst others *anchored* off-shore" (ὥρμουν).

How far did the Athenian wall extend to the east, at the south-east corner? I do not think it could have been much further east than as marked (L-M). For this wall must have been even higher than the wall selected for attack by the Spartans (L-G): otherwise the former would have been easier to attack (from the land) rather than the latter, and there would have been no need of any ἀπόβασις. To build such a wall for any distance would very likely have overtaxed Athenian time and resources: it is clear that they were doing the minimum necessary (παντί τε τρόπῳ ἠπείγοντο - - - τὰ ἐπιμαχώτατα ἐξεργασάμενοι, 5.1 : ἃ μάλιστα ἔδει, 5.2). Moreover such a wall would have been built over flat ground, whereas the wall as marked makes some use of the fan-like formation which affords some natural protection.

The present coast-line distance from G to M on the sketch is approximately 80 yards. If we assume something under 20 ft. per trireme,[8] this would allow 9 triremes to

---

7. *ibid.*
8. See Morrison and Williams.

beach at once, a figure which is consistent with what Thucydides says in 26.3 (στενοχωρία τε κτλ.) Given Pritchett's figure of approximately 2.5 metres drop in land-level, the sand-and-shingle *area* at the south-east corner would have been somewhat extended in 425. It is impossible to gauge precisely how much larger it would have been, even with exact measurements of the present water-depths: first because the figure of 2.5m. is uncertain, and secondly because of other hydrographical difficulties which we have mentioned elsewhere.[9] But the coast-*line* itself would not have been much longer.

The southern coast of Pylos itself at present drops sheer, though from no great height, into deep water, until we come to the sand-and-shingle area to the south-east (G-M), as shown on the map. It would still have dropped sheer in 425: a land-rise of 2.5m., or even double that figure, would make no significant difference here: though it would of course have affected the sand-and-shingle area as described above. The same point applies to the south-west and west shores (including Brasidas' landing-place): though the drop here is not sheer, a land-rise would not have made Brasidas' task any easier than it would be today.

The west or south-west wall

There must have been some kind of wall connecting points R to S (see map C). It is inadequate to say that it " ... extended from the southeast corner to the sea" [10]: for if it did not connect with the cliff-line on the north-west coast (point R), it could of course have been avoided by Spartans landing anywhere on that coast. As 9.2 and 13.1 make plain, there *was* a wall which the Spartans had to face if they attacked Pylos from the west, but it was ἀσθενεστάτου (9.2), and lower than the κατὰ τὸν λιμένα τεῖχος, which is said ὕψος ἔχεω (13.1). Where did this wall run?

First, it is unlikely to have been built actually along the rocks or shore-line of the west coast at any point. Certainly at *some* points it was not so built: for in 9.2 Demosthenes leads his men ἔξω τοῦ τείχους : this is reinforced by 13.4 and 11.1. Moreover, it would have been hard (though *pace* Pritchett [11] not out of the question) for men who were only λογάδην φέροντες λίθους καὶ ξυνετίθεσαν ὡς ἕκαστον τι ξυμβαίνοι (4.2) to build along the rocks at any point. Burrows' discovery of rocks 'smoothed... to receive a fortification wall' [12] is irrelevant, for Thucydides specifically states that they had no iron tools (4.2 σιδήρια λιθουργὰ οὐκ ἔχοντες).

A little help may be gained (though not much) from a close consideration of 9.4 and 11.1. To the casual reader it may seem that Thucydides writes carelessly here:

---

9. See p. 77.
10. Pritchett, p. 21.
11. *ibid.*
12. Burrows, *ibid.*

60

πρὸς αὐτὴν τὴν θάλασσαν χωρήσας ἔταξε τοὺς ὁπλίτας looks much like ἐπικαταβάντες ἐτάξαντο παρ' αὐτὴν τὴν θάλασσαν: unnecessary repetition. But we must take the difference between πρός and παρά seriously. In 9.2 Demosthenes takes his men outside the wall, going (in 9.4) *towards* the sea, and forms them up in order to make the speech in 10. In 11.1 they then go further down (ἐπικαταβάντες) and take up a *new* position actually *along* the shore-line: παρ' αὐτὴν τὴν ῥαχίαν, as Demosthenes had enjoined in 10.5, 'where the waves actually break'. These movements may be thought to imply a fair distance between the wall and the shore-line.

We have two basic alternatives for this wall. Either the Athenians wished to follow the coast-line and built a wall running parallel to the Sikia Channel, more or less due west, curving round at the south-west corner, and then running north to join the cliff-line at the north-west: or else they cut off some of the south-west corner, and joined the two points by a shorter route, if not actually by a straight line of wall. Of these I prefer the second. For if, as is clear, the Athenians did not build actually on or very close to the shore-line, there would have been no point in their following the line at a distance. They would most naturally have followed the contours of the land in a gentle curve, as suggested on map C.

This makes sense, because the southern coastline offered no chance of a landing: the shore here rises sheer, rather like a small cliff. It is only when we reach the south-west corner that landing becomes possible. So the Athenians would have had no need to defend the line of the Sikia Channel: and this is the only place at which they might have tried to build on the shore-line - they certainly did not do so on the west coast. It is not impossible that they built along the line of the Sikia, and then turned sharply north at some distance from the western shore-line: but very unlikely. [13]

---

13. There is of course the point that more or less the only level ground at Pylos is in this south-west area, so that the Athenians might have wished to enclose it in order to have enough space. But then Thucydides specifically stresses the στενοχωρία (26.3); and in any case, after the Athenian victory in the harbour, they would not have feared to camp outside the walls on the seaward-facing part of the island.

C. THE ATHENIAN PLAN

The general picture presented by Thucydides in sections 3-8 seems at best full of gaps and at worst implausible. We are asked to believe (1) that both the generals and the soldiers refused to fortify Pylos (4.1); (2) that nevertheless the soldiers out of sheer boredom undertook and completed the impressive task of fortifying it without iron tools, hods or other equipment (and Thucydides stresses the physical labour involved) (4.3), and that they did so with great speed so as to make it impregnable before the Spartans arrived (4.3); (3) that - although no change of policy of the part of the generals is mentioned - Demosthenes was allowed to have his way and occupy it as a fort, retaining five ships (5.2); (4) that the fleet continued towards Corcyra, presumably knowing that the Spartans would attack Pylos, but nevertheless returned immediately on receiving Demosthenes' message about the impending attack (5.2, 8.3-4).

It is at least clear that there was no plan made at Athens, either agreed unofficially between Demosthenes and the generals, or laid down by the Athenian government, to fortify Pylos (or anywhere else). The decree in 2.4 is extremely indefinite, allowing Demosthenes only χρῆσθαι ταῖς ναυσί ταύταις, ἢν βούληται, περὶ τὴν Πελοπόννησον; but the decisive point is that the Athenians brought no tools for fortification with them (see Gomme's note[1]). Demosthenes himself, as ἠξίου τειχίζεσθαι τὸ χωρίον (ἐπὶ τοῦτο γὰρ ξυνεκπλεῦσαι) (3.2) makes clear, had this intention clearly in mind, but was evidently unable (perhaps owing to his inferior status as a private citizen with no official position, ὄντι ἰδιώτῃ (2.4)) to arrange for fortification-tools to be brought. The original plan, then, was for Sicily and Corcyra, as Thucydides says in 2.2-3 : probably in that order of importance, since they were supposed to deal with Corcyra en route (ἅμα παραπλέοντας, 2.3). Nevertheless these plans were changed at Pylos: our task is to see how this can most plausibly have happened, in regard to the difficulties mentioned earlier.

So far as the first two difficulties, (1) and (2), are concerned, we may hope for some improvement by emending the text (generally regarded as corrupt) of the first sentence in section 4:- ὡς δὲ οὐκ ἔπειθεν οὔτε τοὺς στρατηγοὺς οὔτε τοὺς στρατιώτας ὕστερον καὶ τοῖς ταξιάρχοις κοινώσας, ἡσύχαζον ὑπὸ ἀπλοίας, μέχρι αὐτοῖς τοῖς στρατιώταις . . . ὁρμὴ ἐνέπεσε περιστᾶσιν. . . Most commentators have been concerned (a) with the odd mention of ταξιάρχοις and (b) with the apparent non sequitur of

---

1.   pp. 438-9. But the point cannot be strengthened by contrasting "the careful preparations made for the Megara expedition, 69.2". On the contrary, the Athenian expedition, already at work and trying to capture Megara, had to be supplied from Athens: this must be the meaning of παρεγένετο δὲ σίδηρός τε ἐκ τῶν Ἀθηνῶν ταχὺ καὶ λιθουργοὶ καὶ τἆλλα ἐπιτήδεια, otherwise ταχὺ makes no sense.

ἡσύχαζον (or ἡσύχαζεν[2]) after the ὡς clause, expressed by Gomme[3] thus: "...
inactivity due to stress of weather cannot be the consequence of failure to persuade
the generals and the soldiers". We may deal with these briefly:

(a) It is not odd that taxiarchs should be mentioned: it is only odd that they
should be mentioned as they are: i.e. generals, soldiers and *then* taxiarchs,
and in a piece of syntax which is (on any view) peculiar. Correct emendation must depend on facing the real difficulty about the soldiers' change
of mind: this is dealt with below.

(b) This is not a difficulty at all, *pace* Gomme. There are two possibilities:

(i) Taking ὡς causally (the only interpretation Gomme considers), we
may translate: "Since he failed to persuade them, they did nothing
(because of the bad weather)". The logic is: given the bad weather,
there was nothing for them to do except to follow Demosthenes'
suggestion: since he failed to persuade them, they did nothing.

(ii) We may take ὡς in a purely temporal sense: "when Demosthenes
failed to persuade them, they (to begin with) did nothing because of
the bad weather which prevented them from sailing, until (later) the
soldiers were impelled ... "

The real difficulty which should guide our emendation is the implausibility that
Demosthenes should have failed to persuade the soldiers, yet that they should then
have suddenly and voluntarily changed their minds and undertaken this arduous task.
If we keep οὔτε τοὺς στρατιώτας, there is a strong case for taking περιστᾶσιν in a sense
usually applied only to events, fortune, etc. but readily understandable when applied
personally: i.e. 'changing their minds', 'coming round to the opposite point of view'. If
this is thought improbable on linguistic grounds (for it makes much better general sense),
we shall take περιστᾶσιν in the usual sense of 'standing round' or 'surrounding' - perhaps
a little odd, but I take it that the troops had hitherto occupied one part of Pylos only,
probably the south-east corner. But if we do this (and I think in any case, since the first
sense of περιστᾶσιν only palliates the difficulty) we must certainly do something about
τοὺς στρατιώτας.[4]

---

2. The MSS read ἡσύχαζεν, which may be retained, though most editors change to ἡσύχαζον.
If we retain it, we must understand something like "When he failed to persuade them, he
found himself with nothing to do (because the only other thing to do, namely sail, was
prevented by bad weather), until the soldiers themselves ... ", the implication being that
then he did have something to do, namely organise the building of the fortification. This
seems not too hard. Poppo's and Gomme's suggestions (see Gomme *ad loc.*) seem somewhat
wholesale. If we have to emend, and ἡσύχαζον is not thought acceptable - though I do not
see why it should not be - one might suggest ἀπορίας for ἀπλοίας: though this is perhaps
more original than plausible.

3. p. 440.

4. A third possibility is to take περιστάσιν as a noun, and to translate 'to fortify the place in a
perimeter'. But this use of the word is hardly good classical Greek.

63

By far the most plausible suggestion is to bracket τοὺς στρατιώτας. The first mention of στρατιώται would then be in the phrase αὐτοῖς τοῖς στρατιώταις: and this gives far more point to the αὐτοῖς. Suggestions which include στρατιώται earlier, as Gomme's, miss the point: for we need an interpretation which allows us to hold that the soldiers had sided with Demosthenes, or at least were not against his plan, all along. For only this will make their voluntary fortification plausible. This emendation is also palaeographically plausible: one may easily imagine the muddled repetition οὔτε τοὺς στρατηγοὺς οὔτε τοὺς στρατηγοὺς, corrected into οὔτε τοὺς στρατηγοὺς οὔτε τοὺς στρατιώτας.

We must assume, then, that the generals and taxiarchs were overborne by Demosthenes and the soldiers into at least some change of policy: i.e. they agreed at least to try out Pylos as a fortification. Why then did the fleet leave Pylos, since they must have known that the Spartans would attack? It is not a complete explanation to point to their objectives in Corcyra and Sicily. For if these objectives were regarded as of more importance than Pylos, they would not have returned at Demosthenes' bidding: and if of less importance, why leave Pylos at all? Thus Gomme reasonably asks[5] "But why had Demosthenes never imagined that he would be so much weaker at sea, when the main Athenian fleet had left in a hurry for Sicily?"

We must suppose that though the fleet was indeed 'hastening on the route to Corcyra and Sicily' (ἐς τὴν Κέρκυραν πλοῦν καὶ Σικελίαν ἠπείγοντο), it was doing so partly at least in the hope of meeting and destroying the Peloponnesian fleet, which was known to be in the Corcyra area. Demosthenes would assume, or hope, that this would happen, and hence that he would be safe from a sea-borne attack. When the Spartan troops are on their way, he sends a message to the Athenian fleet (8.3): it is possible that he had information that the Peloponnesian fleet was on its way. The message may have read something like "Spartan army on its way to Pylos: Peloponnesian fleet is proceeding southwards: return immediately". In any case, there must have been a prior agreement that the immediate purpose of the Athenian fleet was to destroy the Peloponnesian fleet in the Corcyra area, or at least to prevent it from returning southwards: and that the Athenian fleet would return if Pylos was threatened.

This gives us the general outline of what happened. It is supported by two other arguments, which will be deployed in the two notes immediately following.

---

5.   p. 445, referring to 9.3: οὔτε γὰρ αὐτοὶ ἐλπίξοντές ποτε ναυσὶ κρατήσεσθαι.

64

D. NUMBERS OF DEMOSTHENES' MEN

This is important in itself, and also gives us the first of the two arguments mentioned at the end of the previous note.

It is reasonable to rely on the assumption that the standard number of hoplite epibatai on Athenian triremes was no more than 10, and that this applied even when there was a chance that hoplite action ashore was needed. In default of contrary evidence, we may assume this to be true of the 40 Athenian ships: we may similarly assume the standard number of archers, which was not more than 4 (more probably 2 or 3) per ship. I shall not argue these points here, since what other writers have said seems conclusive.[1]

Demosthenes was left with 5 ships at Pylos. When he despatched 2 to carry his message, he no doubt stripped them of their hoplites and archers.[2] He had, then, some 50 hoplites, about 15 archers, and the crews of three ships (170 x 3, or about 510). He acquired also (9.1) 40 Messenian hoplites, making 90 hoplites in all. The ships' crews were armed, ἀσπίσι φαύλαις και οἰσυΐναις ταῖς πολλαῖς·οὐ γὰρ ἦν ὅπλα ἐν χωρίῳ ἐρήμῳ πορίσασθαι etc. From this and from ἀόπλων (9.2) we know that the majority of these 510 crewmen were either not armed at all, or armed in a very inferior way. Probably we should not add the non-hoplites from the Messenian privateers. These ships were not dragged up ὑπὸ τὸ τείχισμα with the triremes, and we do not hear of them again: almost certainly the non-hoplites remained on them as their crews, and sailed away before the Spartans arrived. In any case, there cannot have been very many of them, nor can they have been very well-armed.

What is striking about these numbers is that they seem insufficient to keep off a Peloponnesian attack by both land and sea. Despite the natural strength of the place and the fortifications, a land attack was possible on a very broad front (see Note B): I should estimate a minimum of about 120 hoplites, supported by other troops, as necessary to defend the land side against any attack as determined as the Spartans' must have been. And the attack by sea had also to be met. One immediately suspects that Demosthenes must have had more troops.

Fortunately there is a conclusive argument to justify these suspicions. In 9.2 Demosthenes takes 60 hoplites and a few archers to defend the west coast. These he chose out of the whole number: τοὺς μὲν οὖν πολλοὺς τῶν τε ἀόπλων καὶ ὡπλισμένων ἐπὶ τὰ τετειχισμένα .. πρὸς τὴν ἤπειρον ἔταξε ... Plainly the coast-defenders are in a minority, probably a small minority. Yet, on the numbers so far given, he had only 90

---

1. Morrison & Williams.
2. If he did not, the central argument of this note is even stronger: the generals would have had to leave Demosthenes still more hoplites.

65

hoplites to deploy: the remaining thirty could not be called τοὺς πολλοὺς, and could not have defended the landward side.[3]

The other generals must, therefore, have left some of their hoplite epibatai with Demosthenes: a fact which sheds light on their mutual relationships and agreed plans (see previous note). How many? The answer must, logically, be more than an additional 30: for there must have been more than 120 hoplites in all if 60 are to be a minority. Almost certainly it was more: a minority of 60 suggests a τοὺς πολλοὺς of perhaps 120, which would be a minimum for the landward defence. This gives a total of 180, and one might reasonably expect some figure more like 200. Deducting from this figure the 40 Messenian hoplites and the 50 from Demosthenes' own ships, we are left with 110. In other words, of the 35 ships remaining to Eurymedon and Sophocles, either 11 had been totally stripped of their epibatai for Demosthenes' benefit, or the number was made up from more than 11. This hardly matters: what matters is that the generals were prepared to weaken their force significantly, which argues a distinct change of plan.

If we try to argue that the Athenian ships had more than their usual complement of hoplites, we run into trouble. Suppose Demosthenes used only the hoplites of his 5 ships: then their numbers would have had to have been about 100 in all at a minimum, so that (with the addition of 40 Messenian hoplites) the 60 coast-guarding ones could count as a minority. This means a minimum of 20 hoplites per ship, and a total of 800 hoplites in the whole fleet. But in 31.1 we are told that all the hoplites in the Athenian force came to no more than about 800; and this was after the original fleet of 40 ships had been reinforced, the total ship-numbers being rather over 70, and after the arrival of reinforcements from the allies. Plainly we must assume that the numbers of ἐπιβάται were normal.

---

3. This argument was used by Mills (p. 12), who concluded that "the number of ἐπιβάται in Eurymedon's fleet was unusually large". This is improbable for reasons given in the text.
    The argument itself (from τοὺς πολλοὺς) seems conclusive. It has been pointed out to me (by Mr. T. Braun) that the meaning could be: "The majority of the force - consisting as it did of both unarmed men and hoplites - he stationed . . . ". This leaves open the possibility that the 60 coast-defending hoplites are only a minority of the total *force*, not necessarily a minority of the total *hoplites*. But this is an unnatural rendering, and there would be no point in Thucydides' telling us that the force was made up of these two categories: we know this already. It must mean "The majority both of the unarmed and of the hoplites he stationed . . . ".

66

E.   SHIP-MOVEMENTS AND TIME-SCHEME

The Athenians at Zacynthos and the διολκος

Our first point completes the arguments relevant to the penultimate note (*The Athenian Plan*). In 8.2 and 3, the position of the Athenian fleet is given as Zacynthos. It is when they are here that the Spartan fleet evades them, and that Demosthenes sends his message-ships. The point is based on the requirements of the time-scheme, which will be dealt with fully below. Even without the details, however, it is apparent that the Athenian fleet is *waiting* at Zacynthos. It leaves as soon as the fortifications of Pylos are completed: between then and the day on which Demosthenes' ships reach Zacynthos with their message there is a long period, which cannot on any account be less than 5 days and is more probably 7. But Zacynthos is no more than about 70 miles from Pylos.

This distance would normally be covered in two, at most three, days. Of course we may imagine another period of bad weather occurring as soon as they had reached Zacynthos: or the necessity of refitting, taking on supplies, and so forth which might occupy this time. But none of these seem very plausible, particularly since the Spartan fleet was rowing hard for Pylos at the time (see below), apparently in satisfactory weather. It is much more likely that the Athenians were waiting for tactical purposes connected with the Spartan fleet and the Pylos campaign, which I explain below. This still enables us to say that they were *en route* for Corcyra and Sicily (τὸν ἐς τὴν Κέρκυραν πλοῦν, κτλ): that is, following the route: but in their own good time, and for good reasons. Hence the Athenian generals must have changed their plans at Pylos, giving the situation there more (immediate) weight than anything in Corcyra or Sicily. Had they not, they would have covered a far greater distance: indeed, they would have been at Corcyra or near it by the time when, in fact, they received Demosthenes' message at Zacynthos.

Why were they waiting *there*? Why not further north, where they would have caught up with the Spartan fleet more quickly: or further south, which would have made it less possible for the fleet to evade them (as in fact it did)? Not further south, for they needed a friendly base, and there was none (not even Pylos itself) nearer than Zacynthos. Not further north, for tactical reasons. Some places further north, such as Cephallenia, were under Athenian control: but Zacynthos remains the best interception-point. A glance at the map (A) shows a number of possible routes from Corcyra to Pylos, most of the divergencies being in the north part of the Cephallenia-Ithaca area (west of Cephallenia, between Cephallenia and Ithaca, just to the east of Ithaca, or a number of routes among the small islands between Ithaca and the Acharnanian coast). Moreover, the Athenians could not be certain that the Spartan fleet was not already on its way back, or that it would not start back before they reached Corcyra. At Zacynthos they could be sure that it had not passed them (or so they supposed), and that

67

they could intercept it when it did: for at this point there are only two possible routes, east and west of the island.

But then why did the διολκός across the isthmus of Leucas help the Spartans to evade the Athenians? Thucydides says (8.2): τὰς ἑξήκοντα ... αἱ ὑπερενεχθεῖσαι τὸν Λευκαδίων ἰσθμὸν καὶ λαθοῦσαι τὰς ἐν Ζακύνθῳ Ἀττικὰς ναῦς ἀφικνοῦνται ἐπὶ Πύλον. It is hard to see why Thucydides tells us of the διολκός except in order to *explain* the Spartan escape: the information is otherwise gratuitous. And even if it is gratuitous, the event itself requires explanation.

Pace Gomme,[1] the Spartans did not use the διολκός to save time. Compare, on the map, the respective merits of a διολκός and sailing west of Leucas. If they hugged the coastline on their way from Corcyra, the διολκός does not gain enough in terms of mileage to compensate for the time taken in dragging 60 ships over 3 stades: and if they sailed by a more direct route from Corcyra at a perfectly plausible figure of about 10-15 miles from the coast, no mileage at all is saved. So the διολκός must have been for purposes of evasion, as it had been used before.[2]

The Spartans may have had news, or expected, that the Athenian fleet was on its way northwards, and feared to meet it in the Leucas-Cephallenia-Ithaca area. This is sufficient to explain the διολκός *per se,* but not to explain Thucydides' implication that the διολκός helped them to evade the ships at Zacynthos. We must surely assume that the Athenians at Zacynthos had not waited there idly: and there is some definite evidence for this, since when they return to Pylos they are accompanied by guard-ships from Naupactos and other vessels (13.2). They no doubt relied on some ships, either from their own fleet and/or from their allies further north, to act as a scouting or watching force during the period - probably a week - when the main fleet waited at Zacynthos. This force was to inform them of Spartan movements: and because it was deceived by the διολκός, the main fleet at Zacynthos was itself deceived and evaded.

This is not to say that the Athenians and their allies were deceived in principle (so to speak) by the διολκός, which would be hard to believe after their previous experience.[3] What probably happened, as the time-scheme below suggests, is that the Athenians at Zacynthos did not have time to organise the scouting force so that it could operate far enough north to bring certain news that the Spartans had actually used the διολκός. By the time any scouts could be in the right area, the Spartans were already across the isthmus: and while the scouts were, perhaps, watching the Cephallenia-Ithaca area, the Spartans were hugging the Acharnanian coastline,

---

1.   p. 368 (Vol. II).
2.   Bk. III, 81.1.
3.   *ibid.*

sheltered from the view of the watching force behind the islands of Meganesi and Kalamos, and later perhaps sailing east of some of the Echinades. They would then have passed close to the Peloponnesian coast, some 15 miles from Zacynthos - far enough for the Athenians, if they had received no warning at all, to have little hope of intercepting them or even of noticing them.

One further point of interest remains. According to our time-scheme below Demosthenes' triremes going from Pylos to Zacynthos almost certainly crossed with the Spartan fleet coming south from the strait between Zacynthos and the mainland. Demosthenes could hardly have known that the Spartans were so close: nevertheless one might wonder why his triremes were not snapped up by the enemy fleet *en route*. But as explained above, the Spartans would have hugged the mainland in this strait so as to avoid the Athenians at Zacynthos: whereas Demosthenes' triremes would have taken the direct route. So the two courses would not have been on the same line. From Pylos, via Prote, to the coast off Philiatra, indeed, the courses are dangerously close; but thereafter they separate rapidly, particularly if the Spartans continued to hug the coast (now of the Peloponnese). Nor must we forget the possibilities of bad weather, poor visibility, or darkness (Demosthenes' triremes might have rowed through the night). In any case, the triremes had a good chance.

The Timing

This is extremely complicated; but fortunately we have enough internal evidence to construct a time-scheme which is at many points virtually certain, and at most others highly probable. The relevant sections are 5, 6, 8 and 13.

It will be best to start with the day on which the Athenian fleet returned to Pylos (13.1), which I shall call D-Day. We then have:-

D – 3   First day of Spartan attacks.
D – 2   Second day of Spartan attacks.
D – 1   Spartans send to Asine for timber: Athenian fleet appears off Pylos, goes to Prote for the night.

All this is quite straightforward.

The Spartan fleet must have arrived, at the latest, on D – 4: and we may put Demosthenes' despatch of the triremes bearing the message to Zacynthos on D – 5. For Demosthenes sent them προσπλεόντων ἔτι τῶν Πελοποννησίων ... φθάσας (8.3). If we put the Spartan arrival, and therefore Demosthenes' despatch of the triremes, any earlier we run into trouble: for the Athenian fleet sailed from Zacynthos

κατὰ τάχος (8.4),[4] and we should have allowed too much time for the two runs Pylos-Zacynthos and Zacynthos-Pylos. Together these total about 140 miles. Even allowing for some bad weather, preparations of the fleet at Zacynthos (though not many, since παρασκευασάμενοι . . . ναυμαχίαν in 13.3 probably implies that on the fleet's first appearance it was not so prepared), and so on, we cannot allow more than four days for this distance. So we have:

D – 5   Demosthenes sends his triremes.
D – 4   Spartan fleet arrives.
D – 3   Demosthenes' triremes arrive: Athenian fleet starts from Zacynthos.
D – 2   (Second day of Spartan attacks)
D – 1   Athenians appear off Pylos.

Our next problem is the arrival of the Spartan army. Some troops came before others (8.1 οἱ Σπαρτιᾶται . . εὐθὺς ἐβοήθουν ἐπὶ τὴν Πύλον, τῶν δὲ ἄλλων . . . βραδυτέρα ἡ ἔφοδος): but by the time the fleet got there, παρῆν ἤδη καὶ ὁ πεζὸς στρατός (8.2). Moreover, we can induce that the army had been there for some little time. In reference to the soldiers stationed on Sphacteria, Thucydides says (8.9) διέβησαν μὲν καὶ ἄλλοι πρότερον κατὰ διαδοχήν, οἱ δὲ τελευταῖοι . . . This certainly implies three shifts or relays of Spartans (including οἱ τελευταῖοι). We do not know how long each shift stayed, but it can hardly have been less than a day or two. On this evidence it looks as if we must place the arrival of the Spartan army (or its first detachments) on D – 6 at the latest: this barely allows time for three (very brief) shifts.

But there are difficulties. First, could Demosthenes have got the triremes off when the Spartan army was in situ? The Spartans must have had some ships of some kind, in order to get their soldiers on Sphacteria. This may be reasonably answered by saying that, even had the Spartan ships been more powerful than Demosthenes' two triremes, he might still have escaped notice in getting the triremes off: indeed, the ὑπ- in ὑπεκπέμπει (8.3) suggests secrecy or evasion of just this kind. Secondly, would Demosthenes have done so? Would he not have sent the ships off before the Spartans arrived? To this the answer is that he might well have had no certain news that 'the place was in danger' (8.3,τοῦ χωρίου κινδυνεύοντος) until the Spartans' actual arrival. Further, the best reading of the order of events in 8.2-4 suggests that, in fact, Demosthenes' action was not taken until after their arrival. These rebuttals, and the likelihood of the Spartan forces spending not a little time in preparation (8.4, παρεσκευάζοντο), allow us to retain D – 6 as the latest date for the Spartan army's arrival.

4.   In its context, the sentence καὶ αἱ μὲν νῆες κατὰ τάχος ἔπλεον κατὰ τὰ ἐπεσταλμένα ὑπὸ Δημοσθένους must surely refer to the Athenian νῆες to which reference has been made in the previous sentence. Otherwise most of the sense is otiose. For we already know that Demosthenes' ships sailed, and that they sailed according to Demosthenes' instructions (Thucydides has just told us).

We turn now to the rest of the timing, in particular that concerning the Spartan fleet. Gomme,[5] though in various other ways mistaken, points correctly to the tense-differences in 8.2: the Spartans sent orders (περιήγγελλον) round the Peloponnese for land reinforcements, and they had already (ἔπεμψαν, with pluperfect sense) sent a message to the fleet. We may note further that the part of the sentence relating to the fleet seems to be, as it were, in brackets: that is, from καὶ ἐπὶ to ἐπὶ Πύλον. With παρῆν δὲ ἤδη καὶ ... we are back again to 'normal' time: the fleet has not arrived, but the army has. We continue in 'normal' time: whilst the fleet is still on its way, Demosthenes sends off his triremes (under the Spartan army's nose): the Athenian ships at Zacynthos start their journey: the Spartans make preparations, and so on.

If the fleet arrived on D − 4, when did it start? Here we must make some allowance (a) for the διολκος, which must have slowed them down somewhat, but also (b) for the likely assistance of the (prevailing) wind on the course from Corcyra to Pylos. The distance is about 200 miles: we do not know how urgently they were summoned, but almost certainly with considerable urgency. A likely guess is D − 9, which must of course also have been the day on which they received the Spartan message.

Most of our remaining problems involve guesses about the transmission of messages by the Spartans. We are told (5.1) that the Spartans in Sparta did nothing when they heard of the Athenians' enterprise, but (6.1) that the Spartans in Attica immediately returned to Sparta. On their return, and not till then, the first troops left Sparta. Assuming the fastest possible transmission (by mounted messenger direct from Pylos to Attica) of news to the Spartans in Attica, we cannot possibly allow less than about 9 days in all between the sending of the news and the arrival of the first Spartan troops: probably more like 12. For the fleet, the fastest transmission would have been by sea direct from Pylos: but there are two difficulties here. First, the message-ship might well have been snapped up by the Athenian fleet at Zacynthos: and secondly, nobody at Pylos or nearby would have had sufficient authority to convey such a message. We must rather assume that either the Spartans in Attica, or the Spartans in Sparta - and probably the former - relayed the news with instructions to the fleet to return. I cannot see how this could have taken less than about 9 days. Allowing 5 days for the Corcyra-Pylos voyage (see above), this gives us 14 days between the sending of the news from Pylos and the fleet's arrival.

These last figures are, of course, only approximations: but they would be correct to within a day or two. We conclude that the first detachments of the Spartan army arrived about 3 days before the fleet, i.e. about D − 6. This fits snugly with our previous suggestion: also with the idea that, as soon as he could after the army's

---

5.   p. 442. Mistakes are: (1) πέμψαντες does not exist (he means ἔπεμψαν): (2) the fleet did not arrive 'as soon as the first hoplites from Sparta': 8.2, παρῆν δὲ ἤδη καὶ ὁ πεζὸς στρατός expressly rules this out: (3) an unsubstantiated mention of 'Knemos'.

71

arrival, Demosthenes sent off his triremes - on this timing, he did so the next day (D − 5). We can now argue back to the timing of the Athenian fortifications. We assume that news that the Athenians had *started* the fortifications began to come from Pylos almost as soon as the Athenians did start them. While the Athenians were completing them (in six days, 5.2) the news travelled. The first day of Athenian fortifications must be D − (6 plus 12): that is, the day of the arrival of the Spartan army (D − 6), plus the twelve days needed for that arrival and the previous news-spreading: D − 18.

This completes our time-scheme. Some of it is guesswork, but the general outline and order of the events seems reasonably clear. I will set it out (including the chancier guesses) in full:-

D − 18   Athenians start fortification. News travels to Spartans in Attica, and to Spartans in Sparta.

D − 12   Athenians finish fortification: main Athenian fleet sails to Zacynthos.

D − 10   Athenian fleet reaches Zacynthos, waits for Spartans, and gets in touch with allies further north (see p. 68 above).

D − 9   News reaches Spartans in Corcyra: they start for Pylos.

D − 8   Spartan expedition in Attica reaches Sparta: first detachment of Spartan troops sets out for Pylos.

D − 6   First Spartan troops reach Pylos. First relay of troops to Sphacteria.

D − 5   Demosthenes sends off his two triremes. Spartans prepare for attack.

D − 4   Spartan fleet arrives from Corcyra. Second relay of troops to Sphacteria.

D − 3   Demosthenes' triremes reach Zacynthos. First day of Spartan attack. Athenian fleet starts from Zacynthos.

D − 2   Second day of Spartan attack. Third relay of troops on Sphacteria.

D − 1   Spartans send to Asine for timber. Athenian fleet appears off Pylos, retires to Prote.

D -Day   Athenians reappear: seafight in harbour: Sphacteria blockaded.

One more thing needs to be mentioned. In 8.1 we are told of two waves of Spartan troops. The first we have shown to arrive about D − 6. It is probable, for military reasons discussed in another Note (see G.), that the second wave arrived *before* the attack on Demosthenes: we might put their arrival on D − 4. But there are also the Peloponnesian allies summoned in 8.2., but first mentioned in 14.5 after the sea-fight: οἱ δ'ἐν τῇ ἠπείρῳ Πελοποννήσιοι καὶ ἀπὸ πάντων ἤδη βεβοηθηκότες ἔμενον κατὰ χώραν ἐπὶ τῇ Πύλῳ. It seems certain that these contingents did not arrive before the attack on Demosthenes: not only because they were not mentioned earlier by Thucydides, but because the summons in 8.2 was only made when the Spartans from Attica had got back to Sparta, i.e. on D − 8; and it would have taken at least five days for the contingents to arrive ἀπὸ πάντων. The last contingents could not have come in much before D − 1.

F.   THE SPARTAN PLAN

In 8.4-9 Thucydides tells us about how the Spartans proposed to cope with the situation. Any hope of making satisfactory sense of the Spartan plan rests in tackling first that part of the plan which, according to Thucydides, consisted of blocking the entrances. This has been much discussed, as being the chief (perhaps the only) point on which Thucydides seems to have gone seriously astray. Partly for this reason the problems here are even more complicated than usual: and the attempted solutions should be regarded as more than usually tentative.

The first crucial passage to look at is 8.6-7:- ἡ γὰρ νῆσος ἡ Σφακτηρία καλουμένη τόν τε λιμένα παρατείνουσα καὶ ἐγγὺς ἐπικειμένη ἐχυρὸν ποιεῖ καὶ τοὺς ἔσπλους στενούς, τῇ μὲν δυοῖν νεῶν διάπλουν κατὰ τὸ τείχισμα τῶν Ἀθηναίων καὶ τὴν Πύλον, τῇ δὲ πρὸς τὴν ἄλλην ἤπειρον ὀκτὼ ἢ ἐννέα . . . τοὺς μὲν οὖν ἔσπλους ταῖς ναυσὶν ἀντιπρώροις βύζην κλῇσειν ἔμελλον κτλ.

Gomme[1] takes βύζην to mean 'by taking the bungs out of their ships' (and hence sinking them), noting that βύσμα means 'a plug or bung'. However, (i) the verb βύω means simply to 'stuff up' or 'stop up', and neither the verb nor the noun has any particular connection with the bungs of ships; (ii) βύζην could quite straightforwardly mean 'in a stuffing-up or stopping-up way', perhaps adding force to κλῇσειν 'close the entrances by stuffing them up tight'. (The phrase is not a tautology: βύζην tells the reader that they intended to close the entrances in a certain *manner*.) (iii) It is hard to see how the adverb can strictly construe on Gomme's interpretation: it must surely mean 'in a bung-like or stopping-up kind of *way*', rather than '*by removing* the bungs'. None of these points is conclusive: but the weight of probability is against Gomme.

ἀντιπρώροις. Gomme[2] takes this as implying that the triremes were to be broadside on to the open sea. He makes this interpretation seem more plausible by talking only of the *two* triremes (sc. in the Sikia channel) which 'were to face each other': ἀντιπρῷρος he says, 'really means "stem facing stem" '. This will work for two triremes, but Thucydides is talking of the whole blockship plan, which involves many more than two. It is barely conceivable that the plan was (or was thought by Thucydides to be) to have a line of triremes anchored in pairs, one member of each pair being anchored stem-to-stem with its partner: but unlikely. ἀντιπρῷρος naturally (and commonly elsewhere)[3] means simply 'with the prow turned towards . . . ' or 'with the prow facing . . . '. If, as appears from the point just made, the prows are not to face each other, there is nothing for them to face except the open sea or the enemy: either of which would mean that

---

1.   p. 444.
2.   p. 443.
3.   See references in Gomme, *ibid.*

73

they were not broadside on. At the very least, it would be highly misleading of Thucydides to use ἀντιπρῷρος to mean 'broadside on': he would more naturally have used πλάγιος, as elsewhere.[4]

Further, if Gomme is wrong about βύξην, broadside-on ships could be rammed and sunk, and hence provide no effective barrier at all. The example of Syracuse does not tell against this: for there the ships were firmly anchored and very vigorously defended, in a restricted and enclosed area. The Spartans, by contrast, wished to avoid a sea-fight (8.5, ἄνευ ναυμαχίας).

From this it follows that Thucydides tells us of a Spartan plan to block up something with lines of parallel ships. Whatever the width of either ἔσπλους, it is to some extent uncertain just how many ships would be required: but on any plausible view of trireme-dimensions, it is hard to see how the Spartans would need less than one ship for every 20 or 30 feet of space. This obvious point should have worried commentators more than it has, as appears below.

In marrying what Thucydides says with historical fact, commentators seem to have exercised less than their usual care both on the text and on the topography. Two assumptions are characteristically made:

(a)   That, from the number of ships Thucydides gives in 8.6 ('two' and 'eight or nine'), we can infer similar numbers as required for blocking the entrances. This assumption is tacit, and has only to be compared with the text to be seen to be unwarranted. Thucydides says that the location of Sphacteria makes the entrances narrow, allowing on one side a διάπλους of two ships, and on the other a διάπλους of eight or nine. Whatever he means here, there is no reason at all to suppose that his criterion for διάπλους ship-numbers is conceptually the same as, or contingently correlates with, any criterion for numbers of blockships. In fact, διάπλους must mean 'a sailing-through' (sc. of the ἔσπλους): Thucydides is giving the numbers of triremes (two for the Sikia) that could sail comfortably abreast through the channel, and giving them in sufficient detail to be taken seriously. From what we know of trireme-dimensions, we may assume a figure of about 45 feet per trireme for a διάπλους (hull, outriggers, oars, and an adequate space between the triremes), and about 16ft. 6 in. for a block-ship.[5]

---

4.   *ibid.*
5.   Breadth with outriggers about 16 ft. 6 in., and oars projecting perhaps 10 ft. on either side, make up 36 ft. 6 in.: and we may allow 4 ft. 3 in. on either side for a safety margin to make up a round figure of 45 ft. Of course all of this is approximate and some of it guesswork: but the distance is unlikely to have been much less than 40 ft., or much more than 50 ft. The argument would not be affected by any reasonable variations. See Morrison and Williams.

(b)   That there is no problem about the northern (Sikia) channel. It is assumed, not only, as in (a) above, that Thucydides is *saying* that two ships could have blocked it, but also that two ships could *in fact* have blocked it. The Sikia channel is assumed to be about 150 yards wide not only by Gomme but, curiously, by Pritchett, who is himself out to demonstrate that the land has sunk. But if so, it would allow a through-passage for ten triremes, not two, and require about twenty-eight triremes to block it.

The question of the south channel is similarly bedevilled. Thus Gomme:[6] " . . . not only some 1,400 yards wide, but, what is more important, about 200 feet deep and could not have been blocked even by the whole Peloponnesian fleet. It is quite out of the question . . . ". This curt dismissal depends logically on Gomme's implausible view on the meaning of βύζην:the depth is relevant only if the Spartans were planning to sink their ships.

Those commentators who believe in the plan have in effect argued: 'If a channel of 150 yards can be blocked by two triremes, then a channel of 1,400 yards can be blocked by 18'. Here too we meet the assumptions criticized above: briefly,

(a)   Thucydides does not say that a 150-yard channel can be blocked by two triremes;

(b)   nor in fact can it.

Despite the superficial reasoning on both sides, those commentators are nevertheless right who say that the south channel could not have been blocked. For taking ἀντιπρώροις in its more plausible sense, and allowing the generous figure of 18 ft. per trireme, we reach a figure of over 200 triremes: and even if we take ἀντιπρώροις as 'broadside-on', thus giving the somewhat more plausible figure of 30-40 triremes, we still have the difficulty that such triremes could have been rammed and sunk, even if they could have survived bad weather.

Although Thucydides does not specify numbers of triremes required as block-ships, he does have, or conveys, a false picture at least of the south entrance. Nor can this be righted by assuming errors in numeral transmission. Not only is this arbitrary from a palaeographic point of view (in a way in which Burrow's suggestion of εἴκοσι for δέκα in regard to the length of Sphacteria is not palaeographically arbitrary);[7] but, more important, the south entrance allows a διάπλους for far more ships than Thucydides says that it does. The whole Athenian fleet could have sailed through it in line abreast. The fact that Thucydides was mistaken about the southern entrance, however, does not

---

6.   *ibid.*
7.   ΔΠ or ιέ (15) for ΔΔΠ or κέ (25). See Note A.

75

entail that he was mistaken about there being a Spartan plan to block something. We have the following possibilities:

(i)   There was a plan to block the south and north entrances.

(ii)   There was no plan to block anything.

(iii)   There was a plan, or at least some sort of vague intention, to block something: but either Thucydides and/or the Spartans themselves were confused about the various ἔσπλοι and their dimensions.

(i) I hope already to have shown to be absurd, unless we assume that the Spartans responsible for the plan had never actually seen the south entrance: certainly when they had, its impracticability would have been immediately obvious to them.

(ii) is extremely unlikely. Thucydides is both definite and circumstantial: he mentions the plan three times (8.5, 8.7, and 13.4), and gives the details about ship-numbers in conjunction with the first two mentions. We would have to assume a very complex and improbable false source. But Thucydides may well have reached his false notion of the south channel from false inferences: and it is cavalier to postulate a complex false source simply in order to disembarrass Thucydides of the whole idea of the Spartans intending to block something.[8] We are left with (iii).

Since Grundy's suggestion for a second ἔσπλους to the south-east of Pylos has been shown by Pritchett to be baseless, we may either pick the entrance to Voidokoilia Bay as the second ἔσπλους, or assume that the plan was to block one only and somehow Thucydides turned it into two. The latter assumption seems absurd: see (ii) above (also Thucydides speaks constantly of τούς ἔσπλους in the plural). There may, then, have been some confusion between (a) the two ἔσπλοι into the harbour on the one hand, and (b) the Sikia ἔσπλους and the entrance to Voidokoilia on the other. It is thus at least worth considering whether these two latter ἔσπλοι (b) fit Thucydides' figures.

Do these ἔσπλοι fit Thucydides' figures?

The data that follow are from my own measurements, checked by independent observers. They are offered with the reservations mentioned in the footnotes.

---

8.   For what is is worth, Diodorus (XII. 6.3) also mentioned the blockade (but as a reality: τὰς μὲν ναῦς ἀντιπρώρους ἔστησαν τῷ στόματι του λιμέως κτλ.).

(i) The Voidokoilia[9] entrance is approximately 120 yards wide from B to C (see map C). The water is deep over all the entrance, even close to the points B and C, and navigability for triremes of 4 or 5 foot draught would not be affected by a rise in land-level of 2.50 m., nor indeed, by twice that rise. The interior of the bay is sandy, and the depth varies (e.g. over a fairly large area of it the sea-bed rose some 5 to 6 ft. in the course of a year). The entrance, however, remains over 20 ft. deep at all points, and there is no difficulty in landing on the sandy shores, even when strong winds cause surf; particularly close to the cliff (D on the sketch), which is a well-protected point in all weathers.

(ii) The Sikia[10] channel (like the Voidokoilia entrance) is deep throughout, wherever Sphacteria directly faces Pylos (E-F on the sketch). At its narrowest point (E-G) it is approximately 110 yards wide. The shore at E and G is not as sheer as at Voidokoilia, and we should perhaps allow some 10 yards over which a land-rise of 2-3 metres would have made navigation impossible. This leaves 100 yards of navigable water in classical times. Further east, however, the depth diminishes rapidly: that this is not a very recent phenomenon is testified by a number of old nautical charts and maps, which mark depths similar to those marked by Grundy. Briefly, measurements of depths and widths (allowing always for a 2-3 metre land-rise) give us a navigable channel of about 35 yards between points H and I. In classical times it would be either dry or fordable over the line H-J and I-K.

9. Some may be misled here by Leake's description of Voidokoilia (quoted by Gomme, p. 484) as a bay with a 'narrow entrance; it is nevertheless bad, exposed to a continual surf, and capable only of admitting boats'. But (1) the entrance is wider than the Sikia channel (see map); (2) it is usually calm, and its beach is exposed to surf only in strong northerly or westerly winds (certainly not to 'continual' surf); (3) whatever Leake means by 'boats', the entrance is quite deep enough for triremes.

10. Here we cannot be as sure as we should like, because of hydrographical difficulties. Thus, granted a rise of about 2.5 metres, we should have to suppose that the Sikia was completely dry at its eastern end: but both Thucydides and the whole story of the campaign require otherwise. We know that the Normans and Venetians used the south-east corner of Pylos (the part enclosed by the Athenians as their landing-place: see Note B) as a port, which appears on some Venetian maps as Port de Jonc or Zoncio. The eastern part of the Sikia cannot then have been so shallow. The hydrographic probability is that this part has silted up, due to matter being carried eastwards by the west-east flow through the Sikia, this flow being caused by the prevailing westerly or north-westerly winds. The sea-bottom here is indeed 'soft' (sand and silt), and one can virtually observe the building up of sand at the point or spit on the Pylos side (marked J on the map): I myself have seen it increase visibly over a period of five years.
    There seems little doubt that this eastern part, which I take to include one of Thucydides' blockade-lines, has become progressively shallower over the centuries: the depths marked on various ancient maps tend to confirm this, though such maps are too untrustworthy to be quoted as firm evidence. Against, this, however, we have to set the general rise in sea-level of about 2.5 metres. This allows us to maintain that the two processes may have virtually cancelled each other out, and hence that Thucydides' τῇ μὲν δυοῖν νεοῖν διάπλουν (8.6) is acceptable. But it will be seen that we cannot hope for certainty here: particularly since the area is seismic. I doubt whether even a full-scale hydrographic survey could establish such certainty. Fortunately, there is sufficient probability in the matter to allow us to establish the relevant historical points.

77

These measurements fit Thucydides' figures almost exactly. Eight triremes for the Voidokoilia entrance require a distance of 8 x 45 feet, i.e. 120 yards: the entrance itself is 120 yards. A ninth trireme, if sufficiently venturesome, could have sailed between point A on Pylos and the rocks (B). Thucydides' ὀκτὼ ἢ ἐννέα is exactly right. For the Sikia, we require 2 x 45 feet for two triremes, i.e. 30 yards: another very exact correspondence. Even if we grant reservations about the dimensions of the triremes or about shifts in the sea-bed caused by currents, and resist the temptation to extract more accuracy from Thucydides than any author could be expected to bear, the correspondence is striking: and it is, therefore, worth pursuing a theory on this hypothesis.

Commentators have usually failed to consider exactly where the points we have marked as H and I - that is, the end of the proposed Spartan blockade-lines for the Sikia - should be placed. Because of this failure, they have also not appreciated the difficulties for the common view which implicitly or explicitly puts H on Athenian-held territory.

The prima facie difficulties of laying ships sideways on so as to reach enemy territory, and then defending them against fire, or other forms of Athenian destruction, are obvious: but there is in any case the knock-down argument that if this had been possible, the Spartans would certainly have done it (in preference to the dangerous Thrasymelidas landing on the south-west rocks) as a way of reaching Athenian-held territory. There is not much doubt (see note B) that the Athenians enclosed the (comparatively) flat south-east corner within their fortifications, which afterwards served as a base, though an inadequate one. I have marked the possible wall-line here L-M, simply to make the point that the Spartan blockade-end must have been east of this or any similar wall, if it was to be on Spartan-held territory; this virtually forces us to adopt H for this point, and hence profoundly reinforces the significance of the correspondence of Thucydides' figures with the measurements.

Does blocking these ἔσπλοι make any sense?

The crucial passage here is the first sentence of 8.8:

οὕτω γὰρ τοῖς ᾿Αθηναίοις τήν τε νῆσον πολεμίαν ἔσεσθαι τήν τε ἤπειρον, ἀπόβασιν οὐκ ἔχουσαν (τὰ γὰρ αὐτῆς τῆς Πύλου ἔξω τοῦ ἔσπλου πρὸς τὸ πέλαγος ἀλίμενα ὄντα οὐχ ἔξειν ὅθεν ὁρμώμενοι ὠφελήσουσι τοὺς αὑτῶν), σφεῖς δὲ ἄνευ τε ναυμαχίας καὶ κινδύνου ἐκπολιορκήσειν τὸ χωρίον κατὰ τὸ εἰκός, σίτου τε οὐκ ἐνόντος κτλ.

In relation to this passage, and indeed most of what Thucydides says about Spartan intentions (in 8.5 ff.), we may of course be content to say simply that he was hopelessly muddled by his false assumption that the ἔσπλοι were on either side of Sphacteria (as τὴν ἄλλην ἤπειρον in 8.6 clearly shows); and that we have no real hope of seeing through

this muddle to what may actually have been the Spartans' intentions. Thucydides perhaps was told of two ἔσπλους - dimensions noted by some Spartan scout or surveyor: and the rest of what he says may be largely or wholly the result of his own false inference about where the ἔσπλοι were.

However, I think some possibilities at least may be pursued. First, editors take this passage to refer solely to the Spartans' intention to deny the Athenians a *base of operations*. The words ὅθεν ὁρμώμενοι certainly refer to a base: but they are connected syntactically with the τὰ γὰρ . . . ὄντα clause, as the brackets normally inserted by editors indicate, and not with the earlier part of the sentence. Disregard of the syntax could produce some such translation as: "They thought that thus the Athenians would find both the island to be enemy-occupied and the mainland, affording them no chance of landing: so that, since the coast of Pylos itself outside the entrance, towards the open sea, is harbourless, they would have no base of operations to help their troops": or possibly, taking ἤπειρον as the subject of ἕξειν,' . . . the mainland, affording them no chance of landing (since the coast of Pylos . . .), would give them no base of operations . . . '. However, it is plain that the subject of ἕξειν must be τὰ . . . ἀλίμενα ὄντα; and this puts the meaning of the sentence in a new light.

The correct translation is: "They thought that thus the Athenians would find both the island to be enemy-occupied, and the mainland, which gave them no chance of landing [11] (for the coast of Pylos itself, outside the entrance and towards the open sea, is harbourless and would give them no base of operations to help their troops): . . . ". The order of thought is: both the island and mainland would be enemy-occupied, and prevent a landing - *all* the mainland (in case the reader was wondering), since there was no place at Pylos for a base. This leaves open the possibility that when Thucydides talks of ἀπόβασις, he is not thinking of a possible *base* for the Athenians, but of a landing for some other purpose. This is perfectly in accord with Thucydides' use of ἀπόβασις elsewhere in 8-13.

Indeed, the Spartans can hardly have thought that the Athenians would have tried to use anywhere on the ἤπειρος as a *base,* i.e. a defensible and semi-permanent camp. For there already were Peloponnesian forces at Pylos (ready to attack the Athenian wall) which could very quickly have been deployed to attack any attempted Athenian base in the vicinity (e.g. on the coast behind Sphacteria). The Athenians might have tried to use Sphacteria, which partly explains the Spartans sending troops there: but it does not explain why they stationed troops παρὰ τὴν ἤπειρον (in 8.7, immediately preceding this sentence). Stationing troops παρὰ τὴν ἤπειρον would not have prevented the Athenians using Pylos as a base, had it been possible: nor would it have prevented them from sailing into the λιμήν, destroying the Spartan fleet, and thus opening up the south-east corner of Pylos as a base (as in fact they did).

---
11.   Not 'landing-place': there were *places* to land, but no *chance* of landing

79

Nevertheless we are told that the denial of an ἀπόβασις would help the Spartans ἐκπολιορκήσειν. For reasons just given, the reference cannot be to an ἀπόβασις *qua* base: nor can it be to an ἀπόβασις *qua* any point at which supplies might be landed, despite the temptation of οἴτου τε οὐκ ἐνόντος. For, in calm weather and with a friendly shore, supplies may be landed at many points on Pylos - it is not necessary to have an anchorage, or even a proper landing-place, to get supplies ashore. Sense can only be made of ἀπόβασις and ἐκπολιορκήσειν if we take the Spartans to have been afraid of a quick landing by the Athenian ships, designed to take the Spartan troops besieging Pylos in the rear, or by some similar tactical move to make the Spartan assault more difficult. Thucydides is thinking simply of a possible landing-place. If such an ἀπόβασις were possible on Pylos, it would of course *be* a base (because permanently defensible): and that is why Thucydides talks of a base in the bracketed part of the text. That Thucydides has the possibility of such quick tactical landings in mind is itself shown by ὅθεν ὁρμώμενοι ὠφελήσουσι τοὺς αὐτῶν: literally, 'setting out from where they would bring relief to their troops'.[12] Since this putative base is on Pylos itself, where would they go *to* after setting out? The kind of ὠφελία Thucydides has in mind is plainly not in the nature of any general relief, supplies, etc., for Pylos itself: for the ships would be there already. It must be in the nature of the tactical landings already mentioned.

We now have a possible motive for the Spartans blocking the entrance to Voidokoilia: for the bay offers an ideal place for such a landing. The landing is easy, and very close indeed to the Peloponnesian troops who would be besieging Pylos, and whom any such landing would immediately take in the rear. The same point applies to blocking the Sikia channel. It may of course be argued that the stationing of hoplites παρὰ τὴν ἤπειρον would of itself be sufficient protection against Athenian landings: but the Spartans may have wanted to make doubly certain, or may have wished to relieve the hoplites of this guard-duty in order to use them for the assault of Pylos. We might indeed conjecture that one reason why they failed to execute their blocking plan was because enough hoplites arrived to do the job. (See Note G).

We have still to cope with ἄνευ ναυμαχίας. If it be supposed that Thucydides is here thinking in terms of blocking the Sikia and the (impossibly wide) channel south of Sphacteria, then Thucydides is simply reading non-existent Spartan intentions into his own topographical error. On this view, the Spartans (as Thucydides believed) argued as follows: "We do not want a ναυμαχία. We can avoid a ναυμαχία if and only if the Athenian fleet is kept out of the λιμήν. Therefore we must block the entrances to the λιμήν". If this is the way Thucydides thought the Spartans argued, then he is in error: the same error, in effect, as his topographical one. But it should by now be clear that

---

12.   Cf. 1.2, ἐξ αὐτοῦ ὁρμώμενοί (of Messene in Sicily as a possible jumping-off point for the Athenians).

80

the Spartans at least - whatever Thucydides thought - need not have argued along those lines at all. A ναυμαχία would not *only* be necessary to prevent the Athenian fleet from entering the λιμήν. It would be necessary to prevent tactical landings, unless the prevention of such landings could be achieved by some other way. And this is what the Spartans attempted. They argued: "If the Athenian fleet (which will in any case be able to enter the λιμήν, the south entrance of which we cannot block) is going to be able to make tactical landings anywhere it chooses, our siege of Pylos will be more difficult. Therefore we will ensure that it cannot land anywhere on Sphacteria or on the mainland: and we shall block up the Sikia and Voidokoilia entrances, and place hoplites on Sphacteria and the mainland. If we don't do this, we shall have to stop them by a ναυμαχία, which is dangerous to us."

It remains true that the Athenian fleet could (and did) land on the south-east corner of Pylos, after having defeated the Spartan fleet: and that they were thus enabled to blockade the Spartans on Sphacteria. The argument above suggests *one* reason why a ναυμαχία would be necessary, if the Spartans did not take certain precautions: but we may still ask whether the Spartans did not see that it would in any case be necessary for these *other* reasons. In other words, how did they hope to prevent the Athenian fleet from sailing in, landing on Pylos, and blockading Sphacteria without a ναυμαχία, even if they hoped to prevent other difficulties without a ναυμαχία? To this there are two possible answers:

(a)   Thucydides does not say that the Spartans believed that they would certainly be able to avoid a ναυμαχία. The crucial sentence leaves the main verb to be understood; and the phrase κατὰ τὸ ἐικός, which we may take as applying as much to the ἄνευ τε ναυμαχίας as to the rest of the clause, suggests that we may reasonably translate: 'They hoped that . . . ' or 'They thought that they would probably . . . '. Nor was this hope unreasonable. The Athenian fleet would have to enter (by one entrance only, if the Spartans had blocked the Sikia channel) a λιμήν the shores of which were (apart from the small area at Pylos) manned by Spartan hoplites, in face of a fleet half as large again as their own. It would not be clear to the Athenians that they would have anywhere to anchor their ships, or what they would gain by entering the λιμήν.

(b)   The Spartans may well have believed this hope to have been realized when the Athenians (13.3.), after inspecting the area from the open sea, went away in the direction from which they had come: in fact to Prote, though the Spartans may not have been immediately aware of this. The behaviour of the Athenian fleet in 13.2. and 3. might be taken as a ruse. Why did not the fleet sail straight into the λιμήν? It is possible that they needed time, and an anchorage, to prepare for a ναυμαχία (13.3 τῇ δ'ὑστεραίᾳ παρασκευασάμενοι ὡς ἐπὶ ναυμαχίαν), but unlikely: possible too, and more likely, that they arrived towards the evening, and left themselves too little time to make a proper job of the ναυμαχία: but possible also that they found the Spartan

81

fleet alert, and hoped, by seeming to disappear altogether, to be able to return and catch them off their guard. Whether or not that was the Athenian intention, the Spartans may well have thought that they had gone for good (see above, (a)): visibility as far as Prote is by no means always adequate from Sphacteria and Pylos, and darkness may have been coming on.

Some such suggestion is strongly reinforced by the lack of alertness in the Spartan fleet in 14.1. When the Athenians return, they wait for a little to see if the Spartans will sail out into the εὐρυχωρία. ἡσυχάζοντες δ'ἐν τῇ γῇ τάς τε ναῦς ἐπλήρουν καὶ παρεσκευάζ· 'they stayed quietly ashore [13] and *were in the process of* manning their ships and preparing . . . '. As the imperfects show, they had not completed this process. This is why some ships were damaged while still being manned, and before leaving the shore (14.1. ἔτι πρὶν ἀνάγεσθαι ἐκόπτοντο): and others, which must have been on the shore, taken in tow after their crews had been put to flight. Since the Spartans had already gained time for preparation while the Athenians were waiting out at sea, all this indicates a state of extreme unreadiness: more readily explicable if the disappearance of the day before had been taken by the Spartans as permanent. (See also Note I).

This would, I think, in itself sufficiently answer the ἄνευ τε ναυμαχίας problem. But there is a further and more important consideration. For the value to the Spartans of blocking the Sikia channel on the line H-I, *between the south-east corner and the* λιμήν, is plain enough. Most obviously, it has value as a bridge by which the hoplites on Sphacteria could reach the mainland: but it also makes the Athenian position much more difficult. The Athenians required - what after the ναυμαχία (because the Sikia blockade was not executed) they actually gained - a *combination* of an anchorage (i.e. a sheltered area) and a place to land. The former was the λιμήν: the latter, the south-east corner of Pylos. 26.3 gives the picture in brief: the Athenian fleet maintain touch with Pylos by anchoring in the north-west part of the λιμήν, next to the defended south-east landing-place. Had the direct communication between these two been severed so that the Athenian ships would have had to circumnavigate Sphacteria in order to stay in touch with the south-east landing-place, it is doubtful whether there would have been a viable base at all; in the event, indeed, it proved precarious enough. The blockade would justify Thucydides' statement of the Spartan intention (otherwise absurd) to blockade the entrances ὅπως μὴ ᾖ τοῖς 'Αθηναίοις ἐφορμίσασθαι ἐς αὐτόν (8.5). This plan was wholly practicable. If we allow (taking βύζην very seriously) a niggardly 15 ft. for a trireme acting as a blockship, this would require 6 triremes for the Sikia channel of 30 yards, and some 23 or 24 for the Voidokoilia entrance of 120 yards.

---

13.   Not, with Gomme, 'stopping their attacks by land': possible Greek (though unlikely because of the ἐν), but the sense is irrelevant to the context.

Why did the Spartans not carry out the plan?

Despite the obvious merits and practicability of the plan, it would have been surprising if the Spartans had executed it. We need not here rely

(a)   on well-worn remarks about Spartan lack of enterprise: nor

(b)   on their inexperience in nautical matters: nor, more plausibly,

(c)   on the possibility that the arrival of Peloponnesian reinforcements to be stationed παρὰ τὴν ἤπειρον made the plan unnecessary.

More relevant are:

(d)   They needed to use the Sikia channel (if they were not to go a long way round by the southern Sphacteria channel) in order to conduct the assault by sea; and they did not have much time to form their blocks between the end of that assault and the arrival of Athenian fleet (13.1 and 2). Exactly how long they had is unclear from this passage, because the ἐν τούτῳ in 13.2 is uncertain in its reference. The Athenian fleet may have come back whilst the sea assault was just ending, or in that part of the day after it had finished, or on the next day. Nor do we know just how long it would take the Spartans to form the blocks.

(e)   The Spartan plan to use siege-engines on the south-east corner of Pylos would also have needed a free Sikia channel: and this seems to have been the plan with the highest priority in 13.1.

It has to be remembered throughout that the blocking-plan was to operate only ἢν ἄρα μὴ πρότερον ἕλωσι (8.5). In brief, the Spartans simply did not have the time.

Where and why is Thucydides mistaken?

In favour of the view here put forward, it must be noticed that Thucydides is thereby saddled with only one basic mistake: that is, the *position* of the ἔσπλοι. He is correct in referring to two narrow entrances: correct in giving their rough δ ιάπλους – dimensions: correct in saying that the Spartans intended to block them. Further, his reportage in 8.8 and elsewhere enables us to infer their motives. It is simply that he thinks that the ἔσπλοι are at either end of Sphacteria, and that the Spartans intended to block *these* entrances (*sc.* of the λιμήν).

On this view, it is in the highest degree unlikely that Thucydides was told that the entrances on either side of Sphacteria were of the dimensions he gives. He was told of two entrances, told how wide they were, and told that the Spartans intended to block them. This relates importantly to his statement about the Spartan intention. He could not have argued: "The entrances by Sphacteria are narrow: the Spartans intended

83

to block them: therefore their intention must have been to keep the Athenians out of the λιμήν": for he was told nothing about the entrances *by Sphacteria*. How did Thucydides get from his knowledge (1) that there were narrow entrances, and (2) that the Spartans intended to block them, to (3) that these entrances were by Sphacteria? He argued: "The Spartans were going to block these narrow entrances I've been told about - to keep the Athenians out of the λιμήν, of course." (So far, so good.) "Naturally they are the Sphacteria entrances, since Sphacteria stretches alongside the λιμήν."

G. NUMBERS AND COMPOSITION OF SPARTAN FORCES

We cannot hope for exactness here, but we should at least attempt to get as clear an answer as possible to the question "What forces did Demosthenes have to face?"

We know that the Spartan fleet numbered 60 ships: to which we may add some (probably insignificant) shipping used by the Spartans to ferry their troops to Sphacteria. We first hear of this fleet in 2.3: much of it was probably composed of the same ships that had performed ingloriously and ineffectively under the command of Alcidas in 427 (see Bk. III, 80 and 81, and earlier). At Pylos it was under the command of Thrasymelidas, whom Thucydides described by the term ναύαρχος (11.2) and who was no doubt the official Spartan ναύαρχος for that year. The composition of the fleet, however, would as usual have been made up mostly by Sparta's more nautical allies.

Consequently we need not be too surprised that the fleet did not perform efficiently. A strong hint of this is given in 11.4, where the trierarchs are described as ἀποκνοῦντας, and have to be urged on by Brasidas (see also Note H). But the real piece of incompetence comes in 13.4. Granted, as we have argued in another Note (see Note F, p. 81f.), that the Spartans may have been tricked into supposing that the Athenians would not return after their first appearance off Pylos, their failure to act sensibly and decisively is still remarkable. They had neither drawn up their ships on land, nor were they properly prepared to fight. This is not the sort of mistake that can be attributed to lack of nautical skill. We may offer the further excuse that some ships were *en route* to Asine, and others which had been damaged in the attack on Pylos no doubt needed repair: but this is still insufficient. The Athenian fleet, under conditions of normal visibility, would have been seen from Sphacteria (or from a high point on the mainland) as soon as it left Prote: at the very least, the Spartans would have had well over an hour to make preparations, since it is clear that the Athenians delayed before entering the harbour (13.3-4). I am much inclined to suspect lack of discipline, or an inadequate chain of command, in the fleet: less surprising when we remember its mixed composition. (See also Note I).

We have no precise information (*pace* Diodorus' figure of 12,000)[1] of the Spartan land forces. But we have shown elsewhere (Note E) that the third wave of these forces - those contingents coming from the Peloponnesian allies - could not have arrived in time for the attack on Demosthenes. The second wave, however, must have done. For consider what troops the Spartans deployed. They put 420 hoplites on Sphacteria, and others on the mainland (8.7): there must have been many of the latter, for the point was (see Note F, p. 80) to prevent the Athenians using *anywhere* on the mainland as a

---

1.   xii.61.2.

landing-point. This means that there must have been sufficient hoplites to prevent sudden Athenian landings in Voidokoilia Bay, or anywhere in the λιμήν.[2] Further, the 43 ships under Thrasymelidas must have been full of enough hoplites not only to force a landing, but to make it good. I hesitate to assign figures for the last two troop-requirements, but I cannot see that the total (including the Sphacteria contingent) can have been much less than 1000-1,500.

There can hardly have been enough in the first wave for this figure. For the first wave consisted only of οἱ Σπαρτιᾶται αὐτοὶ καὶ οἱ ἐγγύτατα τῶν περιοίκων (8.1). Even for them, it would be a remarkably high figure: but it is in any case contrasted with τῶν ἄλλων Λακεδαιμονίων . . . ἄρτι ἀφιγμένων ἀφ'ἑτέρας στρατείας. Thucydides not clear here, for there must have been Spartiates on Agis' expedition, and these Spartiat fall into both categories. Were they in the first wave qua Σπαρτιᾶται, or in the second qua ἄρτι ἀφιγμένων? We cannot tell for certain: but it is probable that some at least were in the second. In general we can hardly doubt that it was not till the second wave arrived that the Spartans deployed the manpower required by 8.7-9, and by Thrasymelidas' attack.

Besides these requirements, there was also of course the contingent which conducted the land attack on Pylos. As we have argued elsewhere (see Note B, and map C), that part of the Pylos perimeter which was assailable by land extended for nearly a mile: and though much of it οὐδὲν ἔδει τείχους (4.3), there were points at which the Spartans might have hoped to force an entry by a determined attack - particularly since Demosthenes had few men, and had to cope simultaneously with Thrasymelidas' attack. 500 hoplites would not have been too many for the Spartans to use. I should be surprised if the whole hoplite force totalled less than 1500 - too many, surely, for οἱ Σπαρτιᾶται αὐτοὶ καὶ οἱ ἐγγύτατα τῶν περιοίκων.

---

2.   It is true that the Athenians probably had no more than about 240 hoplites to use for this purpose (see Note D, p. 66 : if we imagine 11 of Eurymedon's ships totally stripped of epibatai, for Demosthenes' benefit, we have 24 x 10 remaining). But the Spartans could not rely on this. It is unlikely, however, that the Spartans needed to guard the coastline north of Voidokoilia, or south of the southern entrance to the λιμήν (i.e. south of the modern town of Pylos). For, if the Athenians landed anywhere in this (extremely difficult) terrain, their hoplites could not have attacked the Spartans at Pylos without considerably distancing themselves from their ships, and hence being liable to destruction by a larger Spartan force which could have cut them off from their ships.

H. THRASYMELIDAS' ATTACK

The chief problem here is to determine just where the Spartan ships tried to force a landing. We know from 9.2 (ἐς χωρία μὲν χαλεπὰ κὰι πετρώδη πρὸς τὸ πέλαγος τετραμμένα) that it was on the west coast. We can also be virtually certain that it was not on the northern part of the west coast: for here the cliffs rise more or less sheer from the sea, and both landing and deployment would have been impossible. To this extent we may agree with the tradition of commentary which places it on the south-west shore of Pylos.

However, there are some 500 yards of shore here; and there are good reasons why we should not accept the tradition, derived ultimately from Grundy, that the attempted landing was at one point only - the point often described as 'Brasidas' rocks', facing south-west towards the north-west tip of Sphacteria.[1] For, first, the shore here is in no way more suitable for landing than other parts of the shore in this 500-yards stretch; secondly, and more importantly, there are tactical reasons why the Spartans would not have confined themselves to this point.

The Spartans used 43 ships, and were confronted by only 60 hoplites and a few archers. The position of the Athenian walls was such (see Note B) that they had only to force a landing *anywhere* along the west coast in order to achieve their purpose (9.3, ἐκείνοις τε βιαζομένοις τὴν ἀπόβασιν ἁλώσιμον τὸ χωρίον γίγνεσθαι). A landing confined in principle to the south-west point only makes sense if we envisage a system of fortification which is wildly implausible.[2] For, obviously, in this tactical position the Spartans would wish to extend the diminutive Athenian force as far as possible, by landing with as many of their ships as they could at the same time. Thus (in the extreme case) had they been able to bring all 43 to land at once in different places, the Athenians could have deployed no more than one or two hoplites against each, which would certainly not have kept the Spartans off.

Nevertheless the Spartans were κατ'ὀλίγας ναῦς διελόμενοι, διότι οὐκ ἦν πλείοσι προσσχεῖν. This is perfectly intelligible in view of the terrain. All along this 500-yards stretch there are rocks, similar to the 'Brasidas' rocks'. There are some four or five rocky outcrops or capes, and as many small rock-strewn bays or indentations separating them. Landing is of course difficult anywhere: but at many points it is impossible - not, as has often been implied, because of the rugged nature of the rocks above the waterline and actually on the shore, but because of the rocks under or just

---

1.   See Pritchett p. 23, also map C.
2.   We should have to imagine a weak wall behind the south-west point, and the south-west point itself cut off by two strong walls on either side (otherwise the Spartans could have landed elsewhere on the coast and moved, by land, to face the weak wall). This is obviously ridiculous.

87

above the waterline in the *approaches* to the shore. Triremes trying such approaches would simply get stuck some yards from the land. (On this point see remarks on the Athenian landings on Sphacteria, Note M). On the other hand, there are about four or five areas where this is not true, and where landing is possible. It is difficult to identify these with any exactness: partly because the rise in sea-level[3] would affect the issue, and partly because there may have been other, though more minor, changes in rock-positions. Having taken a number of soundings off this stretch of coast, however, and examined a good deal of it under water, I am satisfied that the above holds good, assuming a draught for triremes of about 4-5 ft.[4]

Two other factors may also have diminished the actual number of landing-points. First, there may have been a sea-swell, if not something stronger. This is common off the south-west coast at the time of year; and it is not clear that the Spartans (unlike the Athenians planning the landings on Sphacteria) could have afforded to wait for a dead calm. For they must have been expecting the Athenian fleet, which indeed arrived two days afterwards (13.1), and were therefore compelled to launch their attack whatever the weather. Secondly, there is a residue of doubt about whether the trireme commanders were not ξύλων φειδομένους (11.4). Thucydides twice bears witness to their enthusiasm (11.3 προθυμίᾳ πάσῃ χρώμενοι, and 12.2 προυθυμοῦντο). On the other hand, Brasidas saw that ἔι που καὶ δοκοίη δυνάτον εἶναι σχεῖν, ἀποκνοῦντας καὶ φυλασσομένους τῶν νεῶν μὴ ξυντρίψωσιν. Since most of the ships probably came not from Sparta itself, but from allied cities, this is less surprising.

We should not, I think, attach much weight to these two possibilities: nor need we, for the topography speaks for itself. The Spartans tried to land *all* along the 500-yards stretch, wherever possible. It was possible only in a few places: and in these, probably not for more than one or two triremes at once, assuming a requirement of about 40-50 ft. per trireme.[5] Hence they had to be κατ᾽ ὀλίγας ναῦς: for ὀλίγας, I should with some confidence guess at about 5 or 6 at most. These, again, would not necessarily actually gain land at the same time: so that Demosthenes' small force would be sufficient to cope. We are, of course, to imagine the Spartan force operating in shifts (ἀναπαύοντες ἐν τῷ μέρει): as Gomme says[6] " . . . if the attempt to drive the boat right on shore and to disembark failed, the boat, or the whole section then in action, was withdrawn from the mêlée and another took its place".

3.   Pritchett *ad loc.*
4.   Morrison and Williams, *ad loc.*
5.   *ibid.*
6.   p. 448.

I. THE ναυμαχία & THE TRUCE

A. Preliminaries & Communications

In the absence of the Athenian fleet, the Spartans on the mainland had every opportunity for communication with their men on Sphacteria. Even had they hesitated to send boats to and from the island at any time when they feared that the Athenian fleet might enter the λιμήν and snap them up, communication of a primitive kind would still have been possible (e.g. by flashing a shield). Moreover, not only is visibility excellent from the heights of Sphacteria, but Spartans posted on the mainland - for instance, on the heights north of Voidokoilia or at the south-east part of the λιμήν - would have been able to discern the movements of the Athenian fleet with ease. There is then little doubt that the Spartans could not have been taken by surprise.

On the other hand, the Athenian fleet was less well placed. Thucydides says that they saw (εἶδον, 13.3) the mainland and the island to be full of hoplites, and the Spartan ships staying in the λιμήν: and describes the Athenians, on the return from Prote, as γνόντες that the Spartans were ἡσυχάζοντες ἐν τῇ γῇ, manning their ships and preparing for a sea-fight (14.1). This requires some explanation in view of the topography. All this time the Athenians are outside the λιμήν. It is not possible to get a clear view of the λιμήν through the Sikia Channel, nor (of course) through or over Sphacteria. The Athenians could only have seen anything in the λιμήν from a point outside the southern entrance which is at least four miles distant from Gialova (or from any other plausible position for the Spartan στρατόπεδον: see below).

What the Athenians εἶδον is plausible. The mainland - or at least the bits of it round Voidokoilia and the Sikia, and as much as they could see of the southern shores of the λιμήν - and Sphacteria itself were both within eyesight easy enough to detect hoplites: some ships might have been visible at Gialova, and others actually sailing in the λιμήν at a closer distance. It is probable that the Athenians arrived late in the day (see Note F), when the westering sun would have increased visibility from the southern entrance of the λιμήν towards Gialova. But the Athenians can hardly have *seen* all that is described in 13.4. All they saw was that the Spartan fleet was *not* afloat and not sailing out to meet them: from this they induced a state of unreadiness. γνόντες must be translated as 'realising', or perhaps even as 'learning'.[1]

---

1.   I suggest 'learning' because it is not impossible that the Athenians on Pylos, who were of course in a much better position to observe what was going on in the Spartan camp, gave the relevant information to their fleet. Units of the fleet would not have had to enter the λιμήν to get this information: any Athenian ship lying just off the west or south-west coast of Pylos, or in the Sikia Channel, could have been informed without difficulty. Yet Thucydides does not say that this is what happened: the impression conveyed is that the fleet are acting entirely by themselves: and γνόντες more usually means 'seeing', in either a literal or metaphorical sense. Thucydides chose γνόντες rather than πυθόμενοι: I prefer 'realising' ('twigging').

In both cases the Athenian fleet must have spent some time deploying in the area west of Sphacteria, in order to see and realise what they did. In the second case, they must have had a good look through the southern entrance, and then (as Thucydides days) split up their fleet, before καθ᾽ ἑκάτερον τὸν ἔσπλουν ὥρμησαν ἐπ᾽ αὐτούς. This adds to the lack of Spartan surprise mentioned above. In Note F (p. 81) I suggest that the Spartans may have been deceived by the Athenian move to Prote into supposing that the Athenians would not return: but in Note H, I point out that this is insufficient to account wholly for Spartan unreadiness, and suggest lack of discipline or an inadequate chain of command, or a command divided amongst Sparta's allies. This last point is strongly reinforced by the course of the battle (see below).

B.   The Battle

This almost certainly took place round the Gialova area. As Pritchett saw,[2] the sea-bottom at Gialova is suitable for the Spartan wading in 14.2. Following the curve of the λιμήν towards the east and south, we soon come to a shore which is much steeper and more difficult for beaching triremes. The Spartan camp could have been further west, on what is now the sand-bar; but it was plainly at or near the place where the Spartan fleet was beached, and the Gialova river is the only perennial source of water which empties into the λιμήν: indeed the only easy water-supply in the whole area. We may confidently place the Spartan camp, and therefore the fleet and battle, near Gialova.

In 14.1-4 the events are as follows:- The Athenians rush in from both entrances, attack and defeat the Spartan ships which are μετεώρους ἤδη, pursue them to the shore and damage them there, and start hauling away other ships whose crews they have already routed. The Spartans see all this happening and then come to the rescue (ἃ ὁρῶντες οἱ Λακεδαιμόνιοι . . . παρεβοήθουν, 14.2). After hard fighting the Spartans manage to save the ships which the Athenians were hauling off. All this shows clearly that, whether or not there were many Spartans in service in the fleet, 'the Spartans' as such were clearly distinguished from those with whom the Athenian fought in the first stage of the battle. These latter, allies of Sparta but not Spartans, were severely defeated, and unable to save the empty ships: it is not till the Spartans come to the rescue that the more equal battle begins, and the ships are eventually saved.

It is reasonable to suppose that the Spartans had few ships of their own and that, though they might exercise a general control for a specific purpose via the ναύαρχος (as in Thrasymelidas' attack on Demosthenes), we should call it 'the Spartan fleet' only by courtesy, as it were. On this occasion, at least, some of the decision-making - like the initial fighting - may have been left to the allies. Since these represented different states, the command may well have been divided de facto if not de iure (as on other occasions during the war), as well as uncontrolled by the Spartans. The chaos is not surprising[3].

---

2.   p. 24.   3.   In Bk. II, 83 the Peloponnesians have a fleet of 47 ships. Each city's contingent had their own generals, and the Corinthians alone had three generals.

In 14.1, as the two pairs of μὲν and δὲ make clear, there are the following categories of ships: (A) the majority, already afloat, under which heading come (i) those which the Athenians pursued and damaged at sea, (ii) four which they captured after the crews had escaped (presumably overboard), (iii) one which they captured with its crew, (iv) those which they pursued to land and then damaged. Then we have (B), the ships which had not yet got afloat: under this heading come (i) those which they damaged on shore, (ii) those which they tried to haul off when they had routed their crews, described as κενάς. All this is complicated but not problematic.

A slight problem arises in 14.4, where the Spartans are described as saving τὰς κενὰς ναῦς πλὴν τῶν τὸ πρῶτον ληφθεισῶν. There are two possibilities. Either τὰς κενὰς ναῦς refers only to (B) (ii), in which case we must take τῶν τὸ πρῶτον ληφθεισῶν as meaning only that the Athenians managed to haul off some of these before the Spartans could stop them: or τὰς κενὰς ναῦς includes (A) (ii) as well as (B) (ii), that is, the ships which the Athenians had captured at sea after the crews had escaped , in which case it is these ships in (A) (ii) which are τῶν τὸ πρῶτον ληφθεισῶν and which the Spartans (naturally) could not save. The second of these reads more naturally to me, but I do not see that any proof is possible. The first would, incidentally, add to the Athenian ship-numbers (see E below), since the Athenians would on this interpretation possess not only the four ships in (A) (ii), but some in (B) (ii).

How much damage did the Athenians actually do to the Spartan fleet? No ships are mentioned as sunk; but they ἔτρωσαν πολλάς (these must be the ναυαγίων of 14.5), captured at least five, and ἐνέβαλλον the rest. Other losses to the original fleet of 60 ships occurred in Thrasymelidas' attack: we must also remember that the Spartans had sent τῶν νεῶν τινάς, i.e. at least 3 or 4, to Asine. All this has to be set against the Spartan desire to rescue their men on Sphacteria at all costs. It looks as if not enough of the Spartan fleet had survived the defeat to attempt this with any hope of success; hence that the Athenian victory must have been a very complete one. On this, however, see C. below.

C. The Truce

It is clear from 15.2 that the Spartans (a) thought it impossible as things stood to rescue the men on Sphacteria, (b) were afraid that the Athenians might make a landing on the island and destroy or capture them. At first sight, (a) seems like panic. For, however complete the Athenian victory, the Spartans must have been able to organise a small, fast squadron of (say) 20 ships to attempt a rescue: either at the eastern end of the Sikia Channel, where the distance from Sphacteria to Spartan-held territory was very short, or perhaps by night to one of the regular landings on Sphacteria further south. They could have selected their best rowers and their fastest ships; and they would not have minded how many ships they lost in the enterprise, provided they could have brought their men safe to land. Alternatively, they could have fought another ναυμαχία

91

with the Athenians: after all, they started with 60 ships to the Athenians' 40, and would take care not to be surprised as they had been before. During such an engagement some ships might have rescued the men on the island.

The Athenians must have damaged or destroyed enough ships to make this latter alternative - another full-scale engagement - impossible for the Spartans. Further, when after the ναυμαχία they sailed round the island and ἐν φυλακῇ εἶχον (14.5), the φυλακή must have been very close indeed, both by day and night: closer than it was during the blockade after the truce (see Note J), and probably closer than the Athenians could have continued to make it over a long period. For the distances from Sphacteria to Spartan-held territory are short (see Note J, p. 98). It is perhaps for this reason that, in the terms of the truce, the Athenians insist that the Spartans hand over τὰς ναῦς ἐν αἷς ἐναυμάχησαν καὶ τὰς ἐν τῇ Λακωνικῇ πάσας (16.1), and refuse on a technicality to hand them back to the Spartans when the truce is over (23.1). With the ships present in a λιμήν whose shores were still entirely under Spartan control, the Athenians could not have been sure of an effective blockade - quite apart from their other blockade-difficulties (see Note J).

For the same reason, the Spartans might well have refused this condition of the truce, if they had appreciated the Athenians' difficulties in maintaining a blockade whilst there was still a Spartan fleet. Perhaps they did appreciate them; but they were frightened that the Athenians would strike first, by landing on Sphacteria. How rational was this fear? In the event, the Athenians waited until they had far more troops (Cleon's expedition: for Athenian numbers see Note L). Before the truce, they could deploy only the epibatai and the crews of 40 ships, plus whatever Demosthenes could spare from the defence of Pylos (not many): they would need to keep the thalamioi on board ship, as they needed to in their actual assault (see Note N). They would have available not more than 500 hoplites and about 4,000 crew-men, virtually unarmed, plus a handful of archers and peltasts: certainly not enough for safety.

But the Spartans could not have had precise information about the Athenian troops: the ships might have carried more hoplites and light-armed soldiers, and allies on the Athenian side might have arrived at any moment, whereas their own troops on Sphacteria could not be reinforced. The Spartans could not be certain of the Athenians' inability to maintain an effective blockade (even in the presence of a Spartan fleet) for long enough. Moreover, although they held the coast-line, the preparation and launching of enough ships to conduct a rescue-operation would not have been easy, in face of the Athenian ships in the λιμήν. Their agreement to the truce is intelligible enough.

About 60 ships were handed over by the Spartans (16.3). 60 had fought in the ναυμαχία; of these the Athenians had already captured 5, and damaged some others sufficiently for them to count as ναυαγίων (14.5). Probably there were not more than a few in this latter group; for the majority, though damaged, would have reached the near-by shore. We might assume something like 10 for the number of total losses. This,

92

therefore, would also be the number of remaining ships ἐν τῇ Λακωνικῇ (16.1), to make up the total of 60 ships handed over: small enough, when we remember that they were supposed to hand over all warships (ὅσαι ἦσαν μακραί, 16.1).

D. Numbers of Athenian ships

In 13.2 the MSS give τεσσαράκοντα. Most editors have argued as Gomme does:[4] "It is very difficult to justify this figure. Forty ships had been sent from Athens (2.2), of which three were with Demosthenes (5.2, 8.3); yet the figure is explained by the addition of some from the Naupaktos squadron and four from Chios. Moreover, after the arrival of twenty more ships from Athens, there were seventy in all (23.2)". Hence they have preferred to read πεντήκοντα: but, I think, wrongly.

Certainly the case for πεντήκοντα is not proved. The fleet at Zacynthos numbered 35, plus 1 or 2 message-bearing ships from Demosthenes: 36 or 37. Some of these, as we have explained elsewhere (see Note E), may well have been engaged in scouting further north. If so, the main fleet would not have waited for them before leaving Zacynthos for Pylos, since it sailed at once on receiving Demosthenes' message (8.4). There *might* have been 6 or 7 of these: and if we take τινὲς in τῶν τε φρουρίδων τινὲς αὐτοῖς τῶν ἐκ Ναυπάκτου καὶ Χίαι τέσσαρες to mean about 6, the total is about 40 (36/7 minus 6/7, plus 6 from Naupactos, plus 4 Chians). Even without the scout-ship deficiency, we must assign τινὲς a figure higher than 5 or 6 if we are to reach a number which is palpably more like 50 than 40. Of course this is possible.

The argument from 23.2 overlooks the fact that in 14.1 the Athenians capture at least 5 Spartan ships. Given the possibility of bad weather, and the lack of mooring space, it is probably that these would have been used, with at least skeleton crews, by the Athenians, rather than left at anchor or on the beach. To these must of course be added the remaining 3 ships of Demosthenes. So to the figure in 13.2 we must add, not only the 20 new ships from Athens, but also 8 more. Plainly, if we are to accept ἑβδομήκοντα in 23.2, τεσσαράκοντα is preferable to πεντήκοντα in 13.2.

The figure in 32.2, where Thucydides speaks of the Athenians invading Sphacteria as disembarking ἐκ νεῶν ἑβδομήκοντα καὶ ὀλίγῳ πλεόνων, is not relevant. For here he is not giving a total of ships at all, but merely saying how many *ships' crews were used* in the assault. If it were a total, it would be too small: for to the 70 in 23.2 we should have to add however many ships Cleon used to convey his force.

In general, I do not think we can hope for anything like certainty here; and the problem is complicated to a hopeless degree by the 60 Spartan ships that were handed over at the truce (see E. below). The MSS reading may as well be retained.

---

4. p. 450.

93

E.   The Spartan ships handed over

The Athenians were in possession of about 65 Spartan (Peloponnesian) ships: about 60 had been handed over, and five captured in the battle. It is, I think, clear enough from the general context of sections 15 and 16 that the negotiations were made and carried out with the Athenian generals at Pylos, not with the Athenians at Athens; and even clearer that the 'Ἀθηναῖοι of 23.1, who refuse to hand back the Spartan ships, are those at Pylos. These 65 ships, then, are almost certainly at Pylos, not at Athens.

What did the Athenians do with them? They cannot all have been pressed into service in the Athenian fleet: there would not have been enough man-power even for skeleton crews without leaving the Athenians' own ships grossly under-manned - and these ships had to preserve the blockade efficiently. Moreover, Thucydides makes it plain that this did not happen in 23.2: if αἱ πᾶσαι ἐβδομήκοντα ἐγένοντο, this cannot have included many Spartan ships; at the most the Athenians manned the five originally captured (see above). Nor would there have been room for them at the south-west corner of Pylos, the only landing-ground available to the Athenians.

It is not likely that the Athenians would have wanted to spare the ships and man-power required to tow them to Athens or to some other friendly territory (Zacynthos was the nearest). To do this would have involved removing a good many of their own ships which were badly needed for the blockade. The Athenians were short, not of ships *per se* - with the Spartan ships they had over 100 - , but of properly-manned ships: hence the need for the extra 20 ships from Athens to help with the blockade. Granted that the truce was in operation, they might have risked it: but I do not think it probable. As the terms of the truce make clear, the Athenians were concerned φυλάσσειν . . . τὴν νῆσον . . . μηδὲν ἧσσον (16.1).

We must assume, therefore, that these 60-odd ships were anchored in the λιμήν: remembering (a) that almost all the shore of the λιμήν was in Spartan hands, and (b) that most areas of the λιμήν do not provide safe anchorage for triremes in stormy weather (on this see Note J), we can see that this must have added considerably to the Athenian difficulties - indeed the στενοχωρία at sea might have been more trouble-some than the στενοχωρία on land.

F.   Timing

Finally, it is clear that it would have taken the Spartans several days to organise the handing-over of all the ships: not, of course, those which had taken part in the battle, but all the other warships in Laconia. Some would probably be at Gytheion, and others still further east. Messages had to be sent, crews found, and the ships them-selves put in a seaworthy condition and rowed to Pylos. All this must have taken 3-4 days at an absolute minimum. This affects the overall time-scheme (Note Q): but

some doubt remains about the precise order of events. Were the ships handed over before or after the truce?

The truce was *agreed* before the handing-over, as the text makes clear. In 16.1 ἐγίγνοντο σπονδαὶ τοιαίδε, and there follows an account of the conditions: then in 16.3 αἰ μὲν σπονδαὶ ἐπὶ τούτοις ἐγένοντο, καὶ αἱ νῆες παρεδόθησαν οὖσαι περὶ ἑξήκοντα, καὶ οἱ πρέσβεις ἀπεστάλησαν. But the truce was not enforced or *in operation* until the ships were handed over, we may reasonably assume. Until then, the Athenians would not have allowed food to be sent to Sphacteria, and the Spartans could not have felt secure against the possibility of an Athenian attack. For these reasons the Spartans would have made all speed in collecting and handing over the ships. The most probable order of events, then, was something like this:-

Day 1:	ναυμαχία: news travels to Sparta.
Day 2:	
Day 3:	Spartan magistrates leave Sparta for Pylos (15.1).
Day 4:	
Day 5:	Spartan magistrates arrive: negotiations begin.
Day 6:	Truce agreed: Spartans begin to collect ships.
Day 7:	
Day 8:	
Day 9:	
Day 10:	Ships handed over to Athenians: ambassadors sent off: truce in operation.

This timing is not, of course, exact. But this would have been the order of events; and it is difficult to see how they could have occurred in less time than the above - though easy to believe that they could have taken longer.

II. SPHACTERIA

J. THE BLOCKADE

The λιμήν During the Blockade

Commentators' views on the shelter afforded by the Bay of Navarino (Thucydides' λιμήν) differ dramatically. (a) Gomme describes the λιμήν as "an 'arm of the sea', and not a very sheltered one at that, for triremes";[1] and other editors express themselves still more strongly, e.g., Mills: "It is far too exposed to have been a refuge for the Athenian fleet in a storm."[2] (b) On the other hand the more topographically experienced Pritchett says that "today, boats of the size of ancient ships anchor and tie up at Gialova in all seasons," and that he has "seen ships anchored for long periods in various parts of the harbour."[3]

Each view has obvious objections. Against (a), we have the fact that the Athenian fleet originally put in to Pylos to escape a storm, and remained somewhere in the Bay after its return from Zacynthos for the whole campaign: against (b), we have Thucydides' remarks on the difficulties to the Athenian fleet of a χειμών (ἐδεδοίκεσαν μὴ σφῶν χειμὼν τὴν φυλακὴν ἐπιλάβοι, 27.1).

The text of 27.1 requires further comment: but the answer is essentially simple. The north-westerly storms can be extremely violent, and since the sea extends uninterrupted for many miles to the north-west, waves of considerable height are easily built up. Shelter from such storms is therefore best at the north end of the bay, i.e., on what is now the sand-bar (and would then have been ordinary land); though vessels beached at the south-east corner of Pylos, or sheltering immediately in the lee of Sphacteria, would also be well placed. View (a) is wrong, therefore, in maintaining that the λιμήν as a whole gives no adequate shelter. On the other hand, view (b) is unconvincing in implying that other parts of the λιμήν (e.g., Gialova) are adequately sheltered. Pritchett's "ships" and "boats of the size of ancient ships" are not good enough. It is not the size but the seaworthiness of triremes that is in question. Modern ships have a deeper draught, more freeboard, and better ballast.

It seems that editors have failed to distinguish between the two essentially different conditions of the λιμήν. (i) When the Athenians first put in to escape the storm, it offered them the northern sand-bar as a landing-ground. (ii) When most of the shore was in Spartan hands, this was no longer true; Spartan troops occupied the whole shore (and Sphacteria), except for a small area on the south-east corner of Pylos. Hence the Athenian difficulties during the blockade. Triremes beached at the south-east corner of

1.   p. 483.
2.   p. 157.
3.   p. 17.

96

Pylos would survive, and others might also survive by anchoring in the comparatively shallow water close to and behind Sphacteria. But a glance at the map will show the difficulties of finding, for seventy-plus triremes,[4] a place which is (a) shallow enough to anchor, (b) not in Spartan-held territory, and (c) sheltered from the waves which pour through the Sikia in a storm from the west. As Thucydides says, there was not room for all the fleet to beach on Pylos (26.3): and there is really nowhere else. Moreover, it would have been impossible to conduct an effective *blockade* in stormy weather, even if the Athenian fleet had been able to find anywhere to anchor. The blockade normally entailed anchoring round Sphacteria at night, and at least two triremes constantly sailing round the island by day. (On this see below.)

Analysis of the text also strongly suggests that (a) there had not yet been a storm; and (b) if there had been the Athenians would not have been able to cope.

(a)   Thucydides nowhere says there was a storm. He says (23.2) that the Athenians could not anchor on the seaward side of Sphacteria ὁπότε ἄνεμος εἴη; that the loyal helots waited for an ἄνεμος and a πνεῦμα ἐκ πόντου; and that if it was calm they were caught (ὅσοι δε γαλήνη κινδυνεύσειαν ἡλίσκοντο). But in these passages there is no mention of a storm. The argument *ex silentio* is strong.

(b)   In 27. 1., the Athenians at home ἐδεδοίκεσαν μὴ σφῶν χειμὼν τὴν φυλακὴν ἐπιλάβοι, ὁρῶντες τῶν τε ἐπιτηδείων τὴν περὶ τὴν Πελοπόννησον κομιδὴν ἀδύνατον ἐσόμενην, ἅμα ἐν χωρίῳ ἐρήμῳ καὶ οὐδ᾽ ἐν θέρει οἷοί τ᾽ ὄντες ἱκανὰ περιπέμπειν, τόν τε ἔφορμον χωρίων ἀλιμένων ὄντων οὐκ ἐσόμενον κτλ.

Why did the Athenians think that ἔφορμον . . . οὐκ ἐσόμενον? Not, surely, because of the supply difficulty. The Athenians are pictured as ὁρῶντες two things: one about supplies, and another about some other difficulty in blockading, which would result in its failure one way or another. These two things are represented by the two distinct clauses τῶν τε . . . and τόν τε . . . . . . The ἔφορμον clause is part of the second, not of the first. We are given two distinct reasons: (1) stormy weather would make it impossible to supply the blockading forces, (2) stormy weather would make the blockade impossible because there was no proper harbour. This second reason must stand on its own feet, i.e., it is the combination of a storm and of the lack of a harbour which would by itself make the blockade impossible, quite apart from any supply difficulty.

But why should it have been impossible for *this* reason? The Athenian fleet was used to πνεῦμα ἐκ πόντου and ἄνεμος, and had continued the blockade nevertheless. The answer must be that the fleet could survive the weather-conditions of ἄνεμος and πνεῦμα, *but not a proper storm.* And this in turn argues strongly that there had not yet been a storm, and that the fleet was thought not to be able to survive storms, in the λιμήν at the time of the blockade, i.e., when most of the bay was in Spartan hands.

---

4.   At the stage described in 4.32.2 there were more than 70 triremes. Numbers of ships at earlier stages are disputable: but at least 40 in 4.13.2. See Note I.

Athenian and Spartan Tactics

The Athenians had to blockade about six miles of coastline. For this they used, during the daytime, δυοῖν νεοῖν ἐναντίαιν (23.2). The nearest lines of escape for the Spartans were (1) from the north-east corner of Sphacteria to the sand-bar (perhaps 200-300 metres),[5] and (2) from the south-east corner to the mainland (1200 metres). To prevent escape along these lines, two ships so placed would not have sufficed. For, as some brief mathematical thought will show, there would inevitably be times when *neither* ship was *nearer* than 1½ miles from any single point, assuming that the ships remained at a constant distance of 3 miles round the coast from each other; and if, as is likely, they did not keep perfect station, then the minimum distance would be more than 1½ miles.

Since the Athenian fleet probably anchored, for the most part, in the north-west corner of the bay (by the south-east corner of Pylos), this may have been enough to deter the Spartans from using the first and shorter escape route. But the second would still be viable. If we call the point referred to in the above paragraph P - that is, the nearest point at which the Athenians would be *certain* of having a ship at all times - then the distance from P to the mid-point of the escape-route is about double the distance of the escape-route itself. Given that we know nothing about what sorts of boats might have been available to the Spartans, it still seems very likely that they could have covered the distance before the trireme could have intercepted them. This would certainly be true if there was a wind from the west: for the circulating triremes would not have their sails rigged.

Why did the Spartans not try this? They had boats, in which the helots had carried the supplies; and in fact the operation would have been even easier than suggested above - the attention of the relevant trireme could have been distracted by a *fausse sortie* from some other point, for instance. The answer must be that the Athenians stationed at least one ship - probably more - at the south of the bay, to command this particular route: and it is quite possible that other ships not mentioned by Thucydides performed similar duties elsewhere - though all other escape-routes involve much greater distances, and may well have been sufficiently commanded by the circulating triremes.

Relevant to this is the question of why the Spartans did not take advantage of other difficulties (i.e., besides the inadequacy of the circulating triremes), in particular (a) darkness, and (b) bad weather. (a) is easily dealt with: the Athenians ἅπασαι περιώρμουν (23.2), and it would be far too dangerous to make the attempt. The fact

---

5.   Much of this would have been fordable (see Note F); but this would not have greatly helped the Spartans.

that they could not anchor on the seaward side in a westerly wind is irrelevant, since it was not towards the sea that the Spartans needed to escape. They might perhaps have attempted to leave from the seaward side and come to land. But first, under windy conditions small boats would have been dangerous (we are not told how many helots drowned); secondly, if they then went south, they could not have re-entered through the channel (which the Athenians would certainly be guarding), and would have been forced to land on an extremely precipitous piece of coastline somewhere between the modern towns of Pylos and Methone; if they went north, they would have to get past Pylos itself, and the Athenian ships near the Sikia, before reaching Voidokoilia Bay. About (b), Gomme says in his note on 27.1 (where the Athenian fear is expressed that the Spartans will sail off in the helot boats χειμῶνα τηρήσαντας): "one wonders why the Spartans had not already made some such attempt, ὁπότε ἄνεμος εἴη. Courage at sea seems to have been expected only of helots."[6] But an ἄνεμος is not a χειμών. As has been argued above, a proper χειμών would obviate the Athenian fleet, in a way that an ἄνεμος would (and did) not. So far there had been nothing in the nature of a χειμών; nor, fortunately for the Athenians, was there to be during the campaign.

To return briefly to the situation in calm weather and daylight, we might suppose that the reasons just mentioned would be sufficient to prevent the Spartans making the attempt then, even if no more than two circulating triremes were on the watch; and this would obviate the need for other triremes stationed by the southern escape-route. But I do not think this is likely. There had been plenty of time (Gomme allows over two months) for the Spartans to have collected enough boats from the helots to take off the bulk of their force. Well-planned diversions with boats - manned by expendable helots - leaving the north end of the island would have put about three miles distance between the escape-route and the nearest trireme; and even landlubberly Spartans should have been able to cover 1200 metres before the trireme reached them. We prefer to believe that the Athenians took precautions, of the kind already described, against this, and that here too we cannot blame excessive Spartan ἡσυχία.

A further reason is also important. Even if the boats evaded capture, they would almost certainly have been noticed. Hence, if the Spartans sent a few of their men off at a time, the Athenians would realise that their numbers had lessened, and attack the depleted force with a good chance of success. On the other hand, if they tried to take off their whole force at once, this would have been a considerable operation: even if only the 420 hoplites went, and left the attendant helots behind. Moreover, if they *were* caught, the disaster would have been total. It was not worth the risk; and I do not think we can blame the Spartans for excessive ἡσυχία.

---

6.   p. 468.

K. DEMOSTHENES AND THE FIRE

In 29.2 we are told that the fire gave Demosthenes confidence (ῥώμην) for planning an attack: and there follows an explanatory section, down to the end of 30.3. What were the advantages accruing to the Athenians?

A. Better intelligence

After the fire, as Thucydides says (30.3), Demosthenes saw that there were more Spartans on the island than he had thought: also that the island was εὐαποβατωρέραν. But this was not the only, nor perhaps the most important, gain to Athenian intelligence. For by 31.1, when the Athenian invading hoplites ἐχώρουν δρόμῳ ἐπὶ τὸ πρῶτον φυλακτήριον, the Athenians plainly know how the Spartans are tactically disposed: hence they knew where to land, with what troops; and how to plan their tactics in general.

This vital knowledge must also have been the result of the fire. First, the summit of Pylos is not sufficiently high to overlook Sphacteria: one can see Mt. Elias and everything north of the ridge running along the short north coast, but that is virtually all. Nor did the Athenians have any other vantage points on land, since the mainland was in Spartan hands. Secondly, the amount visible from the blockading Athenian triremes was less than might be supposed by one unfamiliar with the terrain. The ὕλη concealed much; and the cliffs surrounding most of the island are such that a trireme near to the shore would have its angle of vision cut off too soon, whereas a trireme farther out to sea would be too far away for detailed visibility.[1] In the course of the long blockade the Athenians would of course have gained *some* idea of the Spartan dispositions (particularly on the clearly-visible Mt. Elias): but not a clear and distinct idea.

The fire itself is wholly believable, particularly if we assume that we can pin down Thucydides' vague τοῖς ἐσχάτοις (30.2) to one point of origin. The extreme north-west corner is highly probable. First, it was safe (especially διὰ προφυλακῆς): for the terrain is such that the Spartans could not have descended on them from Mt. Elias, nor from anywhere else, without a long and arduous climb. This applies also to the extreme north-east corner, but not to any other areas. Secondly, the prevailing north-west wind would have been exactly what was required to spread the fire over the whole island. (Winds from the north-east are rare, and make the north-east corner an unlikely candidate).

Thucydides actually says that much or most of the ὕλη was burnt (το πολὺ); and we have supporting evidence from 34.2, where ὁ κονιορτὸς τῆς ὕλης νεωστὶ κεκαυμένης ἐχώρει πολὺς ἄνω. This occurs somewhere towards the middle of the island, when the Spartans are still hoping for a face-to-face battle. If the fire got that far, it probably covered nearly all the island: revealing not only the central Spartan camp, but (most

---

1. Readers to whom this seems incredible should try circumnavigating Sphacteria at various distances from the coastline.

important for the Athenian landing) the southern picket. In the absence of the ὕλη, the Spartan dispositions would have been clear to patient and eager viewers from the triremes, even at long range.

B. The size of the army

In 29.3 Demosthenes is represented as thinking that the wooded and pathless nature of Sphacteria would be an advantage to the Spartans, who knew the area better than the Athenians, πολλῷ γὰρ ἂν στρατοπέδῳ ἀποβάντι ἐξ ἀφανοῦς χωρίου προσβάλλοντας αὐτοὺς βλάπτειν. About this Gomme says: "as Wilamowitz saw, we cannot have the simple πολλῷ in this position; it would imply that the large numbers of the force would be the cause of their losses. He proposed καὶ πολλῷ γάρ: either this or πολλά will serve."[2]

There is, in my view, virtually no force in the argument that the *position* of πολλῷ causes any difficulty. A leading position in a sentence is not always indicative of causality, or indeed of any particular importance to be attached to the leading word. But in any case there would be no point in πολλῷ *anywhere* in the sentence, unless it plays some significant part in the sense: on Wilamowitz' and Gomme's view, it would be purely gratuitous - "for when he landed with his (incidentally) large force, . . . ". So if we need to emend, καὶ πολλῷ will not do the job.

However, not only is there no need to emend: to do so would be to miss the point, which is precisely the point that Gomme finds intolerable. πολλῷ γὰρ does have a causal sense. The point is that, since Demosthenes' force would be large, it would not be capable of concealment, whereas the smaller Spartan force could attack ἐξ ἀφανοῦς χωρίου. στρατοπέδῳ is perhaps deliberately chosen here to imply a large force, and repeated with the same intent (twice) in the next sentence. We should translate with some such phrase as 'with a whole army of troops'.

In 29.4, the phrase τὸ ἑαυτῶν στρατόπεδον πολὺ ὂν διαφθειρόμενον is surely decisive. πολὺ here must go with στρατόπεδον, and we cannot emend to πολλά, or take it as meaning anything like 'to a considerable extent', without also getting rid of the ὄν. The point now is that the size of his force would necessitate splitting it up, and that these groups could be destroyed by the Spartans individually and secretly, without the other groups knowing. We thus have two points: (1) in the first stage of disembarkation (ἀποβάντι) the large force would be all in one place, and because of its size could not be ἀφανοῦς, whereas the Spartans could: (2) in the second stage, when the force was split into groups, the groups could be destroyed individually.

---

2.   p. 471.

C. εὐαποβατωτέραν

30.3 οὕτω δὴ τούς τε Λακεδαιμονίους μᾶλλον κατιδὼν πλείους ὄντας, ὑπονοῶν, πρότερον ἐλάσσοσι τὸν σῖτον αὐτοῦ ἐσπέμπειν, τήν τε νῆσον εὐαποβατωτέραν οὖσαν κτλ. In this passage, the phrase εὐαποβατωτέραν οὖσαν is normally taken in the sense of "easier to disembark on (than he had thought hitherto)." But our suspicions about the meaning of this phrase may be initially aroused when we wonder how the fire could make the *places of disembarkation* more easily visible. It is not as if there were hidden creeks over-shadowed by giant and concealing trees: at most there were probably some stunted bushes growing by the landing-places. If Demosthenes was interested only in the actual landings, these would have been equally as visible (from the slope of the beaches, the rocks or shingle on the shore, etc.) before the fire as after it. We must, then, interpret εὐαποβατωτέραν more widely, to mean something like 'easier to disembark and enter' or 'easier to move about on after disembarkation'. In other words, Demosthenes is concerned not just with the actual landing-places, but (at least) with the terrain of Sphacteria immediately behind them.

This suggests a better sense for the whole phrase. The chief advantage of the fire for the Athenians - an advantage which, on the normal interpretation of this phrase, Thucydides passes over in complete silence - is that it actually *made* movement on the island easier. Throughout 29.3 and 4 Thucydides stresses that the dense undergrowth (δασὺ, ὕλης) favoured the Spartans. This would not only be due to lack of visibility, but also because the Athenians would not be able to move about tactically with any ease. (The difficulties of Sphacterian terrain in this respect today are considerable). We could more reasonably take the phrase in the sense of "easier (than it had been before the fire)". It is true that this would not give an exact logical parallel to πλείους ὄντας earlier in the sentence: but since there is an intervening clause which specifies that Demosthenes had thought the Spartan numbers to be less (ὑπονοῶν . . . ἐσπέμπειν), I do not think this is a real difficulty.

As has been shown elsewhere,[3] the undergrowth or 'wood' on Sphacteria was at least man-high, and could hence give the Spartans the advantages mentioned in this passage by Thucydides (basically, the advantage of concealment). But Thucydides does not bring out clearly the advantage to the defenders of the difficulty of movement on Sphacteria. This is hinted at in πρότερον μὲν γὰρ οὔσης αὐτῆς ὑλώδους ἐπὶ τὸ πολὺ καὶ ἀτριβοῦς διὰ τὴν ἀεὶ ἐρημίαν ἐφοβεῖτο (29.3) and again in εὐαποβατωτέραν (30.3), but the difficulty is not overtly stated.

Readers of Pritchett[4] ("On one occasion . . . I could go no more than 25 meters in an hour") will have some inkling of the situation. There are today large areas of the

3.   Note A.
4.   p. 27.

island where it is, indeed, virtually impossible to move at all. In 425 it would have been worse: first, because the island would have been uninhabited for longer; and secondly, because the comparatively recent planting of small trees (to discourage the thickets) has to some extent succeeded. Thus there would have been no chance whatsoever, before the fire, of the Athenian hoplites attacking the southern picket δρόμῳ. It would have been as much as they could do, even without full hoplite equipment, to fight their way through the undergrowth at all.

Those familiar with African or Asian jungles (I am not) may think that, armed as they were (at least in some cases) with swords, Athenian troops would have made their way more quickly through the undergrowth. Having tried it with a machette, I think otherwise. Possessing such a tool (and it has to be very sharp, probably sharper than the average Athenian or Messenian sword would have been), one finds the going easier and less uncomfortable: but not *quicker*.

D.   A query

More surprising is the element of chance: why did not Demosthenes start a fire deliberately? Thucydides' informant here is plainly either Demosthenes himself or someone close to him: there is virtually no chance of the facts being mistaken. Yet Demosthenes might have taken his cue ἀπὸ τοῦ 'Αιτωλικοῦ πάθους, ὃ διὰ τὴν ὕλην μέρος τι ἐγένετο. For part of the point of the disaster (III.98.2) was, not just that there *was* ὕλη, but that the Aetolians *set fire to it*. It is hard to believe that Demosthenes was too stupid to think of this.

Did Demosthenes try once but fail, and give it up as a bad job? Did he not try because, until that occasion, there was not the right (or enough) wind? Or did the accident happen early on, before Demosthenes had had time to assess the situation fully? Or, after all, has Thucydides missed something - was the soldier acting under Demosthenes' orders? Perhaps the last is the least implausible: but I can feel no confidence in any of these suggestions.

L.   NUMBERS OF ATHENIAN SHIPS AND TROOPS

Crucial passages here are 28.4: Λημνίους δὲ καὶ Ἰμβρίους τοὺς παρόντας καὶ πελταστὰς οἳ ἦσαν ἐκ τε Αἴνου βεβοηθηκότες καὶ ἄλλοθεν τοξότας τετρακοσίους. (This was Cleon's requirement; we know he got it from 30.4, ἔχων στρατιὰν ἣν ᾐτήσατο.) In 31.1 the whole (πάντας) hoplite force is embarked, about (μάλιστα) 800 hoplites, and subsequently landed. After that (32.2) ὁ ἄλλος στρατὸς ἀπέβαινεν, ἐκ μὲν νεῶν ἑβδομήκοντα καὶ ὀλίγῳ πλεόνων πάντες πλὴν θαλαμιῶν, ὡς ἕκαστοι ἐσκευασμένοι, τοξόται δὲ ὀκτακόσιοι καὶ πελτασταὶ οὐκ ἐλάσσους τούτων, Μεσσηνίων τε βεβοηθηκότες καὶ οἱ ἄλλοι ὅσοι περὶ Πύλον κατεῖχον πάντες πλὴν τῶν ἐπὶ τοῦ τείχους φυλάκων.

How many ships did Cleon bring with him? We know that there were 70 before he came (23.2), and at least ἑβδομήκοντα καὶ ὀλίγῳ πλεόνων afterwards. This is not much help; but it is some, since some other ships must have been deployed in preventing any possible Spartan escape - perhaps particularly from the north-east corner of Sphacteria, which was the shortest distance to safety - and as look-outs (Peloponnesian intervention by sea was possible, if not likely). We should allow at least 5 or 6 ships for this purpose (see Note J).

As I shall show later (see below), Cleon must have brought at least 1,500 troops with him. It might be supposed on general grounds of economy that these troops also acted as crews for the ships: but this is contradicted by 32.2. For there, as the μεν and δε make clear, the crews are sharply distinguished from the τοξόται and πελτασταί. Even if we thought that none of the crews of Cleon's ships were disembarked (since there were no crewmen who were not also part of his land-army), we should still be worried by the ὀλίγῳ πλεόνων: there were some ships, at least, in excess of the 70 already there (and therefore part of Cleon's force), whose crews are distinguished from the regular land-forces. We must, therefore, suppose that Cleon's 1,500 were transported and did not row themselves. For such transportation we might suppose a figure of about 20 ships, though of course we cannot hope for exactness here.

This figure, however, would permit us to make sense of the hoplite-numbers, which must have been about 920. For though Thucydides says πάντας (31.1), it is not to be believed that no hoplites were guarding Pylos itself. I have suggested elsewhere a figure of about 120 as an adequate force, which together with the 800 Sphacteria-invading hoplites makes up the 920. To reach this figure, we take the epibatai from the original 65 Athenian ships (for we cannot count the 5 Spartan prizes: see Note I) and from Cleon's 20, making 850: plus the 40 hoplites acquired by Demosthenes in 9.1: plus any more that had trickled in as a response to Demosthenes' summons in 30.3 (στρατίαν τε μεταπέμπων ἐκ τῶν ἐγγὺς συμμάχων). Naturally all this is very uncertain: but the suppositions are fair ones, and to stray too far from them would produce serious difficulties of one kind or another.

The light-armed troops disembarking in 32.2 are clearly distinguished from the ships' crews, the Messenians, and οἱ ἄλλοι ... περὶ Πύλον. They numbered 800 archers and at least 800 peltasts. Some of these archers - perhaps about 250 - may have come from the standard allocation of 2/3 per trireme, since there were probably over 80 triremes in the whole Athenian force at this time (see above). We need therefore to make up about 550 archers and 800 peltasts: and this must be made up from Cleon's force, since the other troops are all catered for under separate categories in 32.2.

In 28.4, whatever may be the correct MS reading, are 400 archers. Again, whatever the reading, we may assume 800 peltasts from Ainos. We have now only 150 archers to make up, and must suppose that these were to be found among the Lemnians and Imbrians. This suggests that an emendation such as ἔκ τε 'Αίνου βεβοηθηκότες καὶ ἄλλοθεν καὶ τοξότας ... is implausible. For that would imply the sense of "Lemnians, Imbrians, peltasts from Ainos and elsewhere - and 400 archers", i.e. that there were no *other* archers in this force. It is better to take Gomme's first alternative[1] and suppose a lacuna after 'Αίνου (or perhaps better, after βεβοηθηκότες): the sense then being "Lemnians and Imbrians, peltasts from Ainos and (somewhere), and an *additional* 400 archers from *other* places".

Of course this is doubtful: and even more uncertain (within limits) is the composition of the Lemnians and Imbrians. They may have included some hoplites, which would make us adjust our figures above : almost certainly they included slingers (cf. 32.4 σφενδόναις): and some may have counted as peltasts and helped to make up the figure of 800. Nevertheless, it seems clear that Cleon's force included at least 800 peltasts, 550 archers, and some Lemnians and Imbrians who were not peltasts or archers - surely at least 150. This gives us a minimum of 1,500: probably something more like 2,000 would be the figure.

Our total figure of the forces used for the assault on Sphacteria, then, seems to be made up as follows:-

Ships' crews (excluding thalamioi)	—	about	8030
Hoplites		about	800
Archers			800
Peltasts			800
Messenians and others		?	500 ?

This last category is rendered still more doubtful by our ignorance of whether Demosthenes' requests for reinforcements (30.3) was made soon enough before the actual assault, or whether it met with any success. But on any account we cannot put the Athenian numbers much lower than 11,000.

---

1.   p. 469.

M.   SPARTAN DISPOSITIONS AND ATHENIAN LANDING-PLACES

These are interconnected: for where the Spartans would think it sensible to put their troops must have depended on where the Athenians could have landed.

We do not know the exact number of the Spartan forces, because we do not know the number of attendant helots. There were 420 Spartans: perhaps we can assume at least one helot per Spartan - probably more. A reasonable minimum force seems to be about 1000 men. Against this the Athenians had 800 hoplites and vast numbers of other troops (for details, see Note L.)

Whatever else they did, it was obviously sensible for the Spartans to hold Mt. Elias: not only or even chiefly in case they had to face an ἀναχώρησις βιαιοτέρα, but because it was a defensible position which the Athenians might occupy. An Athenian party would be able to reach Mt. Elias' summit, from the north-east shore of Sphacteria facing Pylos, in under half-an-hour;[1] and once there, it would have been hard to dislodge them, for much the same reasons as it was hard for the Athenians to dislodge the Spartans when they made their last stand (see Note P).

The remaining dispositions suggest that the Spartans had decided not to try to contest Athenian landings on the shore, in the way that Demosthenes had successfully contested the Spartan attempt. According to most commentators, there were not more than four points at which the Athenians could have landed.[2] If this is right, the Spartans should have contested them. They could have deployed at least 200 men at each landing-point: and Demosthenes had already shown what could be done with smaller numbers in such a case.

But it is not right. Commentators[3] have been deceived into supposing that the

---

1.   A rough estimate but a generous one. When climbing myself through fairly dense waist-high thickets for the first half of the ascent, and virtually impenetrable thickets more than head-high for the last half, I took over two hours. Nevertheless the climb is a walk and not a mountaineering expedition: and after the fire had cleared the undergrowth it would present no difficulties. I should guess something like twenty minutes for able-bodied and determined men.

2.   See particularly Grundy and Burrows. But this is common to all commentators I have come across.

3.   Even Pritchett (p. 27) mentions a place, shown in his Plate 27a, where " . . . all have concurred that no landing is possible . . . " I have landed there twice in a small boat, in a fairly calm sea: even with some surge it would have been possible (I do not say comfortable) for triremes, since there is enough depth of water for them to make the approach. (Depth of water is the only really crucial point in this context. Triremes drew about 4-5' of water. Had the Athenian ships been unable to get near enough for the troops to disembark without struggling through many yards of sea with rocks underfoot, they would indeed have been unable to land. But there are few places of which this is true. In most, either a direct approach to a rocky shore is possible, or else the triremes could have been grounded on a sandy or shingle shore, the troops wading to land without difficulty.)

only possible landing-points for the Athenians were places which would, today, fairly count as 'landings' ('the Panagia landing', etc.): or, at least, places where it would be easy to bring a boat or ship to shore without damage, and disembark without trouble. This misrepresents the Athenian position. All that they needed to do was to get enough men ashore by hook or by crook: preferably, but not necessarily, without wrecking too many triremes. (Though the prize of 420 Spartans was, for the Athenians, at least as valuable as the prize of Pylos itself for the Spartans: and the latter were prepared to wreck their ships to force a landing, as 11.4 makes plain.) Moreover, the Athenians could take their time, wait for a windless day (or night), and make landings at every possible place at once.

The number of such places is in fact limited, not so much by the impossibility of actual disembarkation, but by the terrain immediately behind the disembarkation-points. For instance, various landings are possible along the north and north-east shore: but the steep cliffs immediately behind them would make any landing-party highly vulnerable and virtually immobile. However, this limitation is not severe. As maps[4] (or better, personal observation) will show, most of the west coast is possible, and at least three places on the east and south-east coast. Further detail should be unnecessary, provided we remember that the Athenians needed only to *get their men to land*. The position is similar to that in 26.7, where Thucydides himself implies the existence of several landing-points on the west coast (κατάρσεις where the helots, carried by a πνεῦμα ἐκ πόντου, beached their boats).

There is, then, nothing absurd in the Spartans not trying to contest the actual landings: though this does not mean that their dispositions were in other respects sensible (see below). Why then the thirty or so hoplites in the southernmost position?[5] Because it might have been possible for them to contest, not the landings, but the deployment of Athenian troops immediately after a landing. The thirty hoplites (perhaps plus helots) were intended to observe the Athenian landings, inform the main body of Spartans, and if possible hold up the Athenian troops (or at least keep them occupied) until the main body came up. The numbers of Spartans in the southernmost position may seem too small for this (as, equally, they seem too large if their job was merely to keep a look-out and bring information to the main body): but, though actual landing is easy at many points, rapid deployment is another matter. Had the first stage of the Athenian plan (the immediate destruction of the thirty) not succeeded perfectly, things might well have gone differently.

---

4. See Map B.
5. Almost certainly at the point marked on map B. This commands the best position; moreover it is virtually equidistant from the west and east coast of the island, and the text in 31.1 makes it plain that *both* Athenian landing-parties, from the west as well as the east side, ran to attack the position.

The thirty were placed in this position because it commands (insofar as any such position commands) the landing-points at the southern end of the island. Other landing-points further north on the west and east coast would be commanded by the main Spartan force. The intention seems, then, to have been to contest the immediate deployment of the Athenians. We have 30 hoplites in the southern position: perhaps 70 (μέρος οὐ πολύ, 31.2) on Mt. Elias, for reasons already given: and the remainder, some 220, in the central position. Was this sensible? What alternatives were there?

Occupying a permanent defensive position on Mt. Elias was impossible, since there is no water. Nor was any other defensive position possible. It is true that they would have had time (between the sea-fight in the harbour and the Athenian landing) to build a wall round the well in the central position. But the Athenians could still have starved them out, much more easily than they could when the whole island was in Spartan hands (see 26. 5-9); moreover, the central position[6] is not naturally strong, and would have required a good deal of masonry for an adequate fortification - more, probably, than would be easily available on an island where mobility (before the fire) was so difficult. The Spartans rightly preferred to bet on an open fight.

Another possibility was to decentralise still further. We may imagine, say, 100 hoplites in the central position, with two or three other bodies (like the southern picket) waiting in or near the natural deployment-areas to attack the Athenians on landing. Such dispositions would not have been silly; but the obvious risk is that the Athenians, with their numerical superiority, would have evaded and cut off these bodies, leaving an insufficient number of Spartans in the central position to make a proper fight of it. In fact, Athenian tactics prevented any pitched hoplite battle: had the Spartans known this, they might sensibly have preferred the alternative we are now considering, which at least offers the chance of driving the Athenian landing-parties back into the sea. But they did not know and could not have known.

In fact the Spartan dispositions seem not only intelligible but sensible. Their plans to hold up Athenian deployment were vitiated partly by the ingenious Athenian strategem of the night-landing (see Note N) and partly by the incompetence of the thirty hoplites in the southern position: and their hopes of a pitched battle were thwarted by Demosthenes' tactics as described in 32. 3 and 4. These tactics were still unusual in a Greek world accustomed to thinking of battles in terms of opposing lines of hoplites, and accustomed to accepting Spartan invincibility in these terms (hence popular surprise at the Spartan surrender, well answered by the anonymous Spartan, in 40.2).

---

6.   I can add nothing to Pritchett's excellent account of possible water supplies in the central part of the island (pp. 25-27): in any case, the general location of the main body of Spartans is not in doubt.

Where did the Athenians actually land? We have to remember that this involves two questions, not one. The first wave, carrying the 800 hoplites, presumably on as few ships as possible, would have wanted to land as near to the southern picket as possible. I have marked the most plausible positions on the map. The eastern position is virtually certain. I have followed Pritchett[7] rather than Grundy in regard to the western position, because the landing is indeed easier and the distance to the southern picket no greater than from Grundy's landing. But Grundy's position, though difficult, is possible (see above): *pace* Pritchett and " . . others, including Professor Vanderpool".[8]

The second wave, involving more than 70 ships, would not necessarily have confined itself to these positions. They might have done so, but Demosthenes and Cleon would have wished to get them ashore, and properly deployed, as swiftly as possible. Probably they landed at several other positions, whilst still keeping southerly of the main body of Spartans. All places not marked as 'cliff' on map B are possible.

---

7.   p. 27.   8.   *ibid.*

N. THE ATHENIAN ASSAULT ON SPHACTERIA

Due to topographical insensitivity, the biggest problem here has not been noticed. As has been demonstrated in Note B, the only place available to the Athenians for beaching ships or embarking troops was a narrow piece of coastline at the S.E. corner of Pylos, probably not more than 80 yards wide. This piece of land was separated from Spartan-held territory only by an Athenian wall. It was hence liable, at least in principle, to observation from Spartans to the east. Further, the Spartan outpost on the northern heights of Sphacteria would have commanded a perfect view, at no great distance, from the south. Athenian preparations for the assault - that is, the embarkation of about 800 hoplites (31.1) for the first wave, and much larger numbers (32.2) for the second - would thus normally have been both visible and audible. Yet the Spartans were taken by surprise (32.1), even though they must have been anxiously watching for this embarkation (particularly after Cleon's arrival).

A.   The first assault

It is easy (and correct) to say that the embarkation must have taken place at night. But at once another problem arises. We know what the regular Athenian practice was at night from 23.2: τῆς δὲ νυκτὸς καὶ ἅπασαι περιώρμουν. They did this in order to prevent any passages to or from Sphacteria during darkness. It seems certain that, to do this, the Athenian ships would have taken up their station *before* nightfall. Now the Spartans who were taken by surprise thought that (32.1) τὰς ναῦς κατὰ τὸ ἔθος ἐς ἔφορμον τῆς νυκτὸς πλεῖν. This does not of course mean ' . . . were sailing at night to their stations', but rather ' . . . were sailing to their night-time stations': νυκτὸς might allow the former sense, but τῆς νυκτὸς (and the word-order) only the latter. Putting these two points together, we might think that the start took place before dark, because it was seen by the men on the island, and because the start of the nightly blockade always did take place - κατὰ τὸ ἔθος - before dark . But now, we seem obliged to say that the embarkation of the troops also took place before dark: yet this would have made concealment impossible.

A possible solution may be perceived by considering 31.1: μίαν μὲν ἡμέραν ἐπέσχον, τῇ δ' ὑστεραίᾳ ἀνηγάγοντο μὲν νυκτος ἐπ' ὀλίγας ναῦς τοὺς ὁπλίτας πάντας ἐπιβιβάσαντες κτλ. Most translators take νυκτὸς with ἀνηγάγοντο, thereby falling foul of the problem mentioned above: i.e. that it could not have been κατὰ τὸ ἔθος for the Athenians to do this. We should rather take νυκτὸς with ἐπιβιβάσαντες, 'having embarked all the hoplites . . . at night'. But - and here lies the point - Thucydides does not mean *on the same night as the actual assault.* We now see the purpose behind μίαν μὲν ἡμέραν ἐπέσχον. No doubt various reasons might be given for this delay; but the most plausible, and the only one which makes sense of our problem, is that the Athenians wanted an extra night to conceal the embarkation.

The timing for the hoplites therefore looks like this:

Day 1:   Athenian generals call on Spartans to surrender: the Spartans refuse.
Night 1: Embarkation of hoplites.
Day 2:   Nothing happens until end of day, when Athenian fleet sails to night-time stations κατὰ τὸ ἔθος.
Night 2: Hoplites wait till just before dawn and then attack.

This still leaves one apparent loose end. On which ships did the hoplites embark, if τῆς νυκτὸς ἅπασαι περιώρμουν? But there is no problem here. The ἅπασαι of 23.2 refers to the Athenian fleet before it received the supplement of the ships of Cleon's force. These latter no doubt were beached at the S.E. corner of Pylos, and took no part in the nightly blockade: and this would be accepted as natural by the Spartans. The hoplites embarked on these.

B.   The second wave.

We now face a problem of the embarkation of the other (non-hoplite) troops. Their numbers may be induced from 32.2: ἐκ μὲν νεῶν . . . τοξόται δὲ . . . φυλάκων: see Note L. There is no problem about the embarkation of the normal ship's crews. But the other troops (as the δὲ makes clear) are in addition to these: we may assume, about 2,000 or more.

Here the problem of concealment is mitigated by two factors. First and more important, it was not *these* troops that took the Spartans by surprise: so there is no reason why their embarkation should have been concealed at all, unless failure to do so would also have taken the element of surprise from the hoplites landing. Secondly, despite their numbers, they were not armed as hoplites: and it would have been in principle easier for them to embark, even by day, without making it obvious that an invasion force was being embarked. They could have masqueraded as ordinary sailors or epibatai, and concealed their (light) arms and armour. On the other hand, the problem is aggravated in another way. For if the embarkation took place at the same time as the hoplites' (i.e. on the *previous* night), the absence of these 2,000-plus troops from Pylos would surely have been noticed by the Spartans on the following day.

We should regard this last consideration as decisively against either embarkation on night 1 with the hoplites, or embarkation on day 2. It may be granted that they might not have been noticed going on, or being on, the ships (the numbers work out to only about 30 troops per ship): but they would certainly have been noticed *not* being on Pylos. Thucydides specifically says that the only troops left on Pylos were the guards on the walls: everyone else (including any ἐκ τῶν ἐγγὺς συμμάχων (30.3) who had managed to arrive) took part in the assault. The absence of 800 hoplites, among so many troops, would not have been remarked, if the Athenians had taken pains to con-

111

ceal it: but the absence of *all* the troops is another matter. We are therefore left with the possibility that they embarked on night 2.

As we have shown, it was essential to the Athenian plan that the blockade should appear normal. Hence the blockading ships, which would be the vast majority of the total fleet, would have left before nightfall (and without the 2,000 troops, whose absence would otherwise have been noted). Later at night, either some few ships returned to Pylos to embark the troops, or the troops embarked on the few ships still beached at Pylos; these ships then took up stations just off Sphacteria. There might, indeed, have been time for this between the landing of the hoplites (πρὸ δὲ τῆς ἔω ὀλίγον, 31.1) and the landing of the other troops (ἅμα δὲ ἔῳ, 32.2). The distances involved are very small, and earlier embarkation might, even at night, have been noticed by the Spartans; whereas Spartan observation of any embarkation *after* the hoplite landing would not have mattered. To use more than the minimum number of ships would have been foolish and complicated at night, in an area where there was very little searoom. Nor is there any reason why we should think that these troops came from many ships: the crews of course came from all the ships, but Thucydides says nothing about where all the troops from τοξόται δε onwards came from.

Night 2 in our time-scheme will thus most plausibly read as follows:

Night 2: Hoplites wait till just before dawn and then attack. Troops on Pylos immediately embark on a few ships still beached at Pylos, take up stations with the blockading fleet, and attack at dawn.

One further point: why were the θαλάμιοι not used in the assault? Not because they were deemed inferior, for Cleon and Demosthenes were prepared to use any and every body of men they could lay hands on. The θαλάμιοι were needed to control the triremes: not that so small a number (60 out of a normal crew of 170) could have rowed fast or far, but that they would have been able to propel the ships that had already landed a little off-shore and keep them there, so that others could land. This would have been necessary, since the landing-places are far too cramped for the simultaneous landing of 70-plus triremes. Hence the Athenians could not simply have beached all their ships, used the whole crew of each, and left the ships where they were: there was no space.

O. THE OPENING BATTLE

A. Athenian and Spartan tactics

The general picture in 32.3 - 35.3 is fairly clear: but it is topographically vague, and there are some problems.

In 33.1, when the main body of Spartans saw τό τε πρῶτον φυλακτήριον διεφθαρμένον καὶ στρατὸν σφίσιν ἐπιόντα, ξυνετάξαντο καὶ τοῖς ὁπλίταις τῶν Ἀθηναίων ἐπῇσαν, βουλόμενοι ἐς χεῖρας ἐλθεῖν·ἐξ ἐναντίας γὰρ οὗτοι καθειστήκεσαν, ἐκ πλαγίου δὲ οἱ ψιλοί, καὶ κατὰ νώτου. By the end of this sentence, part of the στρατὸν ἐπιόντα, namely some of οἱ ψιλοί, are *already* κατὰ νώτου. We must assume, therefore, that they were deployed before the Spartans moved. How did Demosthenes manage to do this?

We are told in 32.3 that Demosthenes had arranged them in groups of 200 or more (sometimes less), and that they occupied τὰ μετεωρότατα. This need not imply that Demosthenes organised them in this way *after* landing: nor is this likely. For then he would have had to deploy over 10,000 men (see Note L) from one base-point: presumably from the southern picket-position which the Athenian hoplites had just overrun. Some may well have been deployed from this position: these would have used the high ground which runs along the eastern side of the island from the picket-position, northwards to the Panagia landing. But others, perhaps the majority, would not have landed at the same points as the two earlier hoplite landings: they would have landed further to the north, as marked on map B, in order more easily to take up positions ἐκ πλαγίου καὶ κατὰ νώτου.

The Spartans then closed their ranks (ξυνετάξαντο), as for hoplite warfare, and advanced against the Athenian hoplites who were ἐξ ἐναντίας. These hoplites must have been a little to the north of the southern picket-position, as marked on map B. It was necessary that the Athenian hoplites make a showing, for neither the morale nor the efficiency of οἱ ψιλοί was in itself sufficient to destroy the Spartans. But, since they did not wish ἐς χεῖρας ἐλθεῖν, they kept at a safe distance. Their position was ideally chosen: fully in view of the main body of Spartans and of their own troops, yet about half a mile away from the Spartans, and with an advantage in height of perhaps 100 feet. This gave the Athenian ψιλοί ample opportunity: ἑκατέρωθεν βάλλοντες εἶργον (33.2). For hoplite armour did not give the Spartans adequate protection from flank and rear.

When the ψιλοί attacked, the Spartans must have adopted an 'open order' formation, though Thucydides does not specify this: plainly because such a formation lessened damage from the Athenian missiles. Nevertheless as the Spartans tired of trying to drive οἱ ψιλοί away, and the Athenian morale increased (34.1), their difficulties increased as described in 34.2-3 (for two particular difficulties, see below). In particular, we are told that many were wounded διὰ τὸ αἰεὶ ἐν τῷ αὐτῷ ἀναστρέφεσθαι (35.1). This area

113

is the (comparatively) flat central part of the island, about three-quarters of a mile in length: to this area they were confined, and were easy targets for οἱ ψιλοί.

In 35.1 the Spartans close their ranks again (ξυγκλήσαντες) and retreat to Mt. Elias. They needed to adopt a 'tight' formation in order to avoid, as far as possible, the danger of some of their number being cut off - though this still happened (35.2 ἐγκαπελαμβάνοντο). We cannot tell the exact point in the flat central area from which they began this retreat: they may have been still trying to get at the Athenian hoplites and therefore to the south of their base camp by the well, or they may by now have been driven further north. In any case they would not have had to cover much more than half a mile to reach Mt. Elias (35.1, οὐ πολὺ ἀπεῖχε). But the last part of this retreat involves a steep ascent in the face of οἱ ψιλοί, who would of course be using the high ground to the south of Mt. Elias: so it is hardly surprising that some were cut off and killed. The exact course of the retreat, like its exact starting-point, is hard to determine: for much would have depended on the precise positions of various groups of οἱ ψιλοί, which we cannot hope to know.

It is very difficult to see how either side could have acted more sensibly. Athenian tactics were plainly exemplary. The time of real danger for them was when the Spartans were trying to come to grips with the Athenian hoplites: had they done so, and routed them, the result might have been different, for there is no telling how the ψιλοί alone would have behaved. On the Spartan side, it is possible that they remained too long in the central area: as soon as it became clear to them that they could not come to grips with the Athenian hoplites, there was no point in their remaining. But they did not retreat until τραυματιζομένων ἤδη πολλῶν: probably too long, but they might still have been hoping for a hoplite battle, and would have been reluctant to leave the water supply.

B. Spartan difficulties

All the Spartan difficulties mentioned by Thucydides in 33-35 are readily intelligible except the one in 34.3: οὔτε γὰρ οἱ πῖλοι ἔστεγον τὰ τοξεύματα, δοράτιά τε ἐναπεκέκλαστο βαλλομένων. The unintelligibility is due to the difficulty of translation

What are οἱ πῖλοι? Gomme says "the regular Laconian round steel cap (so Arnold and Steup) rather than cuirasses, as many have supposed". I take him to be right about πῖλοι being caps rather than a protection for some other part of the body: it is true that πῖλος means 'felt' in general, but it is nearly always a felt cap, and felt cuirasses or other body-armour would be insufficient for standard hoplite equipment in first-rate Spartan troops. But he is surely wrong about 'steel': whether or not the caps were strengthened with iron (not steel), they were basically of felt. For otherwise πῖλοι would have no proper sense: and no ordinary missile could in fact have penetrated a properly-made iron or steel cap. Since it is precisely Thucydides' point that the caps did *not* offer protection against the missiles, we can hardly agree with Gomme here.

114

How do we translate δοράτιά ἐναπεκέκλαστο βαλλομένων? Editors and translators have suggested two possibilities (nearly always without regard for the difficulty): (i) 'javelins were broken off and stuck in (some part of their armour) when the men were hit'. (ii) 'their (sc. the Spartans') spears were broken off short when they (sc. the Spartans) were hit'. Neither of these seem quite satisfactory. Against (i), we observe the lack of any noun following the ἐν of ἐναπεκέκλαστο, such as ταῖς ἀσπίοι (Steup's suggested insertion): more important, it is not easy to see why the heads of javelins sticking in their armour should be a difficulty worth mentioning - they did no damage, and could always have been removed by the Spartans: at the worst, it might slightly impede their movements. If it be thought that the ἐν refers naturally to the πῖλοι, this latter point has still more force: why should a few arrow-heads in their felt caps have worried them? Against (ii), we observe the lack of any sense to this ἐν (we can hardly translate 'broken off in the middle' or 'in their hands'): and it is not clear why their spears were broken off. One might argue that they were broken off by being struck by Athenian missiles, and had Thucydides written βαλλομένα we might accept (ii): but βαλλομένων has little relevant sense - we have to translate literally 'the spears of the men as they were being pelted . . . '. This again is possible but not plausible.

A more satisfactory translation would be: 'when the men were hit, missiles remained broken off in their bodies'. Here the ἐν naturally refers to them, the Spartans: and we have a statement of a serious difficulty, namely the fact that they were wounded, and the arrow- and spear-heads stayed in their wounds - quite different from the trivial fact that they stayed in their *armour.*

C. 'Skirmishing' and helots

In 34.1, having described the difficulties of the Spartan hoplites in trying to come to grips with the enemy, Thucydides says that for a short time οὕτω πρὸς ἀλλήλους ἠκροβολίσαντο.

What Thucydides has described in 33 could certainly be called a 'skirmish' in English: the Athenian light-armed troops pelt the Spartans, the Spartans charge them, the light-armed troops run away, and so on. But he has not described anybody on the Spartan side using any weapons at a distance (bows and arrows, slings, javelins, etc.). This would not matter if ἀκροβολίζομαι could bear the more general meaning of 'skirmish': but I have been unable to find any examples where it does not specifically imply (as the etymology suggests) using long-distance weapons. If Thucydides means what he says, somebody on the Spartan side was doing this, not only Athenians: otherwise πρὸς ἀλλήλους has no sense.

Spartan hoplites were not normally equipped to do it, and we must assume that their attendant helots did it. It is odd, however, that Thucydides gives no details, at least at this point: though we observe that he makes no mention of the helots at *any* point after merely affirming their existence in 8.9. We do not know how many of them there were, how they were armed, or what their casualties were: and apart from the above induction from the single word ἠκροβολίσαντο, we are not told what part they played in the fighting. Yet in this particular fight, which was not σταδαία, they must have been important: not only in the skirmishing, but also in giving the Spartans some protection in their retreat to Mt. Elias, and in helping with the stubborn defence of Mt. Elias itself.

Since the main interest of the campaign, in its wider historical setting, lay in the surrender of the Spartan hoplites, it is understandable that the helots should be forgotten. But had they done anything of obvious or dramatic military significance - in particular if they had severely hampered the Athenian tactics - Thucydides would surely have said something about it. We may draw the tentative conclusion, I believe, that there were not enough helots to do this. They delayed the Athenian victory, no doubt (indeed the prolonged Spartan resistance against such overwhelming numbers is hardly intelligible if we picture 420 Spartans on their own, with no helot assistance): but they could not seriously affect the tactics. I do not believe that there were more than one or two helots per Spartan (even with the addition of the helots in 26.5 and 6, who joined the Spartans as food-bringers).

P. THE SPARTANS' LAST STAND

The problems here are difficult, and so interconnected that it is impossible to break them down into sub-headings. The relevant sections of Thucydides are 35 and 36.

The battle round Mt. Elias went on not only for χρόνον πολὺν, but for τῆς ἡμέρας τὸ πλεῖστον. It was only ἐπειδὴ ἀπέραντον ἦν that the Messenian leader made his suggestion. Why not before? It is possible that the Messenians knew of a path, but withheld this knowledge until the last minute in the hope that the Spartans would yield earlier - thereby avoiding the dangers and possible loss of (Messenian) lives that taking the path would bring. But there are strong arguments against this.

He went κατὰ τὸ αἰεὶ παρεῖκον τοῦ κρημνώδους . . . χαλεπῶς τε καὶ μόλις περιελθών : some indication that he was not following a known route. The route (for reasons given below) would have to be invisible to both Spartans and Athenians, and not guessed at by either: and it is highly improbable that any Messenians used for the campaign were so familiar with the topography as to be certain of it. Sphacteria had long been uninhabited: even today the possible paths are far from common knowledge.[1] At best the Messenian leader might have been prompted by some dim memory on the part of one of his countrymen.

This is supported by the sentence εἰ δὲ βούλονται ἑαυτῷ δοῦναι τῶν τοξοτῶν μέρος τι καὶ τῶν ψιλῶν περιιέναι κατὰ νώτου αὐτοῖς ὁδῷ ᾗ ἂν αὐτὸς εὕρῃ δοκεῖν βιάσασθαι τὴν ἔφοδον. This is normally translated: "If they were willing to give him some of the archers and light-armed troops, to go round behind the Spartans by whatever way he could find, he thought that he could force the approach". Of this Gomme, scenting trouble, says[2] "I should have expected the potential ἂν εὕροι (as well as ἦν, as Classen suggested): 'which I would find by myself . . . '." This change from an indefinite to a potential sense, however, carries slightly more implication that the Messenian commander knew the route, or at least knew that there was one to find. Yet Gomme is right in thinking the sentence peculiar. In particular, περιιέναι as an 'infinitive of purpose' dependent on δοῦναι, which is required by this translation, seems implausible. It would not be absurd to consider the possibility of putting the comma after ψιλῶν instead of after εὕρῃ, and translating: "If . . . troops, he would go round behind the Spartans by whatever way he could find that seemed as if it would force the approach". Granted that it is awkward to take δοκεῖν βιάσασθαι after εὕρῃ (though the infinitive

---

1.   As may be induced from Pritchett, p. 29. My own enquiries produced even more ignorance: neither boatmen, nor actual inhabitants of Sphacteria (there are a few in charge of oil installations), had ever heard of it. Pritchett's shepherd had had grazing rights on the island: I should guess that only somebody in this position would have had first-hand knowledge, and the chances of any of the Messenians preserving that knowledge are remote.

2.   p. 476.

with εὑρίσκω is in order)[3], I am not sure that this (unconsidered) alternative is obviously wrong. If right, however, it gives more sense to the indefinite ἀν, and implies that the commander did *not* know of the route.

In any case, it is most plausible to assume that he did not know. The Messenians, characteristically anxious not to allow the Spartans any chance of escape, were prepared (since all else seemed to have failed) to undertake this do-or-die attempt. ἐπειδή might well be translated 'since', giving the Messenians' reasons.

The route itself is more difficult to determine, and is connected with the Spartans' actual position on Mt. Elias. First some more obvious points about the latter:-

A.   Whether Burrows' account of the actual or possible walls composing the Spartans' ἔρυμα (see Map D) is archaeologically acceptable, is irrelevant: fortunately, because the walls no longer exist.[4] It is irrelevant, because the Spartans must certainly have occupied some such defence-line as that of the main wall (A-A on the map), whether or not Burrows is right in having actually identified the masonry: and of the two supporting walls, the southern (B) is wholly conjectural, and the northern (C) need not have been defended by the Spartans just because it was there. We should rely rather on general topographical and military considerations, together with what Thucydides tells us.

Thucydides says that the Athenians did not have the chance of a περίοδον αὐτῶν κὰι κύκλωσιν, or of κυκλώσεως ἐς τὰ πλάγια. The first is true, the second only true in a sense. As the map shows, the Spartan position necessitated a perimeter of substantially more than a semicircle, containing something more like 270 degrees than 180. The Spartans would certainly have had Athenians 'on their flanks'. But as Gomme rightly says, "they were at the moment on higher ground than their enemies".[5] The approach to the Spartan position from the north is particularly steep, and would make it impossible for Athenians attacking by the cliff-edge at the extreme north-east of the perimeter to get a fair shot at Spartan defenders further west: so too, for the most part, at the western approaches. Briefly, after a good deal of personal investigation, I am satisfied that there was nowhere where the Athenians could, in any real sense, take the Spartans 'on the flank'.

---

3.   Cf. parallels given by Liddell and Scott.
4.   Mt. Elias was much altered by Italian installations in the Second World War. Prolonged searching convinced me that nothing that could seriously be described as a wall, or remains of a wall, now exists: though there are stones, some of which are in the positions of Burrows' walls. However, I see no reason to disbelieve Burrows.
5.   p. 476.

It is, of course, quite clear that the Spartans did not occupy the very top of Mt. Elias. This has been flattened and altered in modern times,[6] but whatever it was like in 425 it could hardly have been large enough to hold more than a fraction of the Spartan force.[7] Moreover, if they had only held this position, they could have been surrounded, contrary to what Thucydides says. The Spartans held a perimeter roughly as marked on the map.

We must not be baffled here by Thucydides' two references to the μετεώρος. In the first, the Athenians are trying to push the Spartans ἐκ τοῦ μετεώρου: that is, off the 'high ground'. The term is used generally, to include the very top of Mt. Elias, but to include more besides. When the Messenians appear ἐπὶ τοῦ μετεώρου ἐξαπίνης ἀναφανεῖς κατὰ νώτου, rattling the Spartans τῷ ἀδοκήτῳ and being visible to the Athenians (ἰδόντας), it is on this very top that they must appear. It must have been unoccupied by the Spartans. This at first sight creates the impression that the Spartans both did, and did not, occupy the μετεώρος. But if Thucydides were defending himself against such stringent criticism, he could say that the Spartans were occupying the μετεώρος, but not all the μετεώρος: in particular, not the bit on which the Messenians finally appeared.

When the Messenians had got to the very top, the Spartans were of course ἀμφίβολοι ἤδη, since the Spartan positions are clearly visible, and within easy range, from the summit. Moreover, a quick Spartan attack on the (now visible) Messenians on the summit would not have been easy. Though the distance is short, the ground is extremely steep in all directions (before the modern flattening of the top, it would have been even more difficult). We do not know how many Messenian there were; but even a few would have been reasonably immune, so long as the Athenians at the perimeter kept up the pressure. In fact, Thucydides' implication is that, as soon as the Spartans were ἀμφίβολοι - that is, as soon as the Messenians arrived - they more or less gave up (οὐκέτι ἀντεῖχον): and this is wholly understandable.

B.   We turn now to the real difficulties, which may be summarised in the two questions (a) did the Spartans hold either or both of the supporting walls (B and C on Map D and Burrows' plan), or any similar positions, as well as the general perimeter? (b) by what actual route did the Messenians come?

The chief difficulty is created by the fact that there had been a Spartan outpost in this position for some time, and that the Spartans were aware that they might have to use the position for a last stand: all this is quite plain in 31.2. It is an obvious infer-

---

6.   See note 4 above. The top has been flattened to take gun batteries, and a winding road or track built up to it.
7.   Of course we do not know the numbers: but a minimum figure would be 292, plus surviving helots. A glance at the map shows the impossibility of fitting this number onto the actual summit.

ence that the Spartans, not being totally devoid of intellect, would have checked at least all the obvious ways by which the position might have been turned: and they would have had plenty of time to do so. Similarly the Athenians, never ones to conduct an expensive frontal assault where treachery or turning the position would do instead, would have done their best to discover whether any path might turn the position. Yet, until the Messenians found it, both Spartans and Athenians actually missed the path.

This means that the path must have been pretty well invisible to both sides. (Indeed Thucydides' words in 36.2 do not actually suggest a *path* at all, in the sense of one particular recognised route. They suggest rather that the Messenians simply managed to get there by hook or by crook.) Now the *end* of the route, placed by Burrows (also Compton and Awdry)[8] in the gully or chimney leading to the southern end of a hollow east of the summit, is beyond question too obvious to anyone in the Spartans' position who is interested in ways up to, or down from, the summit.[9] It is unbelievable that the Spartans would not have known about it. We must therefore assume (a) that the Spartans held some such defensive position as B in Burrows' plan, or at least held men in readiness or on watch in case the route should be used: (b) that the Messenians did not use that route.

By contrast, possible routes ending to the north of this are very far from obvious. Particularly from the top, the cliff looks unclimbable: even from the bottom it looks doubtful. Yet in fact there are several possible routes for the determined climber: Pritchett was the first (historian) to discover one of these:[10] I have myself found two others, and there may be more.

There is, however, a limiting factor. The Messenians would have known (for they would have been able to see before they started) that the Spartans were defending position B on the map, and therefore taken care not to come up that way. But equally they would have taken care not to emerge too far to the north: any emergence significantly to the north of the highest point of the 'notch' would have been too near the Spartan perimeter, or indeed actually inside it. The emergence must therefore have been somewhere on a fairly narrow front (perhaps not more than about 80 yards) - far enough to the north not to fall foul of the defenders in position B, yet not far enough to fall foul of the northern perimeter.

---

8. See refs. in Pritchett, p. 28.
9. On one visit I was in the company of friends who knew nothing of the campaign. One of them, wishing to descend as directly as possible from the summit (having reached it by walking from the Panagia landing), cast about for a possible route, and found Burrows' route within a few minutes. A Spartan could have done no less.
10. See Pritchett, p. 29.

There are, in fact, several possible emergence-points (notably Pritchett's 'skala'[11]) which fulfil these conditions: it seems impossible to identify any one of these with certainty, since the precise route the Messenians took must have been partly a matter of chance. They no doubt started in the way suggested by Compton and Awdry,[12.] reached the fan-shaped scree, and took what seemed to them the likeliest-looking path: it is possible that they had to try more than once to find a viable route.[13]

All this, however, would have been quite impossible had the Spartans held any such position as C on the map. For the Messenians would then have been seen immediately on emergence at the top of the cliff; and there is quite a way to go (I estimate at least 2-3 minutes) from the cliff-top to the true summit, during which Spartans in position C could certainly have intercepted them.[14] But there is no difficulty here: when Thucydides says that the Spartans χωρίου ἰσχύι πιστεύσαντες οὐκ ἐφύλασσον, we may believe him. For *that* degree of trust is perfectly plausible, since the way(s) up could not be seen or guessed at. This is a far cry from not guarding position B, which would indicate a 'trust' tantamount to lunacy.

However, the Spartan perimeter must have been complete on the north side. This means that their line must have extended (as marked M-M on the map) beyond the limits of Burrows' wall (A-A), and substantially to the north of Burrows' wall C. The ground here is at its steepest, and the defence would not have been difficult. It would indeed have been easier to defend this northern sector of M-M than position C, unless we assume that there was no wall at all in this sector and a good wall (including an adequate connecting wall) at C. We cannot feel certain about such an assumption; at the very least, the finds of masonry by Burrows do not entitle us to say that the Spartans *must* have defended C.

One apparent difficulty remains. Thucydides has told us earlier (31.2) of the ἔρυμα . . . λίθων λογάδην πεποιημένον: and when we are now (35.2) told that the Spartans διαφυγόντες ἐς τὸ ἔρυμα μετὰ τῶν ταύτῃ φυλάκων ἐτάξαντο παρὰ πᾶν ὡς ἀμυνούμενοι ἧπερ ἦν ἐπίμαχον, we may be inclined to suppose that *all* that the Spartans did was to defend existing walls: is it not going beyond, or indeed against, the text to suggest that the perimeter extended beyond Burrows' walls? (Unless of course there *were* walls along the northern sector of M-M: but there is no evidence for this.)

11. *ibid.*
12. As Pritchett implies, this is more plausible than Burrows' suggestion that the Messenians used boats.
13. The climb from the scree is not a long one, but there is no immediately obvious route to the top. Thucydides' κατὰ τὸ αἰεὶ παρεῖκον τοῦ κρημνώδους is exact.
14. The distances, as the crow flies, are deceptive. For the Messenians to reach the summit, they had first to enter the hollow, and then undertake a short but stiff climb. Spartans at B or C could have moved much more quickly along (comparatively) level ground, and intercepted them with ease.

But there is some indication that by 35.2 Thucydides may be using ἔρυμα in a slightly wider sense, to mean (as ἔρυμα can of course mean) 'a fortified position' or 'a defence-point', rather than tying the word to actual masonry. For in 35.1 he says that they retreated ἐς τὸ ἔσχατον ἔρυμα τῆς νήσου: and this must surely mean, not 'the defence-walls which were at the end of the island', but 'the last (ultimate, furthest) defence-point of the island'. A fair translation of 35.2 might run: " . . . escaped safely to the fortified position, and together with the guards already there arrayed themselves all along the perimeter, to defend it wherever it was assailable". This allows for defence-positions not actually backed by masonry; and indeed the tone of 31.2 implies that the masonry was, at best, an additional advantage and not a watertight fortification - "a sub-section of them guarded the extreme end of the island facing Pylos, where the cliff was sheer on the sea-side, and the position least assailable from the land side: and, too, there was an old fortification of stones roughly fitted together, which they thought would be useful to them . . . "

Had the Spartans defended Burrows' position C, the Messenians could not have emerged unobserved and reached the summit safely unless the Spartans had *not* defended position B. We rejected this on the grounds that the need to defend it against a cliff-climbing party would have been obvious: but we might also add that the defence of such a position was necessary against the main body of the Athenian attack. The position required for this purpose might, indeed, have been a little farther south than that marked by Burrows: but not much, and not sufficiently so to allow enough space between B and C for the Messenians to complete their task. [15] It therefore seems over-whelmingly probable that the Spartan perimeter was as marked.

Some individual considerations must be added:-

(a)   The Spartan position was in principle hopeless, for they had no water. Yet neither Cleon nor the Messenians would have been happy to allow the fighting to cease at night-fall: they needed a decision before then. For during the night, although not many Spartans could have escaped, yet many might have tried: and they wanted as many as possible alive, as is clear from 37.1 (βουλόμενοι ἀγαγεῖν αὐτοὺς Ἀθηναίοις ζῶντας).

(b)   The reader should be impressed by the great strength of the defence-position on Mt. Elias: remembering not only that, despite the vast disparity of numbers, the Spartans managed to holdout τῆς ἡμέρας τὸ πλεῖστον, but also that the fire would have made the attackers' movements much easier. [16] Nevertheless, much of this strength must have been due to existing walls. The minimum length for the perimeter is c. 200 yards: given only about 300 Spartans, even though assisted by an unknown number of helots, there cannot have been many large gaps.

---

15.   The natural line of defence is not more than 15 yards south of B.
16.   See notes on the fire, p.100f. Modern topographers must not be deceived by the contemporary undergrowth, which makes it difficult to move around freely.

122

(c)   Thucydides twice uses the word ἔφοδος. In 36.1 the Messenian commander hopes to βιάσασθαι τὴν ἔφοδον: in 36.3, when the Messenians have arrived, the Spartans ὑπέχωρουν, καὶ οἱ Ἀθηναῖοι ἐκράτουν ἤδη τῶν ἐφόδων. The latter is not disputable: it must mean 'approaches' or 'ways into' the Spartan defended position. So (despite some translators, who take it as meaning 'force home the attack') also with the former. The singular ἔφοδον, particularly with τὴν, may seem odd: for certainly there was more than one possible 'approach' or 'way in'. It does not mean 'force the (one and only) way in', but 'force an entrance': as in 11.4, βιαζομένους τὴν ἀπόβασιν, where there is no question of any *single* landing-place. [17] The ἔφοδοι would include (i) places where the wall was ἐπίμαχον, (ii) places where there was no wall, at the extreme north-east and south-east of the perimeter.

(d)   The Messenians would have stayed on the summit, using however many archers and javelin-men they had (probably not many), rather than descended to tackle the Spartans at closer quarters. This is not only tactically more probable, but also required by Thucydides' description in 36.3 and 37.1. Had the Messenians started a mêlée, it would have been impossible for Cleon to 'keep his men back'. What happened was that the Spartans manning the perimeter found it impossible to endure the Messenian missiles from behind them, and at the same time to beat off the Athenian attacks from in front. They retreated a little from the ἔφοδοι, not knowing where to turn, but still at some distance from the Messenians. At this point Cleon and Demosthenes ἔπαυσαν τὴν μάχην καὶ τοὺς ἑαυτῶν ἀπεῖρξαν, and made their offer to the Spartans.

---

17.   Cf. also VII, 72: βιάζεσθαι τὸν ἔκπλουν.

III. GENERAL

Q.   OVERALL TIME-SCHEME

One of the bases for this must be the time-scheme for the first part of the campaign in Note E, to which the reader will need to refer. The other is the ἑβδομήκοντα ἡμέραι καὶ δύο (39.1) between the ναυμαχία (our 'D-Day' in Note E) and the final surrender.

We marked the start of the Athenian fortification by D-18. To this we have to add the time taken by the Athenian fleet to reach Pylos from Athens (rather over 200 miles: perhaps five days). We have also to add some delay at Pylos, during which Demosthenes fails to persuade the generals and the taxiarchs; some inaction occurs ὑπὸ ἀπλοίας, until eventually the plan is changed and the soldiers do the job (4.1): perhaps 2-3 days. (So far I am in accord with Gomme's note.[1]) This gives us 18 days, plus 5, plus (say) 3, plus 72, from the start of the original Athenian expedition to the final victory: total, 98 days.

The first problem is to make the Athenian movements square with the Spartan. The Spartans stayed in Attica 15 days (6.2), returning as soon as they had news of Pylos (6.1). This will fit by adding to the time-scheme in Note E thus:-

D – 28	Spartans invade Attica
D – 26	Athenian fleet starts from Athens.
D – 21	Athenian fleet arrives at Pylos.
D – 18	Athenians begin fortification.
D – 13	News of fortification reaches Spartans in Attica: they return at once.
D – 12	Athenians finish fortification.
D – 9	Spartans reach Sparta from Attica
D – 6	First Spartan troops arrive at Pylos.
etc.	

Note that this time-scheme is fairly tight. If, for instance, we put the Spartan invasion of Attica earlier, we shall require more than 15 days' stay in Attica in order to arrive at D – 6 for the first troops reaching Pylos: if later, less than 15. So too with the start of the Athenian fleet. Lack of exactness is to be expected here and there, particularly in the time the news took to travel from Pylos to Sparta (not because the time required by the distance is all that uncertain, but rather because we cannot know on which day of the Athenian fortification the news began to travel: remembering the ἐρημία of Pylos mentioned in Note A). But in general the scheme must stand.

After D – Day (the sea-fight and start of the blockade), there is an interim period when the news has to reach Sparta (15.1) and the Spartan officials go to Pylos (15.1) and negotiate a truce with the Athenians. The Spartans would have wanted the negotiations to go through as quickly as possible, and since the terms of the truce are very much in Athens' favour (16.1) we can hardly imagine that they were unduly protracted

---

1.   p. 478.

by the Athenians. For all this we might allow about 6 days, taking us to D + 6. About four days were needed to put the truce into operation: not till then did the ambassadors leave (see Note I, p. 94) and there began the περὶ εἴκοσιν ἡμέρας ἐν αἷς οἱ πρέσβεις περὶ τῶν σπονδῶν ἀπῆσαν (39.2). This takes us to D + 30, leaving about 42 of Thucydides' ἑβδομήκοντα ἡμέραι καὶ δύο to be filled before the final Athenian victory on D + 72.

Cleon's arrival can be dated on D + 70: on that day he makes overtures to the Spartans, which are rejected (30.4), waits one day (31.1), and then wins the final victory on D + 72. Our only other piece of evidence is Cleon's fulfilled promise (39.3) to "bring the Spartans back within 20 days". That this is the correct translation of ἄγω, the verb Thucydides uses both in the original promise (28.4) and in its fulfilment, is shown beyond reasonable doubt by 37.1 and the context in 39.3: "the Athenians and the Peloponnesians both returned home from Pylos with their expeditionary forces, and Cleon's promise (although lunatic) was fulfilled". The promise must be interpreted as a promise to *have them back in* Athens by a certain date: not a promise to *start* bringing them back *to* Athens, still less one to take them prisoner. If this is right (it is at least the most probable), then Cleon fulfilled his promise although the Spartan prisoners could not have arrived much sooner than five days after the final victory, i.e. D + 77. The promise was therefore made not earlier than D + 57.

Cleon would require about 5 days to reach Pylos, putting his departure on D + 65. There is no indication, in the account of the troops that went with him (28.4), that he would have had to wait for any of them to arrive in Athens: indeed there are clear statements that some of them were already there (παρόντας, βεβοηθηκότες). Nevertheless, he would have required a few days to organise these forces and to prepare the ships in which they were to travel: let us say, 3 at a minimum. This would place his promise on D + 62. This too can stand as fairly exact: we cannot (see above) put the promise earlier than D + 57, or later than D + 62.

Our comparative time-scheme now looks like this:

D + 6   Agreement to truce.
D + 10   Operation of truce (see Note I).
D + 30   End of truce
c.D + 60 Meeting of assembly and Cleon's promise.
D + 65   Cleon leaves Athens.
D + 70   Cleon arrives in Pylos.
D + 72   Final victory on Sphacteria.
D + 77   Cleon arrives in Athens with Spartan prisoners.

The worse problem comes when trying to transfer this to real time. The only clue available is in 2.1: it is τοῦ ἦρος, πρὶν τὸν σῖτον ἐν ἀκμῇ εἶναι that the Peloponnesians

125

invade Attica, and the next sentence (2.2) describes the start of the Athenian expedition. There are general grounds for putting the time at the beginning of May;[2] and we should not follow Gomme's[3] suggested possibility of "a little later if χειμὼν ἐπιγενόμενος κ.τ.λ. (3.1, 6.1), means that the weather was unusually cold for a long time". For in 3.1 χειμὼν plainly means a storm: and in any case the cold weather would have begun *after* the dates we are interested in (that is, obviously, after the Peloponnesian invasion and the Athenian expedition). It would have affected the date of the corn's actually *being* ἐν ἀκμῇ, but not any date πρὶν.

It is clear from the above that we cannot alter the comparative timing of D − 28 for the Spartan invasion and D − 26 for the start of the Athenian fleet. This is quite in accordance with the text of 2.1: the Spartans invaded, and then (almost at once) the Athenians sent off their expedition. We cannot, however, get any closer to the real time: *faute de mieux*, let us postulate May 1 for D − 28. This gives us (inter alia) May 29 for the Athenian victory in the λιμήν and the beginning of the blockade, and August 1 for the final victory.[4] But this is highly uncertain: we must allow a latitude of at least a week either way. Fortunately the 'real time' problem seems of somewhat academic interest: the 'comparative time', as we have seen, fits well and exactly.

---

2.   p. 437, with references.   3.   *ibid.*
4.   It is perhaps just worth mentioning that there had been a new moon on 27 July, reaching its first quarter on August 3. The comparative absence of moonlight would have favoured Athenian preparations and landing on Sphacteria (see Note N), if these occurred soon after 27 July. By August 10 the moon had become full.

R. AFTERMATH

A. Establishing the garrison

41.1: κομισθέντων δὲ τῶν ἀνδρῶν οἱ ᾿Αθηναῖοι... τῆς δὲ Πύλου φυλακὴν κατεστήσαντο, καὶ οἱ ἐκ τῆς Ναυπάκτου Μεσσήνιοι... πέμψαντες σφῶν αὐτῶν τους ἐπιτηδειοτάτους ἐλήζοντο τε τὴν Λακωνικὴν...

The δὲ in this passage picks up the μὲν in 39.3 (οἱ μὲν δὴ ᾿Αθηναῖοι): some have claimed[1] that the intervening section 40 (consisting of an illustrative anecdote, rare in Thucydides) was inserted afterwards by the author. But the ᾿Αθηναῖοι in this passage are not the ᾿Αθηναῖοι of 39.3: they are the Athenians in Athens. This makes τῆς Πύλου φυλακὴν κατεστήσαντο slightly odd: surely we cannot translate "they arranged a garrison for Pylos", as if Pylos were now to be garrisoned for the first time, after the Spartan prisoners had been brought to Athens and the Athenians had had time to make up their minds what to do.

When in 39.3 οἱ ᾿Αθηναῖοι... ἀνεχώρησαν τῷ στρατῷ ἐκ τῆς Πύλου... ἐπ᾽ οἴκου, we must surely assume that a garrison was left behind. Indeed this passage is in a way misleading; for, although Cleon's force returned ἐπ᾽ οἴκου, the force led by Eurymedon and Sophocles (by far the larger part) did not go back to Athens, as 46.1 makes plain (ἐκ τῆς Πύλου ἀπῆραν... ἀφικόμενοι ἐς Κέρκυραν...). It is quite possible that this force remained at Pylos until the permanent garrison had been installed. By τῆς Πύλου φυλακὴν κατεστήσαντο we must understand something like "decreed a (permanent) garrison for Pylos": that is, they resolved formally to garrison it permanently, to use Messenians, and so on. It is still tempting to read τὴν for τῆς, to mean "they set in order/reorganised *the* garrison of Pylos": but perhaps unnecessary.

B. Personnel of the garrison

οἱ ἐκ τῆς Ναυπάκτου Μεσσήνιοι cannot mean 'the Messenians *in* Naupactos' or 'the Naupactus-based Messenians': though most translators take it this way, as if using the English analogy of "Smith is from London", meaning that Smith lives in London.[2] But 'the Messenians from Naupactus' does not square well with the phrase πέμψαντες σφῶν αὐτῶν τοὺς ἐπιτηδειοτάτους. πέμψαντες cannot normally mean 'inviting' or 'sending for': so how could Messenians *from* Naupactus (that is, one might suppose, *at* Pylos) 'send their most suitable troops?'

---

1. e.g. Mills, p. 53.
2. ἐκ (τῆς) Ναυπάκτου is found elsewhere in conjunction with οἱ Μεσσηνίοι, but not with this meaning. Thus in VII.57.8, οἱ Μεσσηνίοι... ἐκ Ναυπάκτου καὶ ἐκ Πανάκτου is governed by παρελήφθησαν.

We may entertain a picture of these Messenians, from Naupactus and now at Pylos, sending *out* their most suitable troops *from Pylos* on these ravaging expeditions; but I find this unconvincing (though not impossible). I should rather assume that some of the Messenians at Pylos returned to Naupactus, sent out some of their fellows as a garrison to Pylos, and then themselves returned to Pylos (this is necessary, since they figure as subjects of ἐλήϊζοντο (and ἔβλαπτον). This seems complicated, but it gives us the most plausible picture. At the time of 41.2 there were probably too few Messenians at Pylos to form a garrison: we know only of the two small boats which provided Demosthenes with 40 hoplites (9.1), and ὁ τῶν Μεσσηνίων στρατηγὸς (36.1) does not imply a large number, any more than Μεσσηνίων τε οἱ βεβοηθηκότες in 32.2. In any case the Athenians would want τοὺς ἐπιτηδειοτάτους, not just the ones who had happened to turn up. So it would have been natural for Eurymedon and Sophocles, or Demosthenes, or whoever was in command at the time or had received instructions from Athens, to say to the Messenians then at Pylos: "Go back to Naupactus and send out τοὺς ἐπιτηδειοτάτους of you, and then come back and get on with the plundering".

In the negotiations following the Peace of Nikias, the Spartans persuaded the Athenians to remove the Messenians from Pylos: they were taken to Kranaoi in Cephallenia and replaced by an Athenian garrison (V.35.7). This was in 421 B.C. In the winter of 419/18, however, they were brought back again (V.56.2-3), and no doubt continued their activities as before. Thus in VII.26.2 Demosthenes, whilst on the way to Sicily, fortified a peninsula on Laconian territory opposite Cythera ἵνα δὴ οἵ τε Εἵλωτες ... αὐτόσε αὐτομολῶσι καὶ ἅμα λῃσταὶ ἐξ αὐτοῦ ὥσπερ ἐκ τῆς Πύλου ἁρπαγὴν ποιῶνται.

C. Function of the garrison

The garrison must have been big enough to defend itself against any Spartan attack, whilst still being able to function as an effective striking force. This sets a lower limit of perhaps 500 men: but the numbers were probably larger, if only because of the deserting helots. It is hard to believe that a garrison of sufficient size could have fed itself by land forays in an area which was ἐρῆμον ... ἐπὶ πολὺ τῆς χώρας (see Note A): or how such land forays would have been effective against the Spartans - if they ranged too far afield, a hastily-assembled force could have destroyed them, and if they restricted themselves to short distances, there would have been nothing worth ravaging. Nor would the Athenians have kept them supplied on such a basis, even if they could:[3] though no

---

3.   The passage in 27.1 (τῶν τε ἐπιτηδείων .. κομιδὴν ἀδύνατον ἐσομένην ... οὐδ' ἐν θέρει οἷοί τε ὄντες ἱκανὰ περιπέμπειν κ.τ,λ.) is not really relevant: for this concerns the feeding of the whole blockading fleet (at this point, 70 ships), not of a small garrison. The Athenians may have sent supplies of food when they could: but they would have expected the garrison to feed itself for the most part by sea-borne plundering.

doubt some supplies came from Athens, in the nature of equipment rather than food.[4]

It is thus probable that the ληστεία which the Spartans οὐ ῥᾳδίως ἔφερον (41.3) was conducted primarily by sea. Travel by sea in this area is considerably easier than by land; and it can reasonably be supposed (see below) that the Spartans did not have enough sea-power to prevent such operations, at least until after the Athenian disaster at Syracuse. We must picture sudden descents in a few fast boats of the kind mentioned in 9.1.

Thucydides thinks it worth while to mention the deserting helots in V.35.7 and 56.2-3, as well as in 41.3 of this book: and it is plain, from the Spartans' insistence in V.35.7, that the presence of a specifically Messenian garrison (as against an Athenian one) encouraged such desertion. We learn from Xenophon[5] that helots deserted from as far away as Malea, probably the city among those which Pausanias tells us that the Arcadians abandoned to the Spartans.[6] No wonder the Spartans were frightened μὴ καὶ ἐπὶ μακρότερον σφίσι τι νεωτερισθῇ (41.3), and no wonder Demosthenes tried to repeat the situation in VII.26.2. But difficulties of man-power (Athenian hoplite-numbers had been much reduced by the plague, and the number of available and suitable Messenians was limited) and supply, for a permanent garrison, probably prevented the strategy being used on a large scale.

D. 'Bouphras and Tomeus'

In the armistice agreement of 423 B.C. the garrison at Pylos was restricted ἐντὸς τῆς Βουφράδος καὶ τοῦ Τομέως (118.4). Most editors have taken the view that one at least of these places is either at some distance inland from Pylos, or at some distance along the coast. Even Gomme says that "it would be interesting to know how far inland Tomeus was to be found".[7] The various conjectures of Leake and others are worth a brief glance for anyone interested in the general topography; but there seems good reason to limit these extended guesses on textual grounds.

The text of the agreement (118.4) is given in the words ἐπὶ τῆς αὐτῶν μένειν ἑκατέρους ἔχοντας ἅπερ νῦν ἔχομεν, τοὺς μὲν ἐν τῷ Κορυφασίῳ ἐντὸς τῆς Βουφράδος καὶ τοῦ Τομέως μένοντας, τοὺς δὲ ἐν Κυθήροις κ.τ.λ. The cases of those in occupation of Cythera, Nisaia, Minoa and Troizen stress, by the use of such phrases as ὅσαπερ νῦν ἔχουσι, the point that each side should stay in that territory which it occupied, in a strict sense of 'occupy': ἔχω in this context cannot mean 'generally control' or 'dominate'. Now the only territory occupied by the Athenians was the head-

---

4. In such matters as fortification, repairs to ships, armour and other things requiring slightly more sophisticated tools, the Athenians would not reasonably have expected the garrison to live by plundering. But this required only an occasional ship-load.

5. *Hell.* I, 2.18.

6. Paus. VIII, 27.4.

7. p. 599.

land of Pylos itself (as Thucydides says, ἐν τῷ Κορυφασίῳ) and perhaps Sphacteria: and the most plausible locations for Bouphras and Tomeus will be locations which demarcate that area. One could only avoid this conclusion by violating the Greek, and taking the μένοντας clause as if it were a separate sentence; enabling a translation along the lines: "Article 1: each side to stay in its own territory. Article 2: those on Koryphasion not to cross the Bouphras-Tomeus line. Article 3 . . . " and so on. But plainly the effect is rather "Each side to stay in its own territory, i.e. (a) those on Koryphasion . . . (b) those on Cythera . . . " etc.

Again, if ἐντος . . . μένοντας referred to a border at some distance from Pylos, it is hard to see how the Athenians would have been sufficiently restrained. The boundary-line, however roughly drawn, must be such as to exclude the Athenians from Messenian and Spartan territory in general. Thus in map B, the lines V-W and X-Y (examples of two suggestions by commentators) would allow the Athenians too much: only some line substantially west of these would do the job. For we may reasonably assume that the Spartans would take care over this article of the armistice. Nor is there any reason to think that the Athenians would expect to occupy more than they already held. Valmin's remark[8] "Ils venaient de vaincre les Spartiates et ne peuvent pas avoir été complètement exclus de la plaine à l'est de la lagune" is misjudged: they had indeed beaten the Spartans at Pylos, but the more important fighting in Thrace immediately before the armistice had gone against them. As Thucydides says (117.1), the Athenians were frightened, and at this stage were losing rather than winning.

Where then are we to put these two places?

(i)   *Tomeus*
    Stephanus says ἔστι καὶ Τομαῖον ὄρος παρὰ τὸ Κορυφάσιον τοῦ Πύλου ἐοικὸς σμίλῃ. παρὰ here is likely to mean 'alongside of' or 'next to', rather than just 'near': partly on straightforward linguistic grounds, and partly because of the argument outlined above. We cannot be certain what Stephanus thought a σμίλη (or a τομεύς) looked like. Moreover, there is a possible muddle here, since τομαῖος is normally passive in sense ('cut', 'cut off') whereas τομεύς is active ('The Cutter'). The only things that could plausibly be described by the word ὄρος which are παρὰ τὸ Κορυφάσιον are the hill or small mountain immediately to the north, on the other side of Voidokoilia Bay, and Mt. Elias across the Sikia Channel to the south on Sphacteria. Whether either of these would look, from some angles, like a pointed shoemaker's tool (τομεύς) seems impossible to say.

Neither of these, however, are very plausible candidates. For it seems clear, on general grounds, that the Athenians would have included Sphacteria within τῆς αὐτῶν: not that they would necessarily have occupied the island with a permanent

---
8.   *La Messenie Ancienne,* p. 151.

130

garrison, but that they would at least have regarded it as within their rightful territory at Pylos. They had conquered it, and it was defensible: and they would not have let the Spartans occupy it again. (Combined with the correct tactics of a bridge of boats from the north-east corner of the island to the mainland just outside the Athenian defences, such occupation would have been safe for the Spartans and, at the least, troublesome for the Athenians: on this see Note F). The Spartans would have accepted this view: Athenian occupation of, or claim to, Sphacteria is very different from Athenian rights over any mainland territory round Pylos, which the Spartans would have found intolerable.

It follows that Tomeus and Bouphras must mark the north (or north-east) limit of Pylos and the south limit of Sphacteria. This eliminates Mt. Elias as Tomeus without further discussion. The hill on the other side of Voidokoilia Bay is possible as Tomeus, but this means placing Bouphras as the south limit of Sphacteria: highly improbably, for there is nothing in that area which has any plausible connection with the βου- root. A much more plausible guess is to refer Tomeus to one of the small islands, tall rocks, or 'elevations' (ὄρος is wide enough in meaning to allow this) immediately to the south of Sphacteria. Two candidates are particularly likely: a smaller island whose shape seems to fit ἐοικὸς σμίλῃ more than any other elevation in the neighbourhood, and a larger, which is bifurcated by the sea (and may also be said to bifurcate it, hence allowing sense either to the passive τομαῖος or the active τομεύς). This allows us to place Bouphras to the north, and seems to me much the most likely suggestion.

(ii)   *Bouphras*
        This word, like βουπρασίον, has almost certainly something to do with the grazing-place of oxen. The temptation to equate it with Voidokoilia, on the grounds that the βου - root appears in both, must be resisted. For the root only appears in 'Voidokoilia' because the bay looks like the *belly* (κοιλιά) of an ox. One would have to make out a case for deriving the φρας - root from some word meaning something like 'belly': but φρην, the only plausible candidate, cannot in fact mean this. If our guess in (i) above about Τομεύς is right, we could put Bouphras somewhere to the north or north-east of Pylos. The small plateau immediately above Voidokoilia Bay to the north is today used for the grazing of sheep: and the lower areas of what is now the lagoon (then dry land), a little further to the south and east, may also then have offered pasture for oxen (despite Pausanias [9]). I have marked a position tentatively on map B, which gives us the kind of boundary-line that the situation requires.

These guesses at least fulfil the prime qualification of being in the right place, and are sufficiently in accord with Stephanus, provided we do not insist on a too-exact

---

[9].   IV, 36.5: ὑποψαμμός τε γάρ ἐστιν ὡς ἐπίπαν ἡ τῶν Πυλίων χώρα καὶ πόαν βουσὶν οὐχ ἱκανὴ τοσαύτην παρασχέσθαι. But this may well be no more than an echo of Homer: his next sentence is μαρτυρεῖ δέ μοι καὶ Ὅμηρος ἐν μνήμῃ Νέστορος ἐπιλέγων ἀεὶ βασιλέα αὐτὸν ἠμαθόεντος εἶναι Πύλου.

interpretation of παρὰ τὸ Κορυφάσιον. Other commentators have suggested hills or mountains at a still further distance, or have thrown Stephanus overboard altogether. The former seems misguided, and attempts to insist on a likeness with a supposed ὁμίλη are usually somewhat desperate (see Valmin's for a good example of this [10]): the latter seems unnecessary, and would in any case necessitate placing Tomeus more or less where our own suggestion places it, i.e. south of Sphacteria.

E.   The Recapture of Pylos

It is clear that the Spartans could not recapture Pylos under normal circumstances: otherwise, in view of its standing menace to them, they would have done so before 409/08. The difficulties of a land attack, or a sea-borne attack in the style of Thrasymelidas, are obvious enough: slightly more curious is the fact that they seem to have made no attempt to follow up their earlier intentions of using siege-engines (13.1). However, no doubt the garrison improved its fortifications too well for the Spartans to think that there was any serious chance of succeeding.

The Spartans' only chance was, in effect, to *blockade* the garrison by sea as well as land: for, as I have argued above, the garrison relied on its ships not only for its offensive ability but also for much of its supplies. Such a blockade would be dangerous if there was any chance of being caught, for the second time, by Athenian ships. All this is exactly in accordance with the only information we have, from Diodorus. [11] The Spartans wait till they know that "all the Athenian forces were in the Hellespont area". They can only rake up eleven ships, of which "five were from Sicily" (shortage of shipping was perhaps another reason why they had not tried before): but they manage to effect a blockade. The garrison gave in, not as a result of any direct assault, but because some were dying of wounds and others starving. Anytus' forces, which failed to arrive, were to relieve the blockade.

---

10.   *La Messenie Ancienne, ad loc.*
11.   Book XIII, 64. 5-7 (printed and translated in full on p. 45).

APPENDIX

THE LITERATURE & THE TOPOGRAPHY

I do not intend what follows as anything like a full and scholarly review of what past historians and topographers have said. Such a review would be inordinately long and, inevitably, highly polemical. I intend only some notes which may be useful for those who wish to investigate τὰ περὶ Πύλον for themselves.

1. Some authors and sources (see also bibliography)

The bibliography contains a short selection of works which the reader will find most useful and convenient, and from which he may glean all the other references he will need. The following brief notes may be found helpful:-

(i) Almost all the required references can be gleaned from Gomme's commentary, though I have also listed Mills' convenient and informative edition of Bk. IV. Gomme is a mine of information, and more or less up to date. Unfortunately his topography is weak, as the reader may have gathered from the preceding Notes. This defect is remedied in the later volumes of Gomme, which are based on his notes but have been superbly well completed by Andrewes and Dover. There are, of course, many books (not editions) on various aspects of Thucydides and the Peloponnesian War: references to these will also be found in Gomme. Apart from these, the reader will do best to check through the relevant classical journals.

(ii) Pritchett, an indefatigable polymath, has done more for modern topography of the classical Greek period than anyone else I know of. It was his essay on Pylos, more than anything else, that inspired the present volume: and it is not his fault that he did not study Pylos in more depth. Future historians and topographers might well base other studies in depth on his other essays, particularly in cases where there are more complexities than the essay can cover.

(iii) We owe Grundy, in a sense the founding father of detailed topography in this period, and also the perhaps more intelligent Burrows, a large debt: but it cannot be said, in my view, that most of their attempted solutions to particular problems are accurate or scholarly. This is not to say that they are not essential reading. Of the scholars of this and earlier generations, one would certainly single out Leake as the most perceptive and sensible on Greek topography in general: though the reader will find Valmin's study of Messenia uniquely helpful, and Papahadzis' commentary on Pausanias at least full and well-illustrated, if not always correct. Some useful topographical notes and references are to be found in Levi's translation and commentary on Pausanias.

133

(iv) Of ancient authors, Thucydides is the only one worth serious consideration: though the reader may want to look at Plutarch, Diodorus and Pausanias, if only for amusement. To give some idea of how unreliable such authors can be, consider the following passage from Diodorus XII, from the beginning of 61 (I have put the grosser errors in italics):-

"*Demosthenes made an expedition to Pylos,* intending to fortify this place as a threat to the Peloponnese: for it is remarkably strong - it is situated in Messenia, 400 stades distant from Sparta. *He had at the time many ships and plenty of soldiers*: and he fortified Pylos *in 20 days.* When the Lacedaimonians learned that Pylos was fortified, they collected a large force both of infantry and ships. In fact they sailed to Pylos with *45 well-equipped triremes,* and marched with an *army of 12,000*; and they thought it a disgrace to them that the Athenians, who did not dare to defend Attica when it was being ravaged, should fortify and hold a place in the Peloponnese. This army was under the command of Thrasymedes, and pitched camp near Pylos. The troops were eager (ἐμπεσούσης δὲ ὁρμῆς) to endure every danger and to take Pylos by storm: so *they placed* their ships in the mouth of the harbour, prows facing the enemy, using them to block the enemy's attempt to enter . . . "

Note that in many of the places where Diodorus is right, he (or his source) plainly echoes Thucydides (e.g. "situated in Messenia, 400 stades distant from Sparta"). Sometimes he seems to have got Thucydidean phrases misplaced: Thucydides' ὁρμὴ ἐνέπεσε (IV.4.1), there of the Athenian soldiers, reappears as ἐμπεσούσης ὁρμῆς, of the Spartans. And there are many other echoes in later passages. One even suspects that 'Thrasymedes' is a mistake for 'Thrasymelidas', though the latter commanded only by sea. (The name 'Thrasymedes' has Messenian connotations: Thrasymedes was the son of Nestor, and his supposed tomb is still visible on the edge of the headland across Voidokoilia Bay from Pylos. His tomb is mentioned by Pausanias, IV. 36.2. The MSS of Thucydides read Θρασυμηδίδας.)

(v) But many modern writers do no better. It is worth briefly quoting a passage from a modern guide-book.[1] It is, in general, a good and reliable guide-book, written by an intelligent man who has read Thucydides, if only in translation: yet it includes the following:-

"There, out in the bay, lies the island of Sphacteria, just as Thucydides described it: there was room for two Spartan ships between its northern tip and the mainland, and for *six on the south.* The Spartans planned to land men on the island and to block the entrances with ships, so that when the Athenians arrived in their ships they would be unable to sail into the harbour or land on the island, except against heavy odds. The garrison was landed on the island, but someone forgot to block the entrances with ships, so that *when Demosthenes arrived with his ships,* he was able to sail in, and the Spartan garrison was cut off in Sphacteria. *The Athenians landed on the mainland* on

---

1. A. B. Christie, *Motoring and Camping in Greece* (Faber), p. 106.

134

the north of the bay *and built a fortress there* . . . They maintained a naval patrol round the island, and *it was the Spartans who had to try to land from the sea* so that, as Thucydides says - 'it was indeed a strange alteration in the ordinary run of things for Athenians to be fighting a battle on land - and Spartan land too - against Spartans attacking from the sea . . .'. "

The moral of this is, that the investigator should trust nobody: not even the authors recommended earlier (nor the present writer). Even Leake, for instance, is not immune from gross errors, as when[2] he talks about the Lacedaemonian (*sic*) garrison in Koryphasion, a mistake which may be part-cause of some of the wilder guesses about Bouphras and Tomeus (see Note R). *A fortiori* the sophisticated investigator will expect to derive amusement rather than help from the modern multi-lingual tourist pamphlets ("cette foudroyante victoire", etc.), some of which will baffle him until he realises that elements of τὰ περὶ Πύλον are introduced into the Battle of Navarino (1827), and vice versa.

2. Modern topography

I have explained the inadequacy of modern maps earlier (p. 2). Ancient maps are, of course, still more inaccurate: but some of them are marginally relevant to the campaign, inasmuch as some tentative inductions may be made from them concerning changes in the topography over the centuries. The investigator who wishes to go into this more fully than I have needed to do may best hunt these down in the libraries of Venice; there are also some useful references in Papahadzis. But, as I have said, the investigator who is centrally concerned with τὰ περὶ Πύλον needs to inspect the terrain himself. Here the following notes may save him time and confusion.

(a) *Nomenclature*

Thucydides uses Πύλος or ἡ Πύλος to refer uniquely to the promontory, which (as he says in 3.2) the Lacedaimonians called Koryphasion. Today this is often referred to as 'Palaeonavarino' or 'Palaeocastro': the latter is the more common among the local inhabitants, and is contrasted with the 'Neocastro', which is the Turkish fort on the mainland at the southern end of the bay. This fort overlooks the modern town of Pylos. Thucydides' λιμήν is now officially known, as it has been for some time, as the Bay of Navarino. 'Koryphasion' is now the name of a small village which is just off the road going north to Chora, on the right, up a steep hill and unmade road. The main northward road goes to Nestor's Palace, sometimes called 'old Pylos', on the hill at Ano Englianos. Sphacteria, the reader will be relieved to hear, is still called Sphacteria or Sphagia. If extending his research further afield, however (e.g. southwards around Methone and Asine), he should beware of the common Greek habit of cashing in on ancient names for the benefit of modern villages, or of other features.

---

2.   p. 416.

135

(b)   *The 'Osmyn Aga lagoon'*
This area is fully described by Pritchett. It was dry land in 425, and I have marked it as such on the maps. I have also marked the extent of the 'lagoon' at the present time, bounded as it is by the promontory of Pylos on the west, the sand-dunes round Voidokoilia at the north-east, the raised sand-bar on the south, and the commencement of ordinary farm-land to the north and east.

The modern reader needs to be aware, however, that (i) it is not a true lagoon: it floods only during the winter season, and is in process of being drained: in the summer much of it can be walked or even (with great care) driven over by car: (ii) it is not always known or marked as the 'Osmyn Aga'. ('Osmyn' itself has variants, e.g. 'Osman' in Pritchett.) Thus the *Karta Nomos* map marks it as Λ (for ΛΙΜΝΗ) DIBARI. To most of the local inhabitants it is known simply as the λιμνή (not to be confused with Thucydides' λιμήν!).

(c)   *'Nestor's Cave'*
This is marked on my maps as a 'classical' rather than a 'modern' name. Readers of Pausanias will remember that in his time there was a town on and around the promontory: καὶ σπήλαιόν ἐστιν ἐντὸς τῆς πόλεως, βοῦς δὲ ἐνταῦθα τὰς Νέστορος καὶ ἔτι πρότερον Νηλέως φασὶν αὐλίζεσθαι. [3]

(d)   *Accessibility*
The modern topographer should be made aware that, save for the asphalt road from Chora which skirts the bay and arrives at the modern town of Pylos, most of the area under discussion is difficult of access. There is a track, just viable for ordinary cars (though they need good ground-clearance), which leads from the asphalt road to Voidokoilia Bay: this is the nearest access-point. From the end of this track, which is only a few yards from the bay, it is possible to walk round the curve of the bay to Thucydidean Pylos without difficulty in about 15 minutes.

From here one may ascend Pylos, by quite a steep climb, to Nestor's Cave and eventually (steeper still) to the Frankish-Venetian castle on the top (Thucydides' ἀκρόπολις, 26.2): or take the rough but comparatively level path which leads round the northern and western part of the promontory to the Sikia, and to sea-level at the south-east corner. Thence it is possible to walk back, at least when the lagoon is dry, under the eastern cliffs of the promontory (where there are remains of an old road), across a thick belt of sand-dunes, to Voidokoilia. All these routes are viable for reasonably able-bodied men and women; but I would not call any of them easy.

---

3.   *Messenia*, XXXVI, 2.

Easier, though less topographically rewarding, access is the normal method used by tourists: to take a boat from the modern town of Pylos. Several boats make a habit of taking small parties across the Bay of Navarino, through the Sikia, and to Voidokoilia Bay, stopping just beneath the north-east part of the promontory and giving them time to see Nestor's Cave and/or the castle on the summit. Boats can of course be privately hired. In general, as throughout Greek history, it is easier for most purposes to go by sea rather than land. But the diligent topographer will need a boat full-time: moreover, one which is of sufficiently shallow draught to go where he will need to go, yet seaworthy enough to cope with the frequent πνεῦμα ἐκ πόντου. [4]

Sphacteria is more difficult. Private or public boats will take you to the Panagia landing: from there an easy path leads to Mt. Elias, and there is also a reasonably good track running southwards. I hesitate to give exact details, because mobility on the island is in fact almost wholly dependent on the state of the undergrowth, which can vary within a very few years. But it is likely to remain extremely difficult for the foreseeable future (see Pritchett[5]), and the topographer will be well advised to dress himself in thorn-proof clothing.

---

4. For information on wind, weather and nautical details the Admiralty Pilot, and the Admiralty charts, are the best written source. But they are no substitute for local knowledge and personal experience.
5. p. 25 ff.

MAPS A – D

There are four maps, A – D. Map A is sufficiently general to give the reader an idea of the setting of the whole campaign: in particular it is relevant to points about the ἐρημία of Pylos and its distance from Sparta, the first Athenian landing, Asine, Prote, and the geography of the Ionian Islands in relation to ship-movements (Notes A, C and E). Map B gives the Pylos-Sphacteria area on a considerably larger scale: Map C, Pylos itself on a scale still larger. Map D, which is based on Burrows' sketch but includes a wider area, is relevant to the Spartans' last stand (Note P).

I have tried to put in all strictly relevant detail, but equally to avoid cluttering them up unnecessarily: clarity is the chief consideration. 'Modern', i.e. all non-classical, names are underlined.

See also the notes and legend relevant to each map.

There was a choice to make between representing the terrain as it is today, and trying to represent it on Pritchett's assumption (which I accept) of a rise in sea-level of about 2.5 metres since 425. I have compromised. The terrain appears as it is today, except for the 'Osmyn Aga lagoon', marked as dry land. To attempt an exact reconstruction of coastlines as they were in 425 would be a great labour. Apart from the 'Osmyn Aga lagoon', no significant historical points are affected, except for details of the Sikia Channel (see Note F): but the reader should be made aware that there would be topographically (not historically) significant differences - much of the (flat alluvial) coastline round the north and north-east of the Bay of Navarino would have to be extended, for instance.

139

MAP A

This map, highly simplified for clarity, is designed to illustrate large-scale distances only. In particular it is relevant to the movements of the Spartan and Athenian fleets (Note E). I have added an inset to clarify the movements of the Athenian fleet on its first return to Pylos, its inspection of the λιμήν, move to Prote, move from Prote, second inspection, and entry into the λιμήν for the ναυμαχία. (Even on this map these movements are oversimplified.)

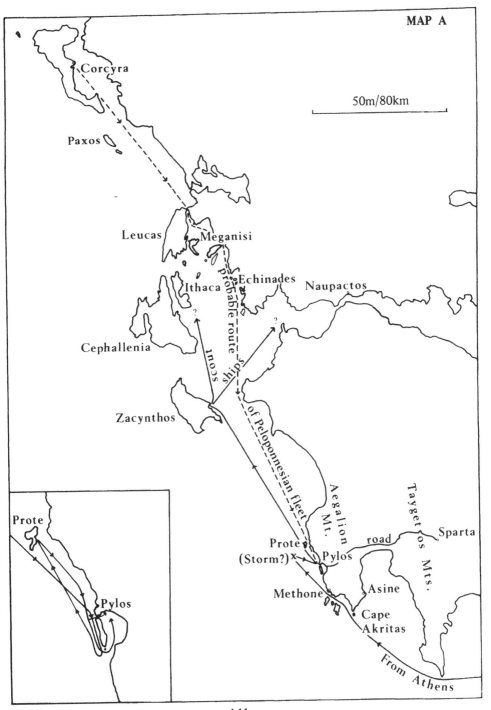

50m/80km

Corcyra

Paxos

Leucas

Meganisi

Ithaca

Echinades

Naupactos

Cephallenia

Zacynthos

scout

probable route

ships

of Peloponnesian fleet

?

?

Prote

Pylos

Prote
(Storm?) x

Pylos

Methone

Asine

Cape
Akritas

Aegalion
Mt.

Taygetos Mts.

road

Sparta

From Athens

141

MAPS B and C

Symbols:		Coastline either consisting of cliff dropping sheer into the sea, or such that, although landing is possible, cliffs immediately behind the landing would make the normal deployment of troops impossible (see notes B, M) I have marked the cliffs on the east side of Pylos in the same way, though not strictly 'coast-line'.
	?	Indicates some historical doubt: see relevant note.
	⊔⊔⊔⊔	A virtually certain line of wall or defence-line.
	∿∿∿	A probable but more doubtful line of wall.
	— — — ⟋	Rough limits of modern 'Osmyn Aga Lagoon' (See Appendix, p. 136).

Letters:	A, B, C	Spartan blockade line (see note F).
	D	Most sheltered part of Voidokoilia Bay (Note F).
	E, F	Length of main part of Sikia Channel (Note B).
	G, L, M	Terminal points of Athenian wall (Note B).
	T	Athenian στρατόπεδον: Demosthenes' triremes here (Note B).
	J, H, I, K	Spartan blockade-line (Note F).
	R, S	End-points of Athenian wall.
	U	So-called 'Brasidas' rocks'.
	N, O. P	Perimeter of Athenian wall.
	Q	Weak point in eastern cliff-face.
	V-W, X-Y	Wrong suggestions about the 'Bouphras-Tomeus line' (Note R).

Numbers:	1	'Nestor's Cave'.
	2	Acropolis of Pylos.
	3	Probable origin of fire.
	4	Summit of Mt. Elias.

142

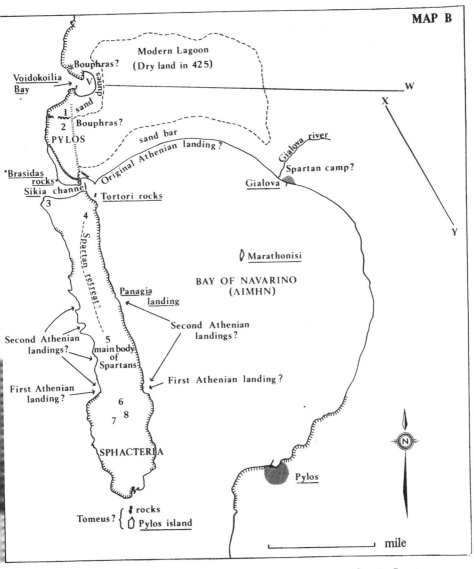

MAP B

Voidokoilia Bay

Bouphras?

Modern Lagoon
(Dry land in 425)

sand

sand

Bouphras?

PYLOS

W

X

sand bar

Original Athenian landing?

Gialova river

Spartan camp?

'Brasidas rocks'

Sikia channel

Gialova

Tortori rocks

Y

Spartan retreat?

Marathonisi

BAY OF NAVARINO
(ΛΙΜΗΝ)

Panagia landing

Second Athenian landings?

Second Athenian landings?

Second Athenian landings?

5 main body of Spartans

First Athenian landing?

First Athenian landing?

6

7 8

SPHACTERIA

Pylos

Tomeus? { rocks
          Pylos island

N

mile

5	'Grundy's Well' (approximate site of main Spartan force on Sphacteria).
6	Probable position of Athenian hoplites.
7, 8	Alternative positions for southern Spartan picket.

Post-classical names are underlined.

143

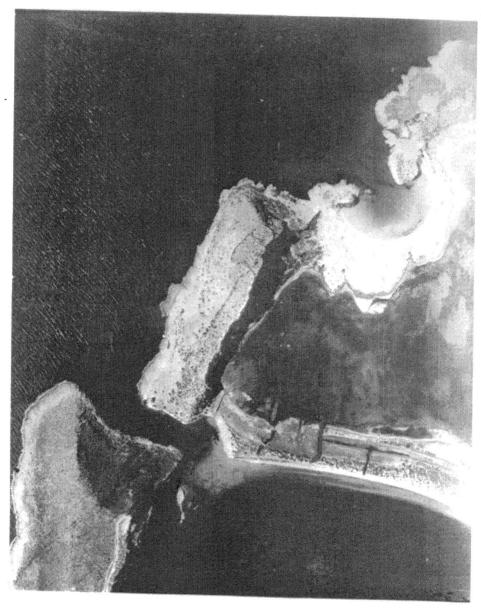

Air photograph taken in 1942 showing Pylos and the northern part of Sphacteria, and corresponding approximately to Map C. (British Crown Copyright reserved.)

144

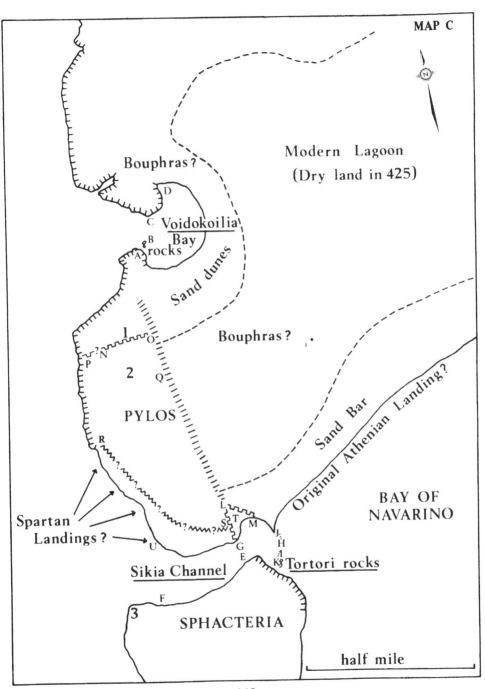

MAP C

Bouphras?

Modern Lagoon
(Dry land in 425)

D

C Voidokoilia
B Bay
rocks
A

Sand dunes

1 O Bouphras?
? N
P

2 Q

PYLOS

R

Sand Bar

Original Athenian Landing?

BAY OF
NAVARINO

Spartan
Landings?

L
S T M
U J
H
G
E K Tortori rocks

Sikia Channel

F

3 SPHACTERIA

half mile

MAP D

This map relates to the Spartans' last stand (Note P). It is based on Burrows' sketch, but slightly extended (particularly northwards) so as to show the complete Spartan perimeter. I have simplified the contour-lines and some other details for the sake of clarity: they should not be taken as accurate in every particular. Even so, the reader may find it hard to grasp quickly how the land lies: the following remarks may assist him.

From the eastern coastline the cliff rises almost sheer, except in one place (marked 'gorge'), where there is a sort of gully - steep but easy to climb - which penetrates about 80' westwards. Here it peters out and connects with a strip of comparatively low-lying terrain (marked 'hollow'), which runs north-south between the summit of Mt. Elias and the high ground on the cliff edge. South of the gorge, and north of the hollow, the land rises fairly sharply again, until it resumes its normal configuration. All this is only visible at close quarters; from outside the area it looks as if there is a continuous area of high ground, from Mt. Elias to the cliff edge.

In the sketch, the solid lines in A-A and at C show the wall, or remains of a wall, which Burrows claimed to have seen. The dotted lines - - - and = = = represent Burrows' conjectures about where the rest of the wall, or other walls, must have been. In the text I argue that A-A is indeed a natural defence-line, and that some line like Burrows' B was necessary to defend the approach via the gorge: but that the Spartans did not defend C, otherwise the Messenians would not have had time to move from the high ground across the hollow to Mt. Elias. The Spartan perimeter, I claim, ran from M-M: that is, A-A plus a northern and southern extension, which I have marked xxx.

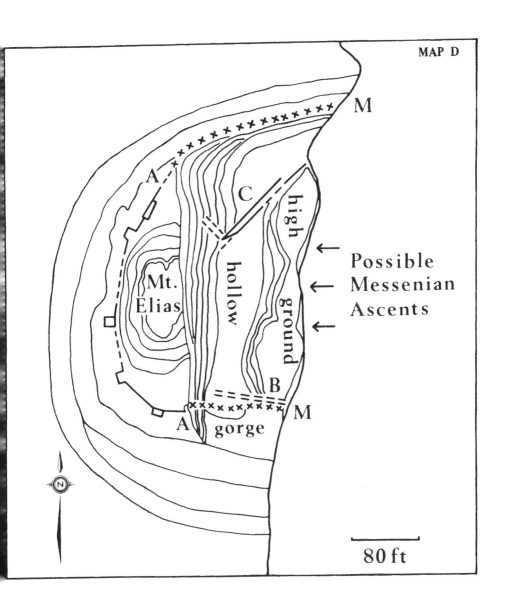

MAP D

M

A

C

high ground

Mt. Elias

hollow

Possible
Messenian
Ascents

B

A

M

gorge

N

80 ft

147

Printed and bound by CPI Group (UK) Ltd, Croydon, CR0 4YY

09/06/2025

14685805-0001